FINALS – THREE GREENS

A LIFE IN AVIATION

BY

WG CDR G.W. (JOHNNIE) JOHNSON
DFC and Bar, CdeG

CIRRUS ASSOCIATES

PUBLISHED BY:
Cirrus Associates (S.W.),
Kington Magna,
Gillingham,
Dorset SP8 5EW UK.

© G.W. Johnson 2000

ISBN 1 902807 09 X

DISTRIBUTORS:
Vine House Distribution Ltd,
Waldenbury,
North Common,
Chailey,
East Sussex BN8 4DR.

PRINTED IN ENGLAND BY:
The Book Factory,
35-37 Queensland Road,
London N7 7AH.

COVER AND PHOTO SCANNING BY:
Duographic Associates,
11 High Street,
Fareham,
Hampshire PO16 7AF.

PHOTOGRAPHS:
Michael Stroud,
Aviation Historian,
82 St. Nicholas Road,
Lavant,
Chichester,
West Sussex PO18 0BT.

DEDICATION

This was written to satisfy the curiosity of family and friends who always wanted to know, but were too polite to ask, and for the rapidly diminishing band that shared the experiences.

CONTENTS

FOREWORD		6
Chapter I:	**O FOR THE WINGS**	7
Chapter II:	**GEORGIA ON MY MIND**	11
Chapter III	**COME FLY WITH ME**	17
Chapter IV	**IN THE STILL OF THE NIGHT**	25
Chapter V:	**TIE ME KANGEROO DOWN, SPORT**	32
Chapter VI:	**SCHOOLDAYS, SCHOOLDAYS**	49
Chapter VII:	**IT'S GOT TO BE THIS OR THAT**	53
Chapter VIII:	**LIFE GETS TEDIOUS, DON'T IT?**	68
Chapter IX:	**BABY, IT'S COLD OUTSIDE**	72
Chapter X:	**I GUESS I'LL HAVE TO CHANGE MY PLAN**	83
Chapter XI:	**SLEEPY TIME DOWN SOUTH**	98
Chapter XII:	**BUSY DOING NOTHING**	105
Chapter XIII:	**FINGS AIN'T WHAT THEY USED TO BE**	108
Chapter XIV:	**ISLAND IN THE SUN**	116
Chapter XV:	**BLUES IN THE NIGHT**	131
Chapter XVI:	**LET'S TAKE IT NICE AND EASY**	134
Chapter XVII:	**THERE'LL BE SOME CHANGES MADE**	142
Chapter XVIII:	**SAND IN MY SHOES**	151
Chapter XIX:	**SONG OF INDIA**	168
Chapter XX:	**PICK YOURSELF UP**	176

Chapter XXI: **THE HAPPY WANDERER**   179

Chapter XXII: **VOLARE**   195

Chapter XXIII: **HIGH HOPES**   206

Chapter XXIV: **AMERICAN PATROL**   215

Chapter XXV: **I'VE HEARD THAT SONG BEFORE**   225

Chapter XXVI: **MIDNIGHT SUN**   230

Chapter XXVII: **SOUTH AMERICAN WAY**   234

Chapter XXVIII: **SWINGING SAFARI**   238

Chapter XXIX: **EAST OF THE SUN**   242

Chapter XXX: **HAPPY TALK**   246

Chapter XXXI: **WINGS OVER THE NAVY**   253

Chapter XXXII: **TOO DARNED HOT!**   260

Chapter XXXIII: **CLIMB EVERY MOUNTAIN**   266

Chapter XXXIV: **THE PARTY'S OVER**   272

FOREWORD

I began this enterprise in a burst of enthusiasm, as a retirement project to fill the long empty days of boredom stretching ahead. I quickly discovered that there were many more interesting things to do and the writing slowed to a stuttering stop. In consequence, many of the friends of whom I have written have departed and, since we were all of an age, it occurred to me that if it was ever to be finished, I had better get on with it.

I hope that I have been able to convey the atmosphere of my times when, although life seemed to be grim and earnest, our youth and optimism allowed us to see that things were not to be taken too seriously. Usually they weren't!

Hemyock, East Devon,
March 2000

CHAPTER I
O FOR THE WINGS

On the 8th January 1941 I reached my eighteenth birthday and the next day, armed with my birth certificate, I called at the Recruiting Office and asked if they had any vacancies for pilots in the Royal Air Force. I had watched the Battle of Britain being fought in the skies over Kent, and had been on the receiving end of bombs dropped in error by Luftwaffe crews with very poor navigators, who mistook the Kent countryside for central London. These factors, and an almost complete lack of interest in walking, had led me to conclude that my part in the conflict would best be conducted in the air.

My interest in aviation started slowly. I have never built a model aircraft in my life, but the disasters forecast during the 1938 crisis led me to think that air power was likely to be decisive if war came, and would be the thing to be in. At the same time, the head boy of my school had gained entry to Cranwell. He was a few years older than me but we had represented the school together in team games and thus formed a tenuous friendship. We wrote to each other during his Cranwell training and this correspondence consolidated in my mind that the air force was the place to be.

There was a short pause before I was ordered to RAF Uxbridge for medical and aptitude testing. This process established that I was literate, numerate and not colour blind, all facts that I already knew and would gladly have told them if they had asked. I was to learn that the service instinctively distrusts newcomers' ability to know anything, a reasonable doubt as any drill sergeant will testify who has tried to persuade a squad to all turn in the same direction.

These hurdles overcome, I was attested and told that my "deferred service" had started, and not to make any plans for extended holidays. The waiting period was not long and in the late spring I boarded a train to Babbacombe, the aircrew reception centre near Torquay in Devon. At this centre we received various inoculations, were blood-grouped, vaccinated and kitted out with uniforms and all the other essentials of service life (button stick and shoe brushes), under the watchful eyes of NCO Physical Training Instructors (PTIs). We emerged, punctured but otherwise intact, from the sick quarters where the only serious competition was to be in the right place in the queue when a new, sharp needle was fitted to the syringe. The PTIs then took over for some violent exercise which they claimed was the best way of dispersing the inert germs now coursing through our bodies. We were vaccinated on the left upper arm, blood sampled from the right arm, tetanus under left chest and typhoid under right chest so that most of the upper body was in shock and much more in need of hot, sweet tea than "arms stretch, hand clapping above the head – begin." After 48 hours we reported back to the weary doctors suffering thumb fatigue after all their labours, to see if the vaccination had "taken." Those without earlier vaccination scars and still not showing that characteristic angry swelling that goes with a successful jab were done again. A local lad, Les Cocking, a Devonian and former schoolmaster, married and with a son, was one of our group whose vaccination was declared a failure and he was given a repeat dose. The next day I was PT-ing in the rank immediately behind him and watched with surprise as a livid red weal spread quickly across his shoulders from left to right just before he passed out. It seems that the first vaccination had taken but was too slow in showing to save him from another. He was the first airman I met who prompted me to think that the country must be in desperate straits if it was forced to recruit people of his age and with his responsibilities; he was probably 26.

We lived in holiday hotels commandeered for the duration and modified to provide extreme discomfort for the maximum number. The Devon coast, whilst extremely picturesque, has no level ground of any kind. Each square yard is on a different level to its neighbours on all sides so that even walking requires some care and agility. We ran everywhere. From early morning to last light we quick-marched or doubled from main lecture halls (cinemas), to smaller classrooms (converted shops). We learned some service history, personal hygiene, and its importance in crowded barracks, the curriculum based largely I suppose, on the experiences of the Crimean War. There was not an aviator in sight, a disappointing start for the budding aces.

This brief period of induction was followed by postings to Initial Training Wings, mostly in the local area. I went to Torquay, together with many of those that I had met for the first time in the preceding weeks. Here the learning pattern changed and, for the first time, our technical instructors began to concentrate on navigation, meteorology, aerodynamics, engines and signals, much of which could be related to our hoped-for future employment. The marching and doubling did not stop, indeed it became a way of life so that walking seemed unnatural. My corporal PTI was Ted Ditchburn, later the goalkeeper of England and Tottenham Hotspur, a gentle giant who found it unnecessary to shout at his charges in the way that some of the others seemed to enjoy. I think that his methods worked because we won the inter-wing drill competition with the squad that he selected and trained. All this work-up stood us in good stead when we completed the practice evacuation exercise, predicated on the need to hide the valuable aircrew trainees when the enemy invaded Devon. Our destination was Cockington, about six miles from Torquay, and the way to get there was 100 yards at quick march followed by 100 yards at the double, then quick march, double until we arrived at Cockington an hour after we had started. Our instructors were simple men but they were not daft, and the focal point of the exercise was a splendid pub where transport awaited us for the return to Torquay, and where I had my first alcohol. Thoroughly dehydrated after this strenuous activity on a very hot summer's day, I drank a pint of sweet cider. Devon scrumpy has probably been the downfall of many young men, and even more young women, and it certainly did for me. It is a very strange sensation to be completely aware of everything that's going on but totally incapable of controlling leg movements.

Lecture followed drill followed lecture for five or six weeks until, after examinations, most of us were declared fit for further training. As a schoolboy, playing whatever game was in season at least three times a week, I was about as fit as it is possible to be and I weighed 158 pounds. After initial training in the Royal Air Force I weighed 147 pounds. This was partly due to the appalling food that we were offered, much of it inedible as far as I was concerned, but even more to very hard exercise on hot, humid summer days. If prisoners were given the same treatment today, the authorities would be charged with cruel and unusual punishment.

As with all things it came to an end and I found myself collecting flying clothing, and writing "Arnold Draft" on my kit bags, together with my name and serial number. There was one other curious thing that occurred at this time; having been forced to send our own civilian clothes home, we were issued with civilian suits. Nobody had the least idea of what was going on and it was quite certain that those in authority were not telling, even if they knew. A small group of us found ourselves on a train, travelling north for 24 hours or so, arriving finally at Gourock where we boarded a ship, the name of which is mercifully blocked from my memory. We were on board for about a week, doing nothing and not allowed ashore for "security reasons" which implies that those in charge thought that we knew where we were bound and were keen to communicate this information to the enemy. We were in fact waiting for a convoy to assemble in order to cross the Atlantic to Halifax, Nova Scotia. We were to discover that Canada was not our final destination however, hence the civilian clothes. This was the autumn of 1941, the United States was not yet in the war but we were to be trained there under a scheme named for General Hap Arnold, the most famous military aviator in America.

We were aboard that wretched boat for three weeks in all and, although Halifax is hardly the Las Vegas of the north, we were all delighted when we finally tied up. Immediately we were on a train bound for Toronto Exhibition Grounds. This vast hall had hundreds of double-tier bunks, all occupied by aircrew under training, waiting to be dispersed to the flying training schools in Canada and the southern United States.

This was my first visit to North America and in Toronto I felt immediately at home, as did my companions. We spoke approximately the same language as the natives, and aside from looking in the wrong direction to check oncoming traffic, which led to one or two near misses, the brief time spent there was good. I discovered hitch-hiking and with several chums visited Niagara courtesy of friendly Canadian motorists. My North American geography and history, formerly limited to colonial wars (Canada – won, United States – lost), also began to improve with the discovery that most of Niagara Falls are not in Canada at all. This blessed relief from life aboard ship passed quickly and enjoyably whilst we waited to learn our fate, still not realising that an issue of civilian clothes could only mean that we were bound for the United States.

CHAPTER II
GEORGIA ON MY MIND

When we boarded the train in Toronto we were not told our destination, but even if we had been it would have meant very little to me and, I suspect, the rest of my group. After about 30 hours on the train, having seen more than enough of the changing face of Canada and the United States, we arrived at dead of night at a railway crossing where we disembarked. We were in civilian clothes, of course, but I very much doubt if we would have been mistaken for anything other than what we were.

To digress for a moment. The "States" as we now recognise them on a map were not always so. By the middle of the eighteenth century, before the Revolutionary War, only the east coast had been colonised, from what is now Maine down to Georgia. Disputes between contiguous territories, usually over the ownership of land or water, were frequent and sometimes bitter. The argument between Pennsylvania and Maryland concerning the precise location of the border almost led to war between them and two of the King's surveyors were sent from England to arbitrate. They were Charles Mason and Jeremiah Dixon and the division which they drew became the Mason-Dixon line, later made famous by Al Jolson whose Mammy came from below it. The train on which I was travelling had crossed that line, carrying me into a world of which I knew nothing.

We had arrived at Souther Field, Americus, Georgia, a private flying club-type airfield. It was already October but the weather was mild and, we were to discover, very hot during the day. The Graham School of Flying was one of several civil schools contracted to train RAF cadets. The instructors were civilians with one Army Air Corps officer with the power of the Almighty since in any cases of doubtful potential he decided whether training should continue or cease.

Our training aircraft were Stearman PT-17s, radial-engined biplanes, now much sought after by private owners who enjoy aerobatics. The instructor to whom I was assigned was a short, lean Texan who was an extremely skilful pilot but who suffered one enormous disadvantage from my point of view – I understood about one word in four that he spoke. My natural politeness and the desire not to be seen as the village idiot limited the number of times that I asked for an instruction to be repeated, and this almost led to my downfall. There were no radios in the aircraft, so orders were shouted into a voice tube, and even the bits that were audible above the engine noise delivered in a Texan drawl meant very little to me. In consequence I did what I thought he had asked for and frequently I was wrong. The thing that saved me was the fortunate chance that the Air Corps officer at Mather Field was a native-born New Yorker, and I could understand every word. I flew a much-dreaded check ride with him, he sent me solo and changed my instructor. Mr Barron, with whom I completed the Primary phase of training, was a big, jolly man with a good training technique which demanded that the student confirm his understanding of what was required before moving on. We got along like a house on fire, the haze cleared and things which I had simply not understood became easy.

We lived in barracks and were allowed off the station from Saturday lunch-time until Sunday evening. With a net income of about six dollars a week, if anyone had the desire to gallivant it was unlikely to be fulfilled, and this must have been known to the good citizens of Americus, who showed us the generous hospitality that I have ever since associated with Americans.

At lunch-time on Saturdays, cars would begin to form up on the dirt roads that surrounded the barracks, full of families offering to open their homes to the British. Indeed there was strong competition amongst the putative hosts who far outnumbered the potential guests, offering increasingly sophisticated diversions. Signs were displayed on windscreens saying "Lake fishing," "Visit to Atlanta," "Tour of Battlefields" and so on – all perfectly proper and much of it sponsored by the Daughters of the Revolution, approximately the very moral equivalent of our Women's Institute. I went with a small group of fellow students to tea at the home of the president of the local Chapter and was astonished at the effort made to make us feel at ease and at home. Conventional tea pots had been gathered by the ladies from somewhere – not a tea bag in sight – and delicate cucumber sandwiches were offered.

Conversation was not easy for us sitting as we were, balancing cups of tea and plates of sandwiches, and I became conscious that our hostess and the other southern ladies had gone very silent. Glancing furtively around to see if one of our number had committed some terrible gaffe, I finally asked my hostess if something was wrong. "Oh! no," she replied, "we are just waitin' to hear you'all talk!"

Georgia, "The Peach State," was rural and backward in those days and the residents lived life at a pace that they would probably like to see again. I saw a chain gang working on the road, men wearing hooped convict uniforms and shackled together, something that until then I had assumed to be fiction. The Civil War was still being fought too. To be a British Boy was one thing, to be a Yankee was quite another. The bitterness felt towards northerners for the humiliating defeat that had been inflicted on the south was tangible and never long omitted from any conversation, even 75 years later. It was all pretty thought-provoking stuff for a young man a long way from home, but was the genesis of the deep affection that I have since held for the United States and the people from there that I have met.

Training continued in the rugged, open-cockpit Stearman, with gradually-increasing skills and confidence as some of the mysteries were explained and practised. There were no forbidden manoeuvres in the Stearman and we were routinely taught snap rolls and outside loops (as far as we could go on the power available), and only later did I realise that we had been lucky to gain this confidence-building knowledge. Frequently, like most of the others, I got it wrong, but with good old Mr Barron there to show me how to recover from whatever extraordinary position the aircraft had assumed as a result of my mishandling, I found the Stearman very user-friendly.

Americus was a typical southern town where the black population outnumbered the white by a considerable margin but, on the surface anyway, they got along amicably and there were no obvious signs of racial tension. As I remember it there was a Main Street, with shops and soda fountains (no bars, Georgia was a dry state), churches and schools and, to be frank, not a great deal else. Many years later I was mildly surprised when reading a profile of President Carter to learn that in his youth his big nights out from Plains, Georgia occurred in Americus! I expect that Americus has changed and, for all I know, could now be the sin city of the South. However it seems more likely, knowing what we now know about the former President, that his entertainment demands were modest and were fully met by Americus. I wonder what Plains was like!

We were in our final days of training at Americus when the Japanese attacked Pearl Harbour and a new urgency became apparent. The declaration of war made no immediate impact on the local people except that we were ordered into uniform and became confused in their minds with pupils at a local military school who wore a Confederate grey uniform, not dissimilar to our Air Force blue.

The failure rate in the primary stage of training was impressive but those that survived moved on to a genuine military establishment for Basic Training in Macon, Georgia. Those that had not stayed the course went back to Canada, mostly to become navigators or other aircrew in the official and rather patronising phrase.

Cochran Field was equipped with Vultee BT-13 low-wing monoplanes with fixed undercarriage but trailing-edge flaps, adding slightly to the list of things to be remembered. When not flying we were subjected to rifle drill American-style, and whilst we never achieved the Guards' standard, we were able to parade without embarrassing anyone.

Training was conducted along normal American lines with a corps of Cadet Officers drawn from the senior course at the school responsible for normal day-to-day discipline. In overall charge was the Commandant of Cadets, Captain Clark of the US Army Air Corps, a West Pointer who made it quite clear that he was not there from choice and neither was he very keen about the British. American cadets use a system of "hazing" in which any senior classman can order any junior classman to perform some humiliating task in order to punish any misdemeanour, real or imagined. One favourite was to order one unfortunate to run backwards around the barrack block and, as soon as he left, despatch another running backwards but in the opposite direction so that they would collide. This may have worked well with American cadets but was not appreciated by the RAF and the system collapsed when a former Queen's University (Belfast) boxer flattened an American upper classman for being so stupid. Demerits were awarded for minor breaches of discipline and for each demerit the offender marched around the sports field in full kit for one hour on Saturday or Sunday when everyone else was on stand-down. Although I kept a clean sheet, the punishment struck me as being not unlike the stocks, humiliating rather than painful.

In Macon, hospitality was just as generous as in Americus and with two others I had the good fortune to be invited to the home of James and Emily Knott for Christmas. They had two young children of their own and simply added us to the family. Nobody could possibly have been kinder to us and there was almost nothing that we could do in return. From Christmas onwards it became routine to be met at lunch-time on Saturday and returned to base on Sunday evening, exhausted by tramping around places of interest and trying to keep up with two small, energetic children.

The flying was straightforward, with Army instructors, themselves recent graduates, detailed for an instructional tour before going operational. Their frustration was sometimes evident and, had I but realised it, a warning of what was in store for me. We learned formation-flying in addition to our other (limited) skills and for the first time flew at night. Cross-countries, led by our instructor, were called navigation training but depended upon a radio compass and a working radio. We drew lines on maps certainly, but in practice flew the beam. Even solo night cross-country flying held no terrors because the radio beam still worked and, in that sparsely populated State, well-lit small towns were hard to miss.

After 70 hours of the Vultee, during which more friends boarded the train to Canada, the survivors were posted to Advanced Training on the North American AT-6A, the Harvard. I left Macon, and particularly the Knott family, with genuine regret and despite the best intentions in the world, I never saw them again. So, still in the "Heart of Dixie," we crossed the border into Alabama.

Napier Field in Dothan, Alabama was to be home for the next three months, assuming nothing untoward happened. The Harvard was a very good training machine capable of just about any manoeuvre, and quite

14

difficult to land tidily. We had some systems management to do too with retractable undercarriage, variable-pitch propeller, mixture control and flaps, all of which provided opportunities for getting it wrong. We were introduced to night cross-countries in formation, which was entertaining but fraught with danger since each of us was concentrating so hard on the leader that, if we had lost contact, we had no idea where we were. Instrument flying also figured prominently and I grew to loathe that black hood that excluded all light and contact with the outside world, but I must have learned something because instrument flying never troubled me later. Best of all were the aerobatic sorties with my instructor, Captain Harry Culberson, who did all the other exercises under sufferance but who loved "acrobatics" as he called them. We continued to be taught and to practise flick manoeuvres and I was surprised to learn later that such exercises were forbidden in RAF Harvards.

At this stage of training the failure rate was low and at Dothan, our upper classmen were all RAF so that the tiresome and slightly absurd cadet officer system did not apply. The one certain way to fail however was to land wheels-up, for which there was only one punishment: back to Canada and "other aircrew." It made such a deep impression on me that I can truthfully say that in more than 30 years of active aviation I never came remotely close to forgetting the wheels. Received wisdom used to be that there were only two kinds of pilot, those that had landed wheels-up and those that were going to, but I think that those least likely to conform to that rule were the graduates of the Arnold Scheme.

When it was all over, with a total of 200 hours in the log book, we assembled in the Cadet Mess and each in turn received a graduation certificate and his wings from a general of the US Army. The wings of course were American and we had no RAF "Flying Badges" until we returned to England, when we bought them at the tailors. That was not quite the end however; an RAF officer was in attendance and several of the new graduates were required to see him for reasons which were unknown until the interview started. He said that the ever-increasing demand for pilots was partially to be met by opening more flying schools in the USA, but operated by the RAF in contrast to the Arnold Scheme. The proposition was to stay in the USA and teach other RAF cadets to fly.

The idea may have been sound, indeed it may have been essential for the future course of the war, but the presentation was appalling. Each of us I think had a guilty feeling about being in the land of plenty when our families and friends were suffering the most awful hardship, and we were now being invited to stay away for another two years. There was no rush of volunteers although the required numbers were presumably recruited since the authorities did not resort to compulsion. What we were not told was that our papers had been endorsed "suitable flying instructor material" or words to that effect, and that when we returned to England, that was to be our fate anyway. At the time the phrase "economical with the truth" was not in common usage but it should have been. So it was back to England and the war which they had kindly kept going in our absence.

CHAPTER III
COME FLY WITH ME

Training in America finished with a last flight at the end of April 1942, and my next flight was in very different circumstances, in Scotland and, to be absolutely precise, at No. 2 Flying Instructors' School, Montrose, Angus. I do not recall anyone asking what we would wish to do and it perhaps is one of those niceties that disappears in wartime. Whatever the case, there I was starting a course for which I was ill-prepared and for which I had little enthusiasm. The school was equipped with two types of aircraft, both manufactured by Miles Aircraft, now long defunct, the Magister and the Master. The theory was that instructors were produced capable of manning Elementary or Advanced Training Schools and, by starting on the Magister, those totally unsuited to the role could be scrubbed without having wasted too much of the taxpayers' money. My fellow students were mostly operational pilots being "rested" and could not have been nicer, but their very presence was a constant reminder that I had not earned a rest. This was the low point of my service life, my morale was at rock-bottom, and it need not have been so if only someone had put a time limit on how long this instructing caper was to last. As it was I had a mental image of years stretching ahead with me climbing into a Master every morning with yet another bone-headed student, and the prospect did not please.

For a month we flew the Magisters, learning instructional technique and how to keep talking whilst demonstrating manoeuvres to those slightly less qualified than I was. It was late summer, the Scottish countryside was beautiful, but it still was not quite what I had planned. The only diversion from the grinding routine came when we joined the search for the aircraft in which the Duke of Kent had gone missing. One of our group excitedly reported wreckage up in the hills, but when a ground party reached the spot it turned out to be an aircraft from the First War that had never previously been seen. This was slightly sobering for those of us that still had a lot of local flying ahead of us. The change to the Masters brought a lift in that they were better-performing and therefore slightly more exciting. The three variants had Kestrel, Mercury and Pratt & Whitney engines, and of these, the Master with its Kestrel was the only one to cause me any grief.

I was giving simulated instruction to a fellow trainee, one Flying Officer Radwanski, a Polish officer who had flown in the Battle of Britain and whom I therefore greatly respected. During a practice forced landing with him as pupil, we found our field and set up the approach, with no intention of landing. He was, in my judgement, clearly going to make it so with a jolly "I have control" I took over from the back seat to overshoot. Unfortunately the Kestrel engine coughed but produced no power and the practice was suddenly for real. I put the thing down but, despite my best efforts, the brakes just were not up to stopping us and we slid gently into the hedge. Neither of us was damaged but the leading edge of the starboard wing was modified to the point where we could not taxy back and take off again. This was very depressing to me although Radwanski, who had suffered similar incidents before, seemed unmoved and saw it as some sort of baptism for me! The course dragged on and, at the end of September, we were declared competent to instruct on Magister and Master aircraft and went our separate ways. I was mildly surprised, on arriving at No. 15 EFTS at Carlisle, to find that there was neither Magister nor Master in sight, but there were a lot of Tiger Moths!

It had apparently been realised that a great deal of time, effort and money was being wasted by sending people with no air experience at all to flying schools where they immediately showed persistent airsickness or a complete inability to assess their height above the ground when landing. The solution was a short course of basic flying to gauge the potential of the students before committing them to serious training. It was called "grading" and led to a sharp increase in the number of instructors required to fulfil the task, which is why I found myself at Carlisle. This was a prewar flying school staffed largely by the Flying Club personnel, now in uniform, who had been doing the job for years. The only bright spot for me was that I met some of my former classmates from America, notably Campbell Kerr and John Bradburn, both Scotsmen who were delighted to be so close to home, a feeling I did not share. The new boys were sent off to operate from dispersal airfields during the day, ferrying the aircraft over in the morning and returning them to the main base in the evening. We operated from Burnfoot and the daily to-ing and fro-ing were good for our formation flying and for some combat, real Red Baron stuff. The job itself was sometimes quite rewarding when a lad with clear ability cropped up and was a delight to fly with, but there were also some terrible turkeys who had chosen the wrong profession.

After three months of this it was a relief to be posted to No. 5 (P) Advanced Flying Unit at Tern Hill to resume my slightly dodgy career on the Miles Master. This school was established to allow people trained abroad to become familiar with the markedly different conditions in England. I had a great sympathy with their problems because navigation was a nightmare, comparatively speaking, since great efforts had been made to conceal landmarks and airfields, usually with some success. On the other hand, maps showed so much detail that considerable skill was required to determine exactly which railway line was below. In most of the training areas of Canada and the United States there was only one railway within a couple of hundred miles and the chances of mistake were sharply reduced.

Once again, the staff were old fighter pilots on a rest tour. Many of them seemed to be enjoying the change whilst others returned to their squadrons at the weekends, busily arranging a return to operational duty. The work was not arduous, usually three one-hour trips a day. When the conversion to type had been done the instructor was virtually a safety pilot keeping the new boys out of trouble until they had started to find their way around without help. I experienced another engine failure with a Kestrel-engined Master, close enough to the runway to land without any drama, and on another occasion had a tyre burst on touchdown which concentrated my mind for a moment. Neither incident was important except that, after the second one, the Wing Commander Flying sent for me to give me a slight pat on the back. During this interview he asked if I was happy in my work which, curiously, was the first time anyone had ever put the question. I stated my case and he obviously took note because a few weeks later he sent for me again, this time to say that there was a posting available to Kidlington, near Oxford, which I might wish to consider. He was not selling it very well and I wondered how it had reached me, about 48th in line for posting. He mentioned something about twins and the penny dropped: nobody from this strictly fighter environment would consider it. Once again I packed my bags and headed south, but this time with a sense of anticipation – at least it would be different.

Kidlington, appropriately, was equipped with Airspeed Oxford twin-engined trainers which were considerably larger than anything that I had flown thus far. After the initial strangeness of climbing into the aircraft rather then putting it on, I took to it like a duck to water. The promise was held out of an operational posting upon the successful completion of the course and for the first time in a long while I had a target again. It was now halfway through 1943, a year since I had graduated with such high hopes from training and, apart from meeting some nice people, in my own estimation I had achieved very little. This was not entirely true because those 'wasted' hours in the air had all taught me something, although at the time that was not clear to me.

By July, with 50 Oxford hours under my belt, it was off to Kinloss on the Moray Firth for Operational Conversion to the Whitley, that extraordinary aircraft that always seemed to be going downhill. This was really entering a man's world with people other than pilots in the aeroplane. It surprises me now to see that after only 1½ hours' dual I was turned loose with a navigator and radio operator who had absolutely no reason to assume that they would ever land safely. Similarly, after 50 minutes of dual at night (two landings), I set off on a cross-country with a full crew. I was not unique, everyone else did the same; it was just the system.

"Crewing up" was a bit like courtship, a careful survey of the field was desirable before leaping into any long-term arrangements. My first choice was Harry Whittaker, based solely on the fact that he was an Observer (as opposed to Navigator or Bomb Aimer), which meant that he been trained in both jobs and had some experience since the two roles had been split for some time. Laurie Howes was Harry Whittaker's chum so we got him, and they acted as my intelligence agents to recruit another navigator and a rear gunner whilst I was away improving my piloting skills. They came up with John Thompson, a quiet, shy Englishman of studious demeanour, and George Ochs, an Australian of quite opposite appearance. Harry decided that dropping bombs entailed far less work than navigating and opted for that slot. George just wanted to shoot things which I put down to his harsh, colonial background. We flew day and night cross-countries, this time with no friendly beacons or brightly-lit towns showing the way but with a man with a sharp pencil telling me where to go. His charts were so neat that they were frequently pinned to the bulletin board as examples of how it should be done. We dropped practice bombs on targets all over the country until finally we were given the real thing which, although only 250 lb, gave a good indication of how much damage could be done. We affiliated with fighters to learn crew cooperation in evading attack and for the rear gunner to get used to the idea of flying with his back to the engines and to remember that his instruction to dive left meant the reverse to me.

Six weeks after starting we were on our way again, by this time an established crew, slowly getting used to each other's foibles and strengths. The bonding was immediate and intense and any one of us would defend any of the others in any circumstances, regardless of right or wrong. I imagine submarine crews were much the same; "interdependence" was not a word in general use at the time, but that is what it was and I revelled in it.

Whitleys were no longer in the front line although they were useful for training and introducing the quite different techniques required to operate aircraft of heavy weight and high inertia.

Our final training was to be done at the Heavy Conversion Unit at Marston Moor, commanded by Group Captain Leonard Cheshire, before he returned to operations and won the Victoria Cross. 1652 Conversion Unit was equipped with Halifax aircraft with four Rolls-Royce Merlin engines, and looked seriously big close up. They were never meant for training and the men who showed us how to fly them were the real heroes. They demonstrated a take-off, flew around for a while showing the effect of opening the bomb-doors, lowering the flaps, losing an engine and so on and then landed. The student meantime was standing alongside with no dual controls, not even a seat. The instructor pilot then handed over his seat to the student and stood alongside whilst the student repeated the exercise. That was bravery of an order not often seen.

Trouble started with taxying for take-off and ended with taxying back to dispersal. Four engines, even at idling, produce a lot of power so that the aeroplane always seemed to be getting away and turning, using differential throttle, seemed to make matters worse. In the air it was easy and had a feel of great strength about it, although manoeuvring of any kind was good for the biceps. "Corkscrewing," the recommended evasive action when under fighter attack, was better than pumping iron, and had rather more purpose too.

The rules were that after his first conversion trip a pilot was allowed to fly with an operational crew of a local squadron. On the 19th November 1943 I flew in a Halifax for the first time with an Australian, Flying Officer Bill Virgo, DFM; the appropriateness of his name did not strike me at the time. On that same night I flew to Leverkusen with Flight Lieutenant Pete Cadman of 77 Squadron, Elvington.

As explained above my net contribution to the operation was as 147 lb of ballast; I could do nothing to help, but was asked politely to move from time to time when the bomb aimer needed access to the nose. I was surprised at the calm that prevailed throughout the aircraft as the crew went through their well-rehearsed routine. There were occasional course corrections from the navigator, and Pete checking the gunners from time to time, but generally, silence.

I was also surprised to learn that it was possible to hear anti-aircraft shells exploding around the aircraft even although they were not very close. The target was under cloud and we bombed on sky markers dropped by the Path Finders who were there ahead of us. Looking down I was impressed by the way the bombers were shown in silhouette as the searchlights played on the cloud, and how easy it should be for the night-fighters to select their targets. I then realised that of course if the guns were firing, any sensible night-fighter would stay well out of the way, and that perhaps the time to start worrying would be when the guns stopped.

The run in to the aiming point, with the bomb aimer directing the aircraft from his position in the nose, required some skill and determination in the light of all the activity going on around us, but "bomb doors open" was followed by a quite distinct surge as the bombs were released and the doors closed. The navigator gave a new heading, the aircraft turned, and we were on our way home. The terse communication of the outward leg was repeated on the way back until, after coasting out over Holland, the flight engineer asked if I would like a cup of coffee. I found it both exhilarating and exhausting. When the attack was over there was an inescapable feeling that the job had been done and that we might as well land now, overlooking entirely the fact that we were three hours flying time from home. Many more capable than myself have tried to convey the feeling of excitement and relief that went with being back in friendly airspace, and better still back at home base, but I have never seen it captured in print. Perhaps it is just one of those things that defy description.

There was a performance hierarchy in Bomber Command which became clear when there was sufficient moonlight or the searchlights were active. At the bottom of the stack were Wellingtons and Stirlings, with Halifaxes above them and Lancasters higher still. If Mosquitoes were operating they were so far above everyone else as to be out of sight. All these impressions were gathered on the Leverkusen sortie and analysed later when I attempted to tell my crew all about it.

After that burst of excitement it was back to the training, and we rapidly increased our crew skills as we flew dummy attacks on bombing ranges reached after the most tortuous routes with very strict timing. We were now seven, having collected a mid-upper gunner, Bob Benton, and a flight engineer, Jack Blackshaw. We all got along well considering our different backgrounds and the unusual circumstances which had brought about our meeting.

Marston Moor is not a congenial spot in winter, and the winter of 1943 was cold. We lived in Nissen huts heated (if that is not a slight over-statement) by a pot-bellied stove fuelled by about three lumps of coal per day. Everything was damp either because rain/snow was penetrating the fabric of the building or because of the condensation caused by a dozen warm bodies. On some of the worst nights we slept in our fur-lined Irving suits, and still shivered. The domestic part of the station was not well administered but the flying side was good because the instructors had all done it and could convey with conviction and authority the reasons for following their advice. The pilots did not instruct in the way that I had been taught, but demonstrated what they required us to do as often as necessary for us to understand. I liked it all and began to feel at last that I was getting to grips with a proper job. Accidents were not infrequent although, having in mind the inadequacy of the aircraft used for training, fewer than might have been predicted. The most curious was a novice crew – like us – finishing a night exercise and going into the overshoot on landing, for reasons unknown, probably a brake failure. The ground was so soft that the Halifax went on to its nose and stayed there. The rear gunner, with great presence of mind, turned his turret on beam and went out backwards, the normal emergency escape route. He fell about 60 feet and was the only member of the crew to be injured.

For recreation we visited York, and particularly Betty's Bar, known locally as "4 Group Briefing Room." It was alleged that any spy who wanted to know the target for the night had only to buy himself a half-pint and stand at the bar. Someone, it was said, had always attended briefing but then been withdrawn from the operation and felt compelled to tell someone else the secret. This may have been true but it seemed to me more likely that when the defences appeared to have been alerted it was because it was difficult to conceal 500 heavy bombers droning across the Continent.

Trips to the villages in the area were less popular because we were obviously resented by some of the local people. There were several theories for why this should be and I favoured the one that said we made serious dents in the limited beer supplies that were available.

The course at Marston Moor was completed in some style with our last training flight, a night cross-country, starting on Christmas Eve and finishing on Christmas morning. An eventful year was coming to a close and, as a crew, we faced the future with great confidence, mostly misplaced.

Before completing our flying preparation for the operational squadron there was the formality of "escape and evasion" conducted at RAF Dishforth. This ground course was designed to assist those unfortunate enough to be shot down to evade capture or to escape. We were introduced to the silk escape maps and compasses made into trouser buttons; we were also advised how to seek help if in occupied territory, and things not to do if in Germany, like – shoot someone. We did a lot of running through muddy ditches and falling on rolls of barbed wire to make a bridge for our companions who took great delight in leaving footprints in the small of the back. It was very like Torquay only with rather more purpose. The graduation exercise was for us to be dropped off in pairs from aircrew buses blacked out for the purpose, at dead of night in the middle of the Yorkshire moors. The police and Home Guard were alerted to the exercise and were on the lookout for us. We were required to wear flying boots, khaki denim trousers with our aircrew battledress jackets and no caps so that we were easily distinguishable. We were each allowed to take two pennies, the cost of a telephone call, in order to contact the Station in case of serious accident.

Harry Whittaker and I formed a team and were dumped in cold, miserable rain in the middle of nowhere. The bus pulled away and we debated what course to take. It seemed sensible to go back the way the bus had come, so we set out, walking at a brisk pace. After a short while I confessed to Harry that I had concealed a 10 shilling note in my flying boot and was not too surprised when he admitted having done the same. You can see that we were beginning to think like a crew.

After half an hour of moist walking I was sure that I could hear voices and we paused, turning to pick up the sound above the wind. It was pitch black but we walked in the direction of the noise and came eventually to a pub. The noise we had heard was the revelling in the bar. We walked in, to be asked by the landlord if we were in the escape and evasion exercise! We bought a pint of beer and he told us that someone on the exercise always found his pub and, if we were prepared to share a room, it would be five shillings each, including breakfast. It was the best offer we were ever likely to get and the next morning we travelled with the milkman to the railway station where we spent the rest of our money on a ticket back to camp. We were not the first ones back by any means but we were better rested than most.

CHAPTER IV
IN THE STILL OF THE NIGHT

We were posted to No. 158 Squadron at Lissett, near Bridlington, and arrived there in early January 1944. It was the first squadron to be rearmed with the Halifax 3 with Hercules radial engines instead of Merlins, and it has to be said that they transformed the aircraft. For the first time we were able to look down on Lancasters because of our greater cruising altitude. The same trick was tried with the Lancaster and, although I never flew one, I believe that the Merlin-engined variants remained superior. The aircraft were all factory fresh and looked very smart, if anything built for such a sinister purpose can qualify as smart.

The Squadron Commander was Jock Calder, a young man already distinguished who, in his mid-twenties, was a Flight Lieutenant Acting Wing Commander. After a brief introduction he invited me to fly with him that night and so I found myself for the first time in the real briefing room. It is difficult to describe the air of nonchalance adopted by the crews, and particularly the captains, as they assembled. I felt a certain apprehension even though I was to fly with the most experienced crew on the squadron, so how come the others were so relaxed? It was pure theatre of course except that even the "audience" were putting on a bit of a show as well as the leading performers.

The Station Commander, Group Captain John Whitley, who had himself been shot down and evaded capture, opened proceedings by welcoming us as though to a discussion in which our views would be sought. He was followed by the Intelligence Officer who had the privilege of opening the green baize curtains which covered the route map to the target. I do not remember why Magdeburg was important, but it certainly looked a long way from Bridlington.

Briefing contained a lot of information on the weather, defences, turning points and target markers which you might expect, but then a lot of other things which perhaps the mind preferred not to dwell on: diversion airfields in case of fuel shortage or damage, emergency airfields in case of bomb hang-ups which could not be cleared and frequencies to be used before ditching – all practical stuff but enough to destroy any idea that it was all for fun. The squadron boss flew with all the other "leaders" so that the senior navigator, wireless operator, gunner, bomb-aimer and flight engineer were all in his crew, and each had completed at least one tour of operations, some of them many more. The atmosphere of calm that I had experienced with Pete Cadman was repeated, but in spades. Whatever was going on inside, externally they all seemed bored to death. For me it was standing room only again but the trip was uneventful. I was astonished to hear on the

BBC News the following day that 55 aircraft were missing and could only wonder how that could have happened without our seeing anyone shot down. At night, with so much going on, unless you happened to be quite close to the stricken aircraft, you saw very little of the sometimes horrendous losses that occurred.

I was now on my own and, a week later, led my crew into the same briefing room with the curtains drawn over the route map, concealing for the moment our night's activity. The procedure was always the same and this time when the curtains parted there was a straight red line leading to Berlin. This was the target that was talked of in awe by those that knew, but I lacked the experience to be daunted.

In the short time that we had been on the squadron there had been some losses, but then there were always losses in wartime flying operations, even in training. It was not long before I realised that things were not good and that a lot of men were not there for the breakfast that followed de-briefing after a trip. Some losses were without doubt due to pressing on when the sensible thing to do was turn back, as those of us that survived such indiscretion appreciated. On our first operation together, in a brand new aircraft, I did all the checks before taxying and take-off but, as soon as the wheels retracted, I lost all contact with the mid-upper and rear gunner. We had an emergency system of lights which enabled the gunners to order evading action by pressing the appropriate direction button for a dive to port or starboard. This brought up an arrow on the instrument panel showing the pilot which way to dive, but it was an emergency system and no one in his right mind would set out for Berlin with only that for the defence of the aircraft. Furthermore, if we were attacked and one of the gunners was injured, I would only know about it by sending another crew member back to check. Overriding all these thoughts was the fear of failing on our first trip. With a bit more experience I would have turned back immediately. We kept going and the trip was a breeze although there was a lot going on all around us and we did see some explosions in the air that did not look like decoys. I reported the defect after landing, but the following night, same aircraft, same target, it happened again. This time my reason for not turning back was that we had done it before – no sweat – but secretly I was fearful that when we landed and the intercom was found to be working (as it was with the wheels down), lack of moral fibre might be suspected, the fate worse than being shot down.

The first few days of February were spent in trying to rectify the fault on what we had come to regard as *our* aircraft, which in every other respect was a good one. The radio fault was finally traced, but another crew took it over for one trip and were lost. For our third trip as a crew we again went to the Big City so that the others were beginning to think that it was the only target in Germany. It was learning the trade the hard way but toughened us up for the months that were to follow.

The Hercules engine was vulnerable to a defect known as "coring" in which the oil temperature and pressure went up together in defiance of all logic and good engineering practice. However, the instructions were firm: if it happened, feather the engine and return. On our seventh operation, to Schweinfurt, east of Frankfurt, it happened to us and we went through the tiresome routine of jettisoning our bombs and returning on three engines. Nearly four hours of flying time wasted. The target was one of those that came to be called "panacea," hit it and the war would be over, but it suffered no damage at our hands. I remember the US 8th Air Force going there several times to destroy the ball-bearing factories, but through no fault of theirs the enemy managed to keep going.

In early March we went to Stuttgart, a fair trip for a Halifax, with forecast winds that made return to North Yorkshire unlikely without refuelling, and our nominated diversion was Hartford Bridge (now Blackbushe). I think that half of Bomber Command was in there, all creeping in with very low fuel states, and calling for priority landing in increasingly high-pitched voices. The station was coping well and had commandeered the NAAFI as a temporary debriefing room, and rounded up every Intelligence Officer for miles around to assist. None of this is important but we found ourselves debriefing next to a Lancaster crew and I was humbled to hear that they had matched our bomb load exactly, plus a 4,000 lb 'cookie'; some aeroplane!

Later that month, targetting changed and we found ourselves going to France and attacking marshalling yards, until that point considered pretty small beer for the heavies, but then we did not know that D-Day was approaching. This proved to be a brief respite, and it was soon back to Frankfurt, Essen and Berlin. We had by now completed 16 trips as a crew and, sad to say, were amongst the most senior on the squadron which, in its worst-ever patch, had lost 16 crews in 4 sorties. This was without doubt the main reason for our being sent down to join the Path Finder Force which drew its crews from the survivors of the Main Force.

PFF had a Navigation Training Unit at Warboys in Cambridgeshire and the title was important because the essence of the entire concept was accurate navigation and split-second timing to ensure that, regardless of weather, there was something to aim at when the main force arrived at the target. This meant that my navigators disappeared for a week whilst the rest of us were gainfully employed in flying around other navigators, in Merlin-engined Halifax 2s! That's progress. Soon however, another pilot and myself climbed aboard a Lancaster 3, with a PFF captain, to be given a quick whizz before trying it for ourselves. The other chap was Ian Bazalgette who was to join 635 squadron with me, and to be awarded a posthumous VC.

Despite my affection for the Halifax, the Lancaster really was something else. It handled better, appeared to have no vices and was a delight to fly. We stayed at Warboys for the rest of April, doing some more day- and night-flying in the Lancaster with full bomb loads, and some fighter affiliation to give the gunners an idea of what sort of manoeuvres we could get away with. In May, we joined 635 (PFF) Squadron at Downham Market, in the county of Norfolk.

The assault on French targets was really under way by now, and what the USAAF missed by day we had a go at by night. It must have been most unpleasant for anyone on the ground. There was the occasional return to Germany, but generally our efforts were being concentrated on anything that might interfere with the invasion, which must surely be imminent. On the night of the invasion I remember the briefing officer saying that, just for once, he was not interested in any shipping in the Channel that we might see on radar or by eyeball.

We worked our way up the PFF ladder, first as "supporters," carrying a normal bomb load and providing company to the more experienced crews that were marking the target, then as "backers-up" or "illuminators" when we carried flares so the visual markers could see the target, or just dropped more target indicators on the aiming point, already marked by someone ahead of us. We were all briefed to fly the same route to and from the target and, although it was unusual to see other aircraft, we were aware of their presence as we hit their slipstream.

The defences sometimes started blasting away as soon as they picked us up, and at other targets it was easy to think that we must be at the wrong address until the first markers or bombs went down. When it was clear to them that they were the object of our visit the lights went on and the guns started. The quiet period was often the time for the night-fighters to try to intercept the lead aircraft, knowing by experience that if they could prevent us from marking the target, the main force coming along behind would have nothing to bomb. I do not believe that they ever succeeded in thwarting an attack.

Returning to Downham Market very early in the morning of June 15th, having attacked yet another target in France, we were at low level crossing the Thames Estuary when something overtook us going very quickly and apparently on fire. At debriefing I mentioned this to the Intelligence Officer who almost put his hand over my mouth. We had seen one of the first V-1 (*Vergeltungswaffe* – "retaliation") weapons and we were sworn to secrecy. There must have been panic in Whitehall at the thought that the long-suffering population was about to be subjected to more brutality, just when

28

things were beginning to look better. Since our intelligence was usually very good I suspect that a plan to overcome this new menace had already been evolved because we were quickly diverted to find and destroy the launching sites, just across the Channel, and in daylight. I had by now graduated to Deputy Master Bomber, the understudy who only took over if the leading performer took sick, but it was quite close to the action.

Operating at night, as I have explained, we saw some other aircraft and felt their slipstream but in daylight, if the skies were not exactly black with aeroplanes they were certainly dark grey. Numbers on the daylight attacks were much smaller too and yet I began to wonder how on earth we avoided each other during those long, dark routes to and from targets at night. I suspect that we shall never know how many collisions occurred because nobody would have survived such an event, and seeing an aircraft explode was reported by witnesses as due to flak or fighters.

It was disconcerting to be flying low over the target in order to mark the aiming point, or sometimes to cancel an errant marker by dropping one of a different colour on it, straight and level under the bomb-aimers' instructions, and to become aware that someone had opened his bomb-doors right above you. The rear gunner had a particularly good view of the bombs going past our aircraft on their way down. When we had completed 45 sorties, those that wished were allowed to retire with honour, since that was the commitment that we had made on joining the Path Finders. My engineer and rear gunner decided that they would exercise this option and this presented me with a slight dilemma since patently we should need to regroup. We had done some "blind marking" as well as "visual" and the consensus was that the latter was more enjoyable since we actually saw the results of our efforts. In blind marking, the markers were dropped over the aiming point suspended on parachutes and were visible for a few minutes until they burned out or entered cloud. The process would be repeated so that following aircraft always had something to bomb. This was possible because, in addition to dead reckoning navigation, we had a pretty basic radar which was quite effective if the target was big enough or close to a coastline or major river system which could easily be identified. Target Indicators were therefore dropped, rather than aimed, by the Path Finder blind markers. The visual crews carried a bomb aimer who took no part in the navigation of the aircraft at all; that was done by two navigators, one with a sharp pencil and the other looking at the radar screen. Ten miles or so from the target, the bomb aimer was given a shake and went forward to the nose armed with photographs of the approaches to the target and the aiming point. With experience, this task was combined with voice control of the attack as Master Bomber or Deputy. The decision having been made, we returned to Warboys for three or four days to pick up some replacements. I should have said our navigator had felt some time before that this was not his line of business and had become an instructor at a navigation school. I put it all down to the fact that on one night attack he had opened the curtains behind which he normally operated in stygian gloom and had seen what was going on outside. He kept going for a little while after that but I sensed that his heart was not really in it. There were periods of silence when I knew from my own briefing that a course change was due, and on one never-to-be-forgotten occasion we were 8 minutes early on the target and received what seemed to be the undivided attention of the entire Luftwaffe night-fighter force. Understandably so, we were the only ones there.

At Warboys we chose a young man called Pat Murphy as Nav1 (the plotter), John Smith as Nav2 (the radar man), and, somewhat confusingly, a Tiny Smith who was returning for yet another tour as a flight engineer. The last choice, to replace our rear-gunner, was Bob Telford; he had the misfortune to be labelled "headless crew," which meant that on one occasion when he was not operating for some reason his crew had been lost, leaving him out of work temporarily. This meant that whenever a crew was short of a gunner they sent for him, and he had grown tired of flying with strangers. I found this rather touching and he was welcomed to the group.

On return to the Squadron we found that the Canadian army was having a certain difficulty at Falaise where the German armour had been rounded up but refused to surrender. Someone who perhaps should have known better decided that this was a job for the heavies, and the C-in-C Bomber Command, realising that his crews were not used to attacking close to friendly troops, ordered No. 6 Group, predominantly of the Royal Canadian Air Force, to take it on. By this time we had air supremacy in the area; all the German fighters had been withdrawn for the defence of the Fatherland, and we were free to roam at will and at any height. After the first wave had dropped their bombs there was so much dust that there was no point in re-marking the target for a while and we simply stopped the attack. Sadly our instructions were ignored and the bombing continued. I fear that many soldiers were killed, and it was a complete waste. We flew around taking note of individual aircraft still bombing, and receiving some fairly unfriendly gestures in the process, but it was inexcusable, and we reported them on our return. Afterwards I realised how shrewdly the C-in-C had selected the force for the attack. I should not leave the impression that I felt this was in any way a deliberate disregard of orders. The probability is that, having heard clear instructions to bomb the target indicators, the pilots switched back to intercom and heard no further messages. Ironically, soon afterwards, the Supreme Commander sent a message saying how cheered the troops were to see our aircraft over the battlefield in such great numbers.

The next month, September, the army were again in trouble, this time with the garrison at Le Havre who had not seen the light and refused to surrender. It was a mistake on their part; we visited them four times in a week, bombing with great care because a lot of French people were trapped in the city. Aside from the odd round of anti-aircraft fire there was no opposition and we were able to minimise the risk to our allies by halting the attack when we lost sight of the precise aiming point.

As we grew in experience we found it less difficult to find casual crewmen when one of the regulars had a cold or some other mild ailment which stopped him flying. One night John Smith was suffering and the Navigation Leader, Bernard Moorcroft, took his place. We went to Kiel and had one of the roughest rides of all time, not only being hit by flak but also collecting some holes from a night-fighter. I thanked the Nav. Leader and told him not to call me, I would call him. We flew a couple of trips in a modified Lancaster with uprated Merlin engines which had been given to the squadron to see how it worked operationally. The improved performance was easily measurable and gave us the not inconsiderable advantage of being first home.

By the end of October we were finished, having flown a few extra sorties to finish off those members of the crew who, for one reason or another, had missed the odd sortie and who, reasonably enough, did not much fancy operating with somebody else. Strangely, on reflection, this was not the signal for a huge party. Pat Connolly, the Flight Commander, joined us for a few beers and the Squadron Commander had us all in for a brief chat, but their war was not over and for us there was a sense of anti-climax. In later years I often thought what a strange way it was to live, going to bed when everyone else was getting up and trying to sleep for a few hours before checking the order of battle for the night to see if we were on again. We stuck to the routine that had worked so far in the hope that some protection was inherent in it. For example, we flew with a toy Scottie terrier which my mother had given to me for luck, and which was always carried by the mid-upper gunner. The dog was also shown on the side of our aircraft with a lead in his mouth on the other end of which was a dachshund with a swastika cummerbund. Climbing aboard one night Bob Benton realised that he had left the toy in the locker room and went back on a petrol tanker to collect it before take-off. I know that it had no magic properties but he was most uneasy about being in his turret without it.

That was the end of Bomber Command for me and in another 25 years in the service I never served in it again although, as we shall see, I got close on one occasion.

CHAPTER V

TIE ME KANGAROO DOWN, SPORT

In October 1944 I flew my 62nd and last operation with 635 (PFF) Squadron and began to wonder what would happen next. My question was quickly answered by my squadron commander, Tubby Baker, who outlined the grand plan to form a VIP squadron of Privateer aircraft (B-24 Liberators extensively modified for transport work with, amongst other things, a single fin), manned entirely by Path Finder crews. The squadron was to operate in support of the British Pacific Fleet, shortly to be reinforced now that the end or the war in Europe was in sight. There may easily have been such a plan because the abrupt end of the Japanese conflict could not be foreseen at that time; true or not, I believed it. None of my crew was similarly posted, the reason given being that Transport Command had lots of navigators and wireless operators, but were short of captains with four-engine experience. This made absolute sense because the York had yet to appear in significant numbers and transport pilots generally flew twins.

The first step in the fulfilment of this plan was to post several dozen aircrew – no aircraft or ground crew – to Stoney Cross in the New Forest where we took over the Nissen huts recently vacated by the Americans who had moved over to the continent. They must have had a monumental party before they left for everything was in ruins. After three miserable weeks with nothing to do, a Wellington appeared in the circuit and landed. This caused little excitement since, as you may suppose, we had all seen a Wellington before. When it was followed by several others which seemed to be settling in for a long stay, we began to ask questions, and were told that they had been provided for us to keep our hands in. It was just as though someone had suddenly remembered sending a crowd of aircrew to Stoney Cross, but such was our relief at having something to do that we set about the Wellingtons with relish. Most days we flew off to another airfield where we had friends, had lunch, and flew back to Stoney Cross. This was a long way from Privateers and the British Pacific Fleet, but it was quite entertaining and kept us out of mischief – well, mostly.

When the Americans left Stoney Cross they had abandoned their motor fuel stocks in handy 5-gallon cans, clearly marked "Property of US Government." Try as we might we could find no US Government representative to assume responsibility for this fuel so we liberated some of it, enough to visit Lyndhurst, Ringwood and occasionally Southampton. I take no pride in this but it provided a sharp lesson in the dangers of leaving fairly bright and highly-trained young men loafing around with nothing to do. At the time it was even more of a blow to our collective pride since a few weeks before we had been involved in a fairly serious war and now nobody had any idea of where we were going and why.

This sad saga came to an end when we were posted *en bloc* to Merryfield in Somerset to convert to the C-47 Dakota. Evidently there had been a change of plan but frankly we were so relieved to be back on a station with all the amenities that nobody cared particularly. We all converted to the Dakota with no idea of what the future held until we were summoned to the biggest building on the station to hear the revised plan. Some change had become inevitable since the "small, elite ex-Path Finder group" had trebled in size and now consisted predominantly of dyed-in-the-wool transport crews, far too many for the planned VIP Privateer squadron.

The word was that the assembled mob would divide into three parties. The majority would form a new squadron to be based in India. The remainder would further subdivide to complete a squadron already formed in Sydney, New South Wales, with the rest forming a Flight in Brisbane, Queensland. We could each state a preference which, as far as possible, would be respected. I really had no strong views but, because I am addicted to cricket and rugby union, and guessed that Australia would offer better opportunities for both, I opted for Australia and was selected for the Sydney squadron.

Those of us destined for Australia crewed up with a navigator and radio operator, in my case Norman Rowell and Jack Allen, both former members of 635 Squadron, although not of my own former crew. The plot was to go to Montreal to collect new Dakota aircraft, carry out a few shakedown flights, and take them to Australia.

The first leg was easy. We joined the Queen Mary at Southampton and sailed at high speed, out of convoy, to New York. The bulk of the passengers were US soldiers, some wounded and some being repatriated presumably before taking on the Japanese. The voyage was not memorable and was an improvement on my previous Atlantic crossings only because it was quicker. Like all wartime journeys, progress was shrouded in secrecy, as was the route, and I suffered some apprehension when it became apparent that amongst the low clouds touching the ocean there were icebergs. There was no orchestra on board so that a complete repeat of the "Titanic" fiasco was not on, but with no women and children on board and, based purely on a visual assessment, I felt it unlikely that the soldiers would give up their places in the lifeboats to their RAF allies.

In New York, the stevedores and tug men were on strike and the Captain, completely unfazed by this, docked the ship unaided and we carried our baggage to the train waiting to take us to Montreal.

We collected our new aircraft at Dorval and the mystery (to me) of how we would cross the Pacific in these range-limited aeroplanes was solved.

Inside the fuselage, ten 100-gallon overload tanks had been installed, more than doubling the fuel capacity. The tanks were manufactured from what appeared to be fibrous material intended to be both cheap and disposable. The tanks were interconnected and gravity-fed to the main tanks so that no action was required by the crew other than to check the dipstick attached to each filler cap to make sure that they were draining properly. The fuselage smelled like a garage, of course, hardly surprising with 1,000 gallons of high octane fuel in a lash-up of tanks which looked suspiciously porous. We resolved not to smoke.

And so, on the 4th April 1945, our passage to Australia began with a gentle first leg from Montreal to Elizabeth City, North Carolina. The tail number of my aircraft was 356 and, although I did not record the letters, they were almost certainly KK or KN, and it was to prove an extremely reliable if not very stimulating mode of transport. The Dakota was a military version of the Douglas DC-3 with the minimum changes that the role demanded. It was designed to have two pilots and some vital actions, post-take-off and pre-landing, just could not be done by the pilot in the left-hand seat. In contrast, the British heavy bombers had only one pilot, and everything vital to the control of the aircraft was within reach. It was a difference in design philosophy caused probably by our shortage of pilots in wartime.

Our night-stop in Elizabeth City provided my first contact with Russians of any kind and I have to say that it came as a surprise. They were naval aviators converting to Catalina amphibians prior to returning to the Soviet Union. From the shape of their extraordinary caps to the toes of their unpolished boots, with their nearly-matching tunics and trousers in between, they did not strike fear into the beholder. For some curious reason, this image returned years later when the invincibility of their airmen seemed to be accepted by a large proportion of the world's politicians. However, as with some other pronouncements, perhaps the politicians were not expressing their true beliefs.

The next day we departed for Dallas, Texas, taking with us (probably quite illegally) some sailors going on leave. We left the following morning for Sacramento, California which was our departure point for the island of Oahu in Hawaii.

Until that time I had never seen such a vast collection of different aircraft types, all waiting for the weather man to produce a forecast wind that would allow the crews to reach their destinations. In our case, if we could flight plan Oahu in less than 15 hours, we could go. This sounded like an eternity, and indeed felt like it, but my sympathies were with the Catalina crews who were off if they could plan less than 20 hours.

Our hope that our wait for the weather would be long enough to allow some exploration of sunny California was unfulfilled and, after one full day on the ground, we left the following night. Using the forecast wind we had planned 14 hours and 30 minutes which was going to exceed comfortably my previous longest trip.

When we crossed the Californian coast we had a lot of ocean to cross before the next landfall, our destination, Hickham Field. Hickham was famous for having almost been eliminated by the Japanese in their attack on Pearl Harbour in December 1941, at which time I was undergoing pilot training in the United States. Newspapers and radio had naturally given enormous coverage to the event and I had heard President Roosevelt deliver his famous "pages of infamy" speech to the American nation. During this mind-numbing flight I have to say that it went through my semi-active brain that I hoped the Japanese High Command had no plans to repeat the exercise during the next few days.

It had been cold on leaving England, even colder in Canada, with temperatures rising slowly as we travelled westwards across the continent of America. Honolulu was my first experience of stepping out of an aircraft and into a sauna, giving fair warning of the sort of weather we could expect over the next couple of years. We had two full days in Hawaii, swimming, sunbathing more than was sensible, and by now accepting as normal the sort of food that had been missing from our diet for a few years past.

I made one visit to downtown Honolulu, a vastly different place from that now shown in endless TV travelogues. After two weeks on the road I needed a haircut and discovered that all the barbers were female. It was so hot that a crew cut seemed a sensible choice and for good measure I had my moustache removed although I am quite sure it had no cooling effect. This clean-shaven individual, hair en brosse, bright red from too much sun, looked unfamiliar to me in the mirror and caused considerable confusion amongst my acquaintances.

Before dawn on the 12th April we boarded 356 again and I was glowing like a medium-rare hamburger. Even a shirt was uncomfortable on my back and shoulders and it was a painful lesson on the strength of the tropical sun. Our destination was Canton Island, 11½ hours away, giving me plenty of time to regret my overindulgence in the sun and sand of the Officers' Club. After a night stop in Canton we continued to Viti Levu in Fiji, a comparatively short leg of 7½ hours, but not short enough to turn the aircraft around and continue the same day. I remember nothing of Fiji and I have never been back to refresh memories and impressions of what I understand to be magic islands, which is rather a shame. At the time I was not anxious to become more familiar with the sea and sand.

We were now in real danger of reaching our destination with an 8-hour leg to Auckland, New Zealand, a night stop, and then across the Tasman Sea to Sydney – or more precisely Camden, New South Wales, which was to be home for the next year.

The trip from Montreal to Sydney had started on the 4th April and finished 73 hours and 35 minutes flying time later on the 16th April. In that time all we did was refuel and check the oil, and we arrived carrying no unserviceabilities of any kind. In my view this was a very convincing validation of the aircraft.

The squadron had the task of moving personnel and equipment from Australia to the neighbouring islands and as far north as the Philippines. Quite frequently our passengers on the return to Australia were RN medical staff joining ships or escorting wounded back for more extensive treatment than ships or field hospitals could provide. The operational pattern was straightforward. Every day an aircraft was positioned at Mascot, the Sydney airport, to be loaded and with manifests prepared for early morning departure. Whatever the final destination, the same crew flew two legs each day and night-stopped somewhere on the north-east coast, usually Townsville or Mackay. The next day's first leg was to New Guinea, generally Milne Bay but occasionally Port Moresby. In both places the heavy lifting was done by locally recruited labour, an impressive sight. If the Americans thought that the Afro hair style originated there I have news for them! It was real 'bone-through-the-nose' stuff and very colourful. The story was told of a USAAF crew that went into Moresby, when one of the passengers offered a local a dollar to shin up a tree and throw down a coconut. The local refused but promised him five dollars if he would do it. They seemed to be gentle people but were reputed still to be cannibals when the authorities were not watching.

From there we went on to Momote on Manus Island in the Admiralties. Flying time each day varied from 8 to 10 hours depending on the route, but always flown in two legs. The only seating for passengers consisted of canvas stretchers along the fuselage sides with leg room restricted by the freight lashed to the fuselage floor. There was no proper catering for anyone so that to stop every 4 or 5 hours was a relief in every sense of the word.

A round trip, Camden–Momote–Camden took four days. Apart from Sydney and Brisbane, the airstrips were pretty primitive compared with a standard RAF station, with no chance of getting lost whilst taxying. Milne Bay was one way only: arrive over the sea, depart over the sea, avoiding the mountains that surrounded the place. We learned to live with the violent turbulence that started as soon as the sun warmed up, from ground level to heights much greater than we could reach. The tropical storms were also a hazard and were entered with some trepidation since their extent was impossible to gauge and, once in, visibility reduced to zero. We all had an uncomfortable awareness of the clouds with hard centres which surrounded the New Guinea airstrips.

When the need arose the operation was extended to Leyte in the Philippines, reached via Biak, a small island off the north-west of western New Guinea, and Peleliu in the Palau Group. These were coral strips, levelled by the bulldozers of the US Navy Construction Battalions (Sea Bees), and capable of operating the biggest aircraft. There were no hangars and the control towers were all of a pattern, about 50 feet high and hammered together from 6" x 6" timber. The most impressive aspects of these airfields were the provision of all the essentials for running a very large air support operation and, in addition, delicious fresh ice-cream and a different movie every night. I may say that this contrasted sharply with airfields under what might loosely be termed "British" control, that is Royal Navy, RAAF or RNZAF.

This routine was quickly established and, although not very exciting, the flying was interesting with new destinations and a wide cross-section of new acquaintances. We averaged about 70 hours a month, with occasional bursts up to 90 hours. This left very little time at Camden which was perhaps as well since it had not much to offer. The town of Camden was really a village, with one pub and not much else.

The pub/hotel was to cause me some anxious days when, following a party in the mess attended by my new radio officer Bill Kendall and his fiancée, the only local taxi failed to show at the appointed time to return Zena DuBois to the hotel. It had been quite a good party, not riotous because we were flying the next day, and when Bill explained the problem I urged him to relax and leave it with me. A quick recce showed three or four staff cars parked around the mess and I borrowed one to drive my crewman and his lady back to the Camden hotel. Departure from the station was uneventful and, the delivery of Zena accomplished, Bill and I were returning to the airfield. Up to this point we had not seen another vehicle, but suddenly we observed a Jeep approaching somewhat erratically with its headlights flashing. I stopped and the Jeep driver proved to be Dickie Dawes, officer-in-charge of mechanical transport, to whom the loss of the squadron commander's staff car had been reported. Bless his heart, Dickie said that he would claim to have found the staff car unattended and persuaded me, who happened to be taking a constitutional nearby, to drive his Jeep back to the garage whilst he led the way in the recovered staff car. You may judge from this which of us had had the better party. I suggested that this would not work and that the only thing to do was declare it a fair cop. No damage of any kind had been done and I should get off with five to ten years.

The next day my crew left with another captain, whilst I faced the squadron boss, a man called Charlie Warren with whom I had, until now, enjoyed a quite friendly relationship. This was a different Charlie and he informed me quite briskly that I was confined to quarters and, dressed in my best tropical uniform with tunic and tie, I would await the pleasure of the Acting Station Commander. It seemed to me at the time that rather a meal was being made of a harmless incident which circumstances had forced upon me although later, when I learned of the existence of King's Regulations and Air Council Instructions, I realised that Charlie Warren did not have a wide choice of actions open to him.

My quarters consisted of a room in a timber-framed hut with one window. The temperature and humidity were matched at 90, my crew were long gone, nobody was speaking to me and I was left stewing for a couple of days before being sent for by the Acting Station Commander. Having been escorted to his door by the adjutant, I knocked and was bidden to enter.

I marched in smartly, saluted and then realised that the Wing Commander had his feet on the desk, a cigarette in his hand, and was smiling. He opened the discussion by saying: "Well, Johnnie, I understand that you haven't been doing so well again." It was the "again" that hurt because until then such misdemeanours as I had committed had gone undetected. He went on to say that the road from camp to Camden was tricky, especially in the dark, and that the bridge was an accident black spot. He could not recommend driving that road after a party and went on to suggest that my driving skills exceeded my intelligence by a significant amount. He concluded by thanking me for ensuring that Miss DuBois had been returned safely to her hotel, and added that my crew were awaiting my arrival at Brisbane if I would care to join them.

Australia is a snake-infested desert surrounded by shark-infested waters with a narrow coastal strip which at that time was inhabited by some of the least attractive people it had been my misfortune to meet. And yet, this unpromising background has produced some rare jewels and William John McLean was one of them. He was then serving in the Royal Australian Air Force and was commanding Camden pending the arrival of an RAF group captain. I spent the next 25 years in the Royal Air Force and never met another man who would have handled such a serious offence with such calm and understanding and I freely confess that, in other circumstances, my career could have stopped there. Like so many Australians who are loyal to their country but can nevertheless see its shortcomings, he transferred to the Royal Air Force and I was to meet him again.

Soon after this event we were detailed to fly a group of British scientists with their RAF minder on a tour of unlikely places that we had difficulty finding on a map, never mind in the Pacific Ocean. We went to Guam in the

Marianas, Eniwetok and Kwajelein in the Marshall Islands and Piva on Bougainville. I never knew what they were reconnoitering but I strongly suspect that Christmas Island finally got the job!

The Japanese war came to an abrupt end following the attacks with atomic weapons against Hiroshima on August 6th and Nagasaki on August 9th. On the 14th the Emperor accepted the terms of surrender and the formal signing of the instrument of surrender took place aboard the USS Missouri on September 2nd. Whilst the morality of nuclear weapons will be argued forever, and the cases for and against are too well-known to be rehearsed here, the certainties seem to me to be that the effect of the two strikes certainly caught the attention of the Japanese and for years afterwards maintained the peace because of their awesome example.

It might be thought that this would have signalled the end of the Far Eastern saga from my point of view but, even as the instrument of surrender was being redrafted for the 'n'th time, I was sent to Tocumwal, New South Wales to convert to the B-24 Liberator. Earlier stories of a Privateer VIP squadron regained currency and no other sensible explanation for this unlikely detachment could be found. Tocumwal had the run-down appearance of most other Australian military installations that I saw, difficult to avoid in near-desert conditions with sand blowing everywhere. We were issued with bicycles for travelling between the mess and the flight line and the order on one of the road signs remains with me to this day: it read "No double-dinking" and, since I had never knowingly 'double-dinked' in my life, puzzled me every time I rode past. Eventually, and half suspecting that the sign had only been erected to catch the Poms, I asked what it meant. It turned out that to 'double-dink' was to carry a passenger on the crossbar of the bicycle and I gave my solemn oath never to do so on the station.

The Liberator was a good pilots' aeroplane which handled nicely and, of course, had a tricycle undercarriage, which increased by a wide margin the amount of concrete required for take-off and landing. I did not experience, nor have I read about, the effect of brake failure on landing a B-24 but, assuming that he did not retract the wheels, the pilot would be well advised to look for a 10,000-yard runway into wind. It was again interesting to compare the design philosophies of the British and Americans in the heavy aircraft field. In the Liberator, great attention had been paid to crew comfort and self-protection, with war load subordinated to those require-ments, whereas in the Lancaster the reverse was the case. The ten days at Tocumwal passed pleasantly enough and I returned to Camden, qualified day and night on the B-24, to await the next move.

We returned to the Squadron routine: New Guinea, Admiralty Islands, Palau Islands, Philippines, until on 25th September I flew to Melbourne with John Shanley (another captain) and the same Charles Warren whose staff car I had misemployed as a taxi. We were to see the Royal Air Force Chief of Air Staff (Australia) in the headquarters which he shared with his navy and army equivalents.

A visit to such a lofty personage with Charlie Warren made sense, although rather disagreeably from my point of view, but I did not understand why John Shanley was with us – he had no staff car for me to borrow. All was eventually revealed; the war was over, everyone was going home except the joint staffs in Australia who would oversee the troops required to retake our possessions and to fulfil our commitments to the colonies and mandated territories. With this in mind, the CAS had been given a VIP Dakota (thought to be one careful owner – Lord Mountbatten), and therefore required a crew to fly it. Shanley and I were the short list of two from whom the choice was to be made; Charles Warren was the token "older, more responsible officer" and also along I suspect to give such views on character as the Air Marshal might request. I was not optimistic.

Returning to the squadron we were off again "up the route" as the expression had it, this time to continue beyond the Philippines to RAF Kai-Tak, the only airfield in Hong Kong. This was a most agreeable prospect because not only was it a new destination but the route home was changed to transit Morotai in the Halmahira Group, Darwin in the Northern Territory and Cloncurry in Queensland. These changes were made to avoid as far as possible American bases where fuel, spares, accommodation and food were now to be charged to the user government since, with the war finished, mutual aid was cancelled. This struck me as strange whilst acknowledging that the United States was by far the greatest donor. Under their accounting system everything that left Stateside was written off, including major items like aircraft. The RNZAF, which operated a squadron of Corsairs from Momote, could not keep going without the steady supply of spares which had flowed from the US Navy. Royal Navy friends told me that they had watched brand-new aircraft being pushed over the side of supply ships whilst their squadron aircraft of the same type were unfit for flight through lack of spares. There were good commercial reasons for this, of course, but the transition from "take what you need" to "show me your money" was so abrupt that operational capability was profoundly affected.

This first trip to Hong Kong was extremely rewarding for us. We carried concentrated orange juice, milk, chocolate bars and all sorts of other treats for the newly-released prisoners of war and internees. Basically they were to be fattened up in Australia before being returned to the United Kingdom or wherever they called home. After landing under the control of HMS "Victorious" which was tied up alongside, we taxied past gangs of orientals apparently repairing craters in the ground adjoining the runway and taxiway. I noticed that the foremen were European, of military bearing and carrying pick-axe handles. The foremen, it turned out, were Royal Marine Commandos, and the labourers were the Japanese guards from the infamous Stanley Camp. Not quite knowing what to do with these former bully-boys, the marines had hit on the idea of forming them into small teams which alternately dug holes and filled them in. This work was to be done vigorously and during the whole of daylight hours, and the pick-axe handles were to ensure compliance. With great insight on someone's part, the amiable Royal Marines assigned to this task were first shown Stanley Camp, and the conditions under which the detainees had been held.

Families were split so that husbands did not see their wives and children until sons reached the age of 10 when they were transferred to the men's camp, after which the mothers lost touch. This sounds cruel (and was), but came about because the young boys were stealing out of the women's camp at night and taking food to the men's camp. Perhaps they saw it as a bit of a lark but without doubt their activities kept the men alive.

The officer temporarily in charge of Kai-Tak was Pat Connolly who had been my flight commander on 635. He was going out with Tiger Force to form the RAF element of the combined air strike force against Japan when the surrender occurred, leaving them jobless. His deputy was a bear of a man, Sam Weller, who like me had survived life on 158 and the rigours of the Yorkshire winter. This was a most agreeable surprise and between them they gave us the grand tour of Kowloon and Victoria Island during our half day and one night there. The next morning we filed our flight plan for Leyte, and for the first time met the passengers who were to be our constant companions for the next three days. There were husbands and wives recently reunited; mothers getting to know sons whom they had not seen for four years and who in that time had passed into self-reliant early manhood; fathers with very young daughters who were still not absolutely confident about their relationship; and young men who had aged considerably in the previous four years but who still epitomised the empire builders that they undoubtedly were. From time to time, when the door from the main cabin to the flight deck was opened, I looked back to see what resembled a badly conducted child's birthday party. Children were rushing up and down clutching paper cups full of orange juice, faces smeared with chocolate, whilst harassed mothers appealed for calm. The adults were invited in turn to sit in the co-pilot's seat, really to escape the bedlam in the back, but also to survey the ocean and to be briefed on our route to Sydney. Several times I turned to see an energetic child seated on the radio officer's lap, pounding away on the Morse key and listening to music on the radio compass. It was all very heartwarming and most satisfying to make a contribution to the rehabilitation of those brave souls.

41

December 1945 found us despatched to Darwin to collect AVM Graham and to return him to his headquarters in Melbourne. I think that this was by way of a final interview for the job of personal pilot; he not unreasonably wished to be assured that I could fly an aeroplane. I believe that my appointment was confirmed soon after that but, before departing Camden we did another VIP trip with Sir Henry and Lady French. I frankly do not know why they were in Australia although I suspect that the British Government had sent them out to visit all the states in the commonwealth and to thank them for their contributions to the war effort which, in men and material, were considerable. We took them to Perth in Western Australia, Adelaide and Hobart, Tasmania, Canberra and finally Newcastle, New South Wales, not to be confused with a city of the same name in northern England. The knight and his lady were absolutely charming and, after a week or so with us, Lady French was almost at the point of checking that our shirts were properly aired before we wore them!

I took up my appointment as personal pilot at the beginning of February 1946 and on the 9th took VIP Dakota KN372 from Camden to Essendon, Melbourne, which was home for the rest of the year. My navigator, Alan Millar who, as a medical student, qualified for early release to resume his studies, did not come with us and was replaced by Norman Ulph, a very good, steady man with a surname I had never seen before and have never come across again. We were also joined by Sergeant Laurie Sutton, one of a very rare breed, a Fitter 1, qualified on airframes and engines, who was to fly with us as crew chief.

KN372 had been fitted out by Canadair and was quite spectacular with maple panelling, deep blue carpeting and lots of sound-deadening material to keep the cabin quiet. There was a full-size executive desk and matching chair, a day-bed and a conference area with four very comfortable chairs. Two 100-gallon overload tanks were installed in the wardrobes immediately behind the flight deck and at the rear of the aircraft there was a refrigerator and a cooking stove. All this meant luxury indeed with in-flight catering to go with the 10-hour endurance of the aeroplane.

Our arrival at the headquarters in Toorak, a leafy suburb of Melbourne, passed unnoticed but within days the senior members of the staff began placing bids for our services, rather like a very small charter operation. We were on constant standby for the Chiefs of Staff but if they had no requirement for the next 24 hours we were offered to descending orders of seniority until someone had a reason for using the aircraft: rather like an auction in reverse. As a result we were kept busy on a variety of tasks, the purposes of which were, and remain, a mystery. The first interesting trip was with the Air Marshal and Major General Hayden, his army sidekick. In the words of the classic Staff College setting: "The CAS sends for you and says . . .": in this case, "take us to New Zealand." Thus we found ourselves crossing the Tasman Sea in foul weather of the kind that I shall forever associate with New Zealand. We were treated with extreme courtesy and kindness wherever we stopped although the radio officer reported an inability to raise anyone at Paraparaumu from 30 miles out, which was most unusual. When I called the tower on joining the circuit it was no better. Only when the controller finally called to ask if the Dakota in the circuit intended to land at "Paraparam" did we realise that "Parra Parra Oomoo" was a mispronunciation.

In April 1946, a similar opening scene was played but this time the boss said that he would like to go to London, leaving the next morning, to attend a meeting called by Lord Tedder, then the Royal Air Force Chief of Air Staff. It appeared that his plan to travel on the BOAC Lancastrian service from Sydney had misfired, probably overbooked! His ADC, John Aitken, would accompany us because he was tour-expired and was taking up a new appointment (he subsequently did rather well in his RAF career).

We planned our route with particular regard to the night stops to try to ensure a measure of comfort for the Air Marshal who was required to arrive daisy-fresh to launch into a great series of meetings. We had six long flying days ahead with a short final day from southern France to Northolt, just outside London. On the first day we crossed Australia from Melbourne to Darwin, refuelling at Charleville in central Queensland. Day Two took us to Singapore via Balikpapan in North Borneo. I had seen neither place before and would have appreciated some free time to look around, especially Singapore which was struggling to return to normality after four years of harsh occupation. In the early morning of Day Three we departed Singapore for Rangoon for a fuel stop before pressing on to Calcutta. That was another 12½-hour flying day so that there was no temptation to explore the treasures of Calcutta, if any. This was pre-partition so that we were in eastern India and needed merely to cross to the west which we did via Allahabad. From Karachi, another long day was spent in reaching Lydda in Palestine, staging through Shaibah in the Persian Gulf, until then known to me only as the subject of a rude song. The last long day took us to Marseilles through Malta, with the final dash to Northolt the next morning. Total flying time was 73 hours and 20 minutes for the week and I cannot imagine a civil operator or even the RAF sanctioning such a workload today. However, they would perhaps provide some jolly good post-trauma counselling in lieu of the few beers that we had to celebrate our arrival.

For the return to Melbourne we were joined by Mrs Graham who was kindness itself and who treated us as part of her family, which in a way we were: a personal flight crew is very much an extended family. The route was almost the reciprocal but we were in less of a hurry and, at the boss's suggestion, we took in some rather more pleasant destinations where these were available. As a result I was able to check New Delhi and, with some exhausting travel, to see the Taj Mahal although alas not by moonlight. It was worth seeing, but not worth going to see. We hit the monsoon between Calcutta and Rangoon and I was compelled to fly quite low in order to avoid the worst of the turbulence and blinding rain. From time to time I opened the flight deck door to make encouraging signs to the two passengers, to see the boss reading quietly with his half-moon spectacles low on the bridge of his nose and Mrs Graham getting on with her embroidery. The aeroplane was taking a terrible hammering and it crossed my mind that he could not possibly steady his book sufficiently to read and that she was in real danger of puncturing herself if she really was sewing. My fervent hope was that the production workers at the Douglas factory in Long Beach, California had been particularly diligent when nailing together KN372.

A couple of months later I was summoned to the presence to be told that our services, aircraft and crew had been offered to the Chiefs of Air Staff RAAF and RNZAF who had to go to London for some doubtless good reason. Thus, on 24th July 1946 we departed Melbourne at a very early hour with the two Chiefs in the back. Two hours into the flight with dawn just breaking, at cruising altitude, auto-pilot 'on' and that feeling of lassitude when you are comfortable and warm after a brief night's rest, there was a most frightening noise as a propeller ran away and achieved more revolutions per minute that the instrument could record. I should have said earlier that, because of its sumptuous fittings and sound-proofing, KN372 reached its single-engine safety weight at about the time that the fuel tanks were empty. So soon after take-off this patently was not the case and we had to find somewhere to land, soon. I made encouraging signs to the rather startled senior officers in the cabin and sent a message via the navigator that we would be landing Mildura. Having closed down the ailing engine I eased into a silent Mildura where the natives had not yet sprung into life. After a cursory examination it was quite clear that we were not going any further for the time being and I set about making contact with RAAF Laverton (Melbourne) to secure a replacement. A65-101 eventually arrived but being a standard Dakota had no overload tanks, causing a brisk revision of our flight plan. By now the two Chiefs were probably doing a Laurel and Hardy "another fine mess you've got me into" routine since all the advantages of flying with us had literally gone up in smoke.

Our limited range compelled us to take in one or two other beauty spots that we might otherwise have missed, like Alice Springs, Koepang on Timor, Penang in Malaya, Habbaniya in Iraq and El Adem in Libya, with of course all our previously planned stops. Landing in the dark at RAF Habbaniya I hit something on the runway with the port wheel which burst the tyre and, by the time that I had regained control, the wheel had broken. We suffered the loss of dignity of blocking the runway until a servicing crew changed the wheel. We had already flown for 10½ hours that day and, with the inevitable delay of the wheel change and undercarriage check, it seemed best to stay overnight and to make an early start the next morning. Having two Chiefs of Air Staff as unexpected guests must have stretched the Station Commander's resourcefulness but the only time that I saw him was early the following morning when he arrived at the flight line on horseback. You just do not find them like that anymore.

To make up time we flew for 16 hours of the next 24 and, on arrival at Istres in southern France, I was so weary that I nodded off in the bar, not one of my usual characteristics.

We returned to Australia without further incident, to learn that we had inadvertently provoked a surge of Australian chauvinism when the Sydney *"Sun"* discovered that their CAS had been flown to London by a Pommie crew. Like all the best tabloid stories it was dead by our return and caused me no loss of sleep.

What proved to be my last trip with the Air Marshal was really R and R for himself and Mrs Graham, both keen amateur naturalists and both keen to visit Bali. They determined to do so whilst they had a private aeroplane and crew to minimise the discomfort of travel. This was a very good trip via Singapore where we stayed for a couple of days. In Singapore, the war crimes trial of the guards from one of the camps on the Burma–Siam railway was in progress and, vaguely aware that this was an important historical event, I was determined to attend a part of it.

The prisoners in the dock, guarded by tall military policemen, were a sorry lot and seemed almost disinterested in the proceedings although they were on trial for their lives. It was afternoon, and it was hot, so that from time to time some of them had to be prodded by a guard to keep them awake. This was in part due to the complicated interrogation process in which the prosecutor, a British Army officer, put his questions in English to a Filipino civilian who translated into Japanese. The prisoner who had been addressed replied in Japanese and the Filipino gave the answer in English.

One exchange which I have never forgotten concerned the camp doctor who was a graduate of a technical school with no medical training, of any kind. The camp was beside a river and the prisoners had a daily water ration of 5 litres for drinking, cooking and washing. The doctor was asked why the prisoners were not allowed to bathe in the river and indeed to use as much water as they wished when it was there in abundance. He answered that the rules stipulated five litres as a daily allowance and he had not considered varying that amount even though prisoners were dying of dehydration. This single-mindedness and unthinking obedience has worked well for Japanese industry since those far-off days but gave me a lifelong reluctance to buy anything from that country.

We were now well into October 1946. My replacement had arrived and been vetted; my radio officer had married the Miss DuBois of the Camden Hotel incident and was in no hurry to return to England; my navigator had already gone.

In anticipation of returning to more normal duties I had been studying the 'situations vacant' advertised in Air Ministry Orders and had become quite excercised about the Empire Test Pilots' School. I met all the listed qualifications and therefore applied in the manner instructed as well as making the course my first choice for next appointment. This latter is a small section of the Annual Confidential Report (F1369) inserted as a joke by whoever designed the form. It is usually ignored completely by the posting authorities but, when the reporting officer is an Air Marshal, perhaps they pay more attention, I really do not know. Whatever the case, my application went forward appropriately endorsed.

I chose to return by sea, reasoning that a 6-week cruise would do me no harm and I should still be home for Christmas. Needless to say, I fell among thieves. This time it was in the shape of three RAN lieutenants posted to Portsmouth for a long navigation course, one of whom I had flown between islands on some occasion, forgotten by me but remembered by him. We discovered simultaneously and to our collective dismay that the ship on which we were embarked was on its final run as a trooper before being returned to its rightful owner, the P&O line, and therefore sailed under the Supreme Commander's dictum that such ships should carry no alcohol. This was a serious blow and we pooled our refreshment resources to see us through to Adelaide where we were due to put in. On arrival we swiftly arranged a visit to the Stonyfell vineyards, taking with us two steel sea trunks. Like most vineyards, Stonyfell had a sampling room where visitors were invited to taste the product and to make purchases, and some of the products were very good indeed. We left with a fine selection of wines and augmented our haul with some beer from grog shops on the way back to the ship.

Crossing the Great Australian Bight was an experience. It is said to be the roughest stretch of water in the world and in those pre-stabiliser days it was an adventure. The ship started to roll as we entered, and continued to roll until we left, causing misery to most of the souls on board. At meal times only four were present and, looking out of the tightly-secured portholes in the dining salon, the horizon changed from brilliant blue as the ship's side pointed skywards to bilious green as the reverse roll took the side under water. The Bight is about 600 miles across so that, at our modest cruising speed, we took two days to cross. During that time others appeared at the head of the dining salon stairs, some even made it down the first one or two steps. Whether it was the smells drifting from the kitchens or the sight of the crockery and cutlery sliding from one side to the other of the tables that upset them I could not determine, but the stewards continued to enjoy quiet mealtimes.

When I reflect on Australia, even 50 years on, I can find few redeeming features. For example, one day I was in a big department store in Sydney and, seeing a young mother with a child in a pushchair, I opened the glass door separating departments and stood aside for her to go through ahead of me. Nothing remarkable about that, you might think and I would agree but, instead of a word of thanks or even a curt nod, she said: "What are yer, queer or something?"

A statute, introduced at the time of the First War, I believe, required pubs to close at 6 o'clock thus reducing the incidence of drunkenness and keeping the streets safe for women and children. As most city people finished work at 5 pm, an event known as the "5 o'clock swill" was staged in all the pubs that had beer. The aim was to down as many schooners as possible in that hour before closing time and, with this in mind, individuals would approach the bar carrying large trays and order as many beers as the tray would hold, perhaps 12 or 14. Each would then retire to a corner and solemnly drink the lot. If he could he would repeat the process until he could no longer stagger to the bar. This led to some uninspiring scenes both within the pubs and without and fulfilled none of the hopes of whoever first drafted the statute.

It is perhaps not widely known, except to airmen and rugby players, that if there is anyone an Australian dislikes as much as a Pommie, it is a "pig islander," or New Zealander as we would call him. The cause of this dislike was never explained, and indeed it is likely that nobody any longer knows, but dislike them they most certainly do. The RAAF then, and now as far as I know, wore uniforms of navy blue with black buttons, whereas the RNZAF followed the RAF pattern. The point of this sartorial review is that in an Australian mess, RAF or RNZAF personnel stuck out like a chapel hat peg. In the last few months of my time in Australia mine was the only RAF crew left, and it was never long into the evening before one of the residents made known his views on New Zealanders and, when the whole truth was revealed, even more so the English. The situation was aggravated by the issue of campaign medals which immediately revealed the theatre of operations in which we had been most active, because for most Australians those that fought in Europe were war-dodgers. I am at a loss to explain this except that there was a general feeling in the country that they had been left in the lurch by the British. I can only report that it was their firmly held opinion and the cause of fat lips and bruised knuckles later in the evening when sense of humour failure was complete.

Because of our close association with some very senior officers we were frequently invited to social functions that otherwise would have passed us by, for example the Melbourne Cup. The Chiefs had a horse called JCOSA, (Joint Chiefs of Staff, Australia – neat eh?), which was competing although not in the main event. I know nothing about horse-racing but Nell Hopman, wife of the Australian tennis coach who was the social secretary at the headquarters, assured me that a beast called Bernborough was sure to win. However, the list of runners included a filly called Flight which I took to be an omen, and I told the fat man with the Gladstone bag that I wanted ten shillings on Flight. When the horses paraded I was disappointed to see that this goat with its front legs metaphorically crossed was carrying my number. Had I known enough about betting to have backed it each way I would have cleaned up because Flight ran second. At this climax of the Melbourne social season there were lots of "debs," or Aussie equivalent, and some of them were absolutely stunning. The only problem was that they spoke; that sound that can be so distressing to hear from some Australian males is even more like fingernails on a blackboard when in the female vocal range!

This chapter of my service life closed without my realising the full effect that it would have on my future. I had now flown nearly 2,500 hours on 23 types of aircraft, and I was 23 years old.

CHAPTER VI
SCHOOLDAYS, SCHOOLDAYS

I arrived in Southampton on 6th December 1946, feeling frozen to the marrow, despite some acclimatisation from the Bay of Biscay onwards. It was to be the coldest winter for years and was a harsh reintroduction to my native land. I had a lot of accumulated leave and disembarkation leave as well so that it was six weeks before I reported to RAF Dishforth. Diligent readers will remember that I had been there before during the "escape and evasion" phase of my bomber training. It held no happy memories for me and I was not wildly excited by the prospect of teaching people to fly Dakotas, which was the point of my being there. A fellow instructor was a man called John McCallum who had trained with me and who had elected to stay on in America as a teacher. It turned out that he had spent the entire war there, which reinforced my suspicion that the authorities sometimes spoke with forked tongue. In almost no time the training stopped whilst the aircraft were filled with bales of hay, which were flung out of the loading doors for the unfortunate animals trapped on the moors in deep and drifting snow. In order to launch the aircraft it was first necessary to de-ice the runways, a thankless task at the best of times, positively demoralising when they immediately froze again. With nothing getting in or out of the station it soon resembled a city under siege, and the only sensible decision was taken, to send home anyone that could go. I needed no second bidding and therefore was at home when the message arrived to report to Thames House, Millbank, to be interviewed by the selection board for the Empire Test Pilots' School.

The Board was chaired by a serving group captain wearing a flying badge and the ribbon of the Air Force Cross plus a black patch over his right eye. None of the members of the Board was named but the others were a mixed bag of serving officers and civilians and they all seemed very friendly. The questions were not very demanding technically and seemed to concentrate far more on motivation and enthusiasm. They thanked me warmly and asked if I would wait in the ante-room whilst they saw some other applicants. I struck up a conversation with another, rather despondent, candidate who I assumed was suffering a hangover. Not so; his gloom was caused by the fact that on leaving the interview he had sought to impress the Board by carrying out a smart "about turn" and saluting before exiting. Unhappily he tripped as he was turning and completed his salute from the prone position! I warmed to him immediately and he became one of my lifelong friends. After a suitable pause I was recalled and asked some further questions before being dismissed. I found it difficult to assess my chances because none of the questions had left me floundering, but on the other

49

hand none seemed closely related to my professional skills, which I had assumed to be vital to the task. I returned to Dishforth and did some more "conversions to type" for people getting into the transport business from other Commands, and it remained bitterly cold in Yorkshire. At the end of February the word came to report to the Empire Test Pilots' School (ETPS) at Cranfield near Bedford. I packed with a light heart.

The reporting date turned out to be a Saturday which struck me as odd, but it had been arranged deliberately so that the new course met the staff in the friendly atmosphere of the mess. A figure at the end of the bar was easily recognised on account of the eye patch as the chairman of the interview board, Group Captain Dick Ubee. My friend who had distinguished himself by his balletic exit from his interview was also there, Red Evans. The rest of the course came from the Royal Navy, Canada, Australia, the United States Navy and South Africa. Topping it off was a very suave civilian, the Chief Test Pilot of Short Brothers who, having been in the business for years, was about to learn how to do it properly; he was Tom Brooke-Smith. This rather jolly start set the scene for the entire course during which, if you expected to be coddled in any way, you were doomed to disappointment.

Ground School started with some fairly basic revision of long-forgotten mathematics and physics, in the middle of which the Commandant sent for me to say that I was to go down to Sunninghill Park to be selected (or not) for a permanent commission in the Royal Air Force. I asked if this could be deferred since, of all those present, my need for the revision was as desperate as anybody's, but "they" refused on the grounds that they had been chasing me for some time and, having caught up with me, it had to be done now. In consequence, instead of swotting up my sums, I was explaining to a psychiatrist the exact impact upon me that a series of blots had, and directing my squad in the transfer of empty oil drums from one side to the other of an imaginary stream. I was not best pleased. At the end of it the chap running it, Group Captain George Beamish, one of a famous family of RAF brothers, interviewed us and asked me what I had thought of the process. I explained that I had just started a course that was going to test me severely and that I could have easily managed without his diversion. He showed some sympathy and even gave me a half-day off in order to get back to Cranfield.

My first flight at ETPS was dual in an Anson with a super QFI (qualified flying instructor), Peter Wingate. We flew around, feathered an engine, carried out a single-engine landing and so on, a normal introduction to a new type of aircraft. At the end of it he complimented me on my handling skills which drove me to ask why he was surprised. Because of some confusion he had thought it was my first-ever trip in a twin-engined aeroplane. Some of the sailors really had flown nothing but singles and were

50

quite keen to have an experienced man with them on the exercises in the Lincoln. Most of the fleet aircraft were single-seat so that dual was impossible and it was very much a case of reading the Pilots' Notes and landing when you felt confident.

I had my first introduction to jet flight via the Vampires and Meteors on the fleet, as well as the distinctly difficult big reciprocating-engined Tempest 2 and Seafire 47. During an exercise measuring level speeds in a Mosquito B.35, a bit tedious since it meant flying very accurately for some time to ensure that the speed was stable before starting to record, I was about a third of the way through my assigned task and turned to head back towards my start point and to set up a new stable speed. In the turn there was a sudden rush of cold air and the noise level increased sharply, both of which were puzzling, as was the reduction in indicated airspeed to zero. The aircraft seemed to be flying alright and I fairly quickly realised that the hatch above my head was missing, and in rather slower time I recalled that the pitot head, fundamental to measuring the airspeed, was in the leading edge of the fin, *ergo* the hatch had taken the fin off when it left. This was not a comforting thought and it seemed best to see if Mr Irvine's parachutes lived up to their reputation. There was a serious snag to this plan however. To get into this particular mark of Mosquito, there was an outward-opening door which gave access to an inward-opening door which could be secured to the cockpit wall by a catch, an action normally performed by the navigator. I had no navigator and the catch was broken. I unlocked my safety harness and tried to hold the inner door open with my right boot, meanwhile flying what was left of the aeroplane and wondering how I could do all this and find another leg to kick the jettison button on the outer door. I concluded that I was not likely to be successful and therefore got back properly into my seat and attempted to resecure my harness in order to land wheels-up in a field somewhere. The locking device refused to function so that scheme B had to be abandoned; I had no wish to assault the front windscreen with my face. Somewhat calmer now (after all it was still flying), I looked ahead and found that I was almost lined up with a runway on a disused airfield then called Twinwood Farm. I lowered the wheels, put down some flap, and steered the thing using a touch of differential throttle to keep it straight, guessing that I was a bit too quick but not prepared to reduce speed and stall if I was wrong. After landing I stopped the engines, got out and had a look at the back end. My diagnosis was absolutely right; the fin and rudder were two-thirds gone, with the pitot head tubing waving in the breeze.

I was relieved to see a car approaching and even more pleased when it proved to contain two RAF officers on their way to work at a nearby headquarters. They explained that they normally drove across the airfield and had seen me on my approach and had a short debate about the latest modifications to the Mosquito of which mine was yet another example.

The awful winter gave way to the best summer that I can remember when the sun shone every day for six weeks. We took block leave at the school; clearly it was not practicable for people to go on leave at any old time, so that for most of July we were free agents. However, the school was to move to Farnborough and the Commandant had found a course for us to attend which he felt would not be too testing. At Thorney Island, a school of air-sea rescue had been set up, designed I suppose for young men joining the aircrew branch. They did dinghy drills and lectured on survival, but most of all they had a fleet of sailing dinghies, and we had a block booking package tour to the south coast basking in Mediterranean weather. Most days we sailed across to the Isle of Wight, had a few beers and lunch in a pub and wove our somewhat erratic way back to Thorney Island. And we were being paid to do it.

At Farnborough, the newcomers were accommodated on what was then a very busy airfield, housing the Experimental Flying Department of the Royal Aircraft Establishment; but the mess had no room, and we took over Warburg Barracks in Aldershot for our living quarters. This was less than ideal since it was some way from the airfield and offered no chance for quiet study when unexpected breaks occurred through bad weather or aircraft unserviceabilities. Interspersed with the flying and lectures we made visits to the aircraft manufacturers to see how they made their aircraft and, if we were lucky, to get a glimpse of what was on the drawing board. These were always jolly occasions, usually including a convivial lunch in a local hostelry, or concluding with a dinner in a high-class establishment. These walkabouts induced in some a painful though not life-threatening condition which we called "factory foot." Tom Brooke-Smith was so afflicted and, when the visit to his parent company was being planned, he cried "enough." Instead of walking around the Short Brothers factory, Brookie arranged that we see Sid Field in "Piccadilly Hayride" followed by dinner at the Savoy. He was a chap with considerable style.

The course ended in December with a splendid dinner at which the McKenna Trophy was presented to the best all-round student. It was not me, but I passed. While the visiting officers (foreigners) went home, the British graduates were distributed about equally between the RAE at Farnborough and A&AEE (Aeroplane and Armament Experimental Establishment) at Boscombe Down in Wiltshire.

CHAPTER VII
IT'S GOT TO BE THIS OR THAT

It is necessary to make clear that on joining the experimental flying side of the military aircraft business, serving officers were seconded to whichever Ministry ran aircraft procurement at the time. In the late forties it was the Ministry of Supply. This led to some strange management and control arrangements at the mixed military/civilian establishments where the work was carried out. Boscombe Down for example was commanded by an Air Commodore, but of equal status, except for the purely military side of the operation, was a scientific civil servant called the Chief Superintendent. The division of labour, roughly speaking, was that boffins dreamed up the tasks and we flew the aeroplanes. At Boscombe our task was to ensure that new aircraft met the criteria for the type laid down in a set of rules. For example, all fighter aircraft had to have a spin recovery procedure established before release to the service. The way to establish the recovery procedure was to conduct a spinning programme. This turned out to be quite sporting on some of the high-performance aircraft then being produced and sometimes Pilots' Notes for the type, under the side-heading "Spinning" said it was forbidden, adding: "However, if you should find yourself in a spin, the following recovery procedure is recommended." This was followed by: "If you have not recovered by 20,000 feet, eject."

In those far-off days, when the operational requirement was written for a new type, particularly for fighters and trainers, more than one company would respond, and there would be a fly-off, leading to a recommendation of which one to manufacture in quantity for the service. Our work stopped there and the Chief Superintendent/politicians took over. In parallel, the Armament Division used us to carry/fire new weapons before they were cleared for service use. The flying wing was divided into squadrons, 'A' for fighters, 'B' for Bombers, 'C' for Royal Navy. 'D' squadron was later established to cover transport aircraft and helicopters. A civil aircraft test section (CATS) was also there to watch over new airliners. However, there was great freedom of movement between squadrons since, in theory at any rate, we were equally well-qualified on all types of landplanes.

On arrival at the establishment, most of the newcomers joined IFDF, the Intensive Flying Development Flight, before going to whichever squadron they were assigned to on a permanent basis. This provided some interesting flying on a mixture of aeroplanes which had just entered or were about to enter service. The Sea Hornet was one, and the main task was to simulate deck landings and their effect upon the undercarriage. In pre-angled-deck days, aircraft approached under the control of a deck landing officer, advising as to height and direction by waving paddles and finally giving the "cut" signal when the aircraft was in the right position to catch a landing wire. With a pitching and rolling deck this must have been a bit of a trick and we were meant to subject the unfortunate Sea Hornet to an "early cut" which dropped the aircraft from a dizzy height on to the runway. It was surprisingly difficult deliberately to drop the pretty little fighter in the manner required since it was contrary to all that we had ever been taught. We all had a go with almost no success, and the last one to try was Dickie Stoop, who raced sports cars by way of recreation, and who admitted failure to the boffins at the side of the runway controlling the test. Saying he would join the circuit for a normal landing, he rushed around again and dropped the aeroplane so hard that he broke the undercarriage.

Interesting chap, Dickie: he was the son of Adrian Stoop, of Rugby Union fame, and was colour-blind. Aware that this defect would soon be discovered during medical examinations on joining the RAF, he learned by heart all the numbers that were hidden in the test cards, and fooled the doctors for years. While at Boscombe, he bought a 1938 BMW chassis and went to the Fraser-Nash factory in North London to have a body of his own design fitted. I went with him to collect it and it was a beautiful piece of work, and they had followed his instructions to the letter. Unfortunately, the colours that Dickie had used, and what he believed to be coffee and chocolate brown, were actually metallic blue and maroon. Not a pretty sight, and what a target for the police! He had a heart attack and died at the wheel of his Porsche during a race at Mallory Park many years later.

The aircraft that made the deepest impression upon me, mostly because of its supreme unsuitability for its operational task, was the Blackburn Firebrand, a fighter intended for the Royal Navy but which I think never saw service. My conviction that it was not suitable stemmed from the fact that even in straight and level flight it was necessary to weave in order to see ahead. It was powered by a Bristol Centaurus radial engine and the cockpit was so far aft that even raising the seat did not solve the visibility problem. Just picture trying to put that down on a heaving deck.

Soon after my arrival at Boscombe a replacement pilot was required for the Tropical Experimental Unit at Khartoum where trials were in progress on the Vampire, the first jet aircraft in Africa I believe, and the Brigand. I flew out by South African Airways DC-6 and arrived, fairly shopworn, at about four o'clock in the morning to be met on the tarmac by Paddy Barthropp who was to be my constant companion for the next month. He said that I had an hour to get organised before we set out on a shooting trip that he had arranged to a dam south of the city. That was the start of another service friendship that persisted. Flying from Khartoum was easy even though the navigation and landing aids were primitive, because the city stands at the junction of the Blue and White Niles and could be found even in the blowing sand that was commonplace. The working day started with first take-off at 6 am before the heat and turbulence made it difficult to fly accurately below 10,000 feet, paused at lunch-time and resumed, after a rest, at 4 in the afternoon. We lived in bungalows and were looked after by a local batman who made tea, laundered and kept the place fairly clean. Following the afternoon rest a strange man appeared every day with things to sell. I never heard him arrive but his goods were always laid out on display when we took tea before going back to work. His name was Ali Osman and he had a store in Omdurman (out of bounds to us) which must have been a sight to see. The stuff he brought to sell us looked very good and I particularly admired a chess set made from "ivory" and teak. We talked most days for three months about all sorts of things. He had one son reading medicine and another reading law in London, and needed another studying dentistry since as far as could be seen he had only one tooth in his head. Occasional references were made to the chess set; I maintained that it was much too expensive, he made a marginal reduction in the price, we shook hands and I went off to fly. This scene was repeated umpteen times until, on my last day, he gave me a carefully wrapped parcel – which of course was the chess set.

At that time they had not shot all the Nile crocodiles and, when low-flying in the Vampire, I could approach without them hearing. There were dozens basking close to the water's edge and it was interesting to see the activity when, having passed them, the noise caught up. The Grand Hotel, with the only flushing loo in the Sudan, The Sudan Club and two "cabarets," the Gordon and the GB, offered a change of menu from the mess food which was pretty terrible. The only commodity that they had in abundance was peanuts and they were used in every conceivable way, and many beyond belief. The speciality was peanut soup, resembling a thin gruel, that even Oliver Twist would have spurned.

The airmen, also detached from Boscombe, were like all airmen when away from base, prepared to work all hours and invariably in good humour. A corporal fitter in the hangar was called "Divvy" for reasons which only became clear when, on pay parade, I learned that his name was Littlewood. The instrument man, Sergeant Gash Howard (a Mancunian), aside from being a very good tradesman, was a devoted cricket follower with Cyril Washbrook as his special hero. The England team was playing Australia and Gash was up all night, having found a radio station giving a commentary. My first question on seeing him in the morning was:"What's the score?" and he always knew precisely. Not only that, he had the bowling and batting analyses and quite often a description of the best shots played. Quite the best bit though was when Washbrook was batting. Gash would produce a school cap from his overalls, putting it on at the same jaunty angle as his hero and, using a crowbar or similar as a bat, execute a cover drive at the same time as he gave Washbrook's score in a broad Lancashire accent: "Our Cyril is 87" – long pause as the makeshift bat followed through – "not out."

During such a detachment it was usual to take a pay-book from the parent unit rather than open a local bank account for the brief duration of the stay; the money drawn was recovered on return. One morning I had called at Accounts to get some money, and continued to the Flight Office to get on with my work. Returning to the bungalow for a rest after lunch, I stripped off and, as usual, threw my clothes into the laundry basket for the batman to wash. I returned to the Flights at four o'clock and was changing into my flying suit when a figure came into view, running hard and with his fist waving above his head. His black robes were flying behind him but I recognised Abdullah, the batman. He had found the money in my shirt pocket and was not prepared to hold it until I returned but felt compelled to run the half mile or so to hand it to me personally. The sum was probably a fiver, which would have been a usual sort of withdrawal at that time, and his pay was ten shillings a month. This greatly impressed me but the Sudanese had a great reputation for honesty and are generally a noble and graceful people. Their suffering in more recent times has been sickening to watch and totally undeserved.

The resident squadron at Khartoum was No. 6, commanded by Denis Crowley-Milling and equipped with Tempest 6 aircraft with Napier Sabre engines. They were a jolly lot of mostly young officers enjoying their first operational tour. One of their number had come to grief at Asmara in Abyssinia, and it was necessary for the Board of Inquiry to be taken there to view the wreckage. The station Anson was available but had no qualified driver, or there was none around, and I was asked to take them over. Asmara was delightful: cool and civilised and still very much an Italian colony in fact if not in theory. It made a pleasant break from the unceasing heat of Khartoum. On the return trip, every spare corner was filled with fruit and potatoes for the mess, which laid on an orgy of eating for the members.

Just before Paddy went home we had dinner in one of the down-town cabarets and were being driven back to camp in a horse-drawn carriage. Paddy saw it as one of his tasks in life to tell the Sudanese at every level that the current British government was a broken reed and would soon be changed. Using the few words of Arabic at his disposal, this political lecture boiled down to "Churchill quois, Attlee mush quois," which translated freely as "Churchill good, Attlee no good." The *tonga* driver so addressed either misunderstood or was a dedicated socialist because he slashed Paddy across the shoulders with his whip. We held him until a policeman arrived and took him into custody. Two weeks later I was required to attend court to confirm the evidence which Paddy, having returned to Boscombe, had submitted in written form. Either the miscreant had "form" or justice was harsher there than I had expected, because he was given five years at hard labour.

The conclusion of my detachment coincided with the completion of the Vampire trial, so that it fell to me to return the aircraft to the Canal Zone to be broken down for shipment back to Boscombe. There were some logistical problems and everything we needed in order to fly had to be pre-positioned or carried in the support aircraft. 40-gallon drums of fuel had been left at the staging points when the aeroplane was flown down from Egypt at the start of the trial, a Mosquito escort was arranged through the PR squadron in Palestine and a Dakota carried the support crew and fuel-pumping equipment. Two 100-gallon drop-tanks were fitted to the Vampire to stretch its legs and, early on the 27th May 1948, the caravan departed Khartoum. The Mosquito, flown by David Reynolds, took off first and I launched immediately afterward, or at least as soon as the dust created by his departure had cleared. The outcome of all this was that on the entire trip to Fayid, the only time that I saw the Mosquito it was on the ground. My starboard drop-tank did not feed, causing an out-of-trim condition which got a bit tiring, and 800 lb dead weight under the wing gave the undercarriage a hard time. We staged through Atbara on the way to Wadi Halfa for the first night-stop. My flying time was only 2¼ hours but there was a lot of waiting for the Dakota to arrive before refuelling could start. They could not leave ahead of us because they were carrying the starter trolley which both Mosquito and Vampire required and, furthermore, had to ensure that we were well on our way and not returning with an unserviceability.

The second day did not begin well. Priming a Merlin engine for start was always a hit-and-miss affair since there was no recommended dose, you just kept priming until the engine fired and settled down to run smoothly. David Reynolds had tried to explain to the local crew at Wadi Halfa that there could be some flame from the exhausts when starting but for them to take no action unless he asked for fire extinguishers to be applied. In theory this was all understood but, strapped in my Vampire, I watched with interest but no surprise as the contents of two extinguishers were discharged into the first engine he tried to start. His frantic waving finally conveyed the right message and they allowed him to get on with the job. The Merlins appeared totally unaffected. The next stop was Luxor where, as usual, the Mosquito caught up with me just after I landed. I taxied as directed and cranked open the canopy to see a man holding an aerosol insecticide can. He climbed his stepladder and released the contents into my face and the cockpit. Not satisfied with that, he gave the air intakes a going-over and then solemnly emptied the rest into the engine exhaust jet pipe. I was glad to observe that he refused to let the Mosquito crew get out until they had been given the same treatment.

The main role of the Egyptian Air Force at Luxor was maritime and there was no sign of any land-based aircraft on the dusty airfield. There was however tension in the air, which was only explained when the station commander took us to his office for a cup of tea whilst we awaited the arrival of our support party. There had been some serious trouble that morning when, as far as I could gather, some Egyptian Spitfires had tangled with some RAF Spitfires and guess who had lost. Hostage-taking was not then in vogue and the Vampire would have been no use to them anyway, but it made for a stilted discussion while we waited. They had not quite finished with us, for when Reynolds taxied out to take off I could hear, but for some reason he could not, that they had changed the runway. Failing to grab his attention by voice they began firing red Verey cartridges at him and I mean *at* him. As far as I could see none struck his aircraft but they were close. I took off on the correct runway without interference.

I was to deliver the aircraft to the Maintenance Unit at Fayid but before landing I asked if I could jettison the drop-tanks, one empty, the other still full of unusable fuel. The duty controller directed me to their sailing club on the Bitter Lakes where I banged off the tanks, one of which sank like a stone, while the other was used forever after as a racing buoy. The final act in the drama was to demonstrate the aircraft to the military in the area. It was planned that three separate events would be staged but unfortunately the sorely-tried starboard undercarriage oleo could only cope with one more landing, after which it lost all its hydraulic fluid and there were no replacement seals. The drop-tank at the bottom of the lake had had the final word.

Return to Boscombe meant assignment to 'B' Squadron, not unexpectedly, but I had acquired a taste for the fast jets and would have quite liked to go to 'A' Squadron. However, there seemed to be more fighter background students selected for ETPS so that bomber experience almost certainly meant the heavy squadron. It was an unpromising time for new aircraft with the change-over to turbine engines well under way and each designer with his own ideas of how best to exploit this new, and apparently unlimited, supply of power.

Our time was occupied with development work on new systems, trials with new weapons and some clearance work on aircraft for the service including the Hastings, Viking, Valetta and Shackleton. We completed the weapons clearance on the Brigand with endless trips to Lyme Bay firing rockets, and hurried through a clearance for the Hastings which was urgently required for the Berlin airlift.

We were from time to time given some very odd ideas to examine and one that I remember clearly concerned the Hastings. When a stick of parachutists drops from an aircraft there is inevitably some separation, which you might think is just as well. However, when on arrival they are meant to rally round the flag and start fighting, it could be fatal to the individual to be separated from the main group, and not so good for the group if some members are missing. The solution to this, thought someone (with impeccable logic but very little understanding of aerodynamics), was to pack the soldiers into a container and drop them all together from one monster parachute. This strange device, called a "paratechnicon," was suspended below the aircraft, and flown around at increasing speeds in an attempt to establish the handling penalties that it imposed. On its final flight the Hastings could be seen at some distance from the eastern end of the airfield, paratechnicon gone, and with it half of the tailplane and elevator. As the aircraft dived it seemed to regain some control in pitch and the nose came up before pitching down again. It finally hit the side of Beacon Hill, hurling flaming wreckage over the farmland and on to the A303 which passes north of Boscombe. It seemed evident that the aircraft had reached a speed at which the nose of the paratechnicon caved in, causing it to swing aft on its rear attachment bolts, striking the tail with catastrophic effect.

The Vickers Viking was in service with British European Airways and, after being fairly well run-in, one of the type was allotted to the King's Flight. When completed, the aircraft was pretty non-standard and had to be checked particularly for ground handling on unpaved and sloping taxiways. On extended forward CG loading there was a suspicion that it might go on to its nose when brakes were applied – and it did. It was the only time I was ever ordered to have a taxying accident.

Accidents were not uncommon, which is hardly surprising considering that there were so many unknowns in the work being attempted and so much untried equipment in the new designs of aircraft. Formerly the golden rule was to change engine or airframe but never to enter the double jeopardy of having everything new. Now that had to be forsaken, involving higher risk technically in order to try to lead the fast developing field, particularly of fighter aircraft.

Martin Baker ejection seats were coming into service and have since saved thousands of lives, but in the early days they were treated with grave and justifiable suspicion because nobody was quite sure how to service and maintain them. There was an accident in the naval hangar and a sailor was seriously injured when the seat in a Supermarine Attacker fired inadvertently. The immediate response was to remove the cartridges from the seat, thus isolating it until the cause of the malfunction had been established. Flying continued on the aircraft and Spike King-Joyce made a cruciform shape in Salisbury Plain when he hit at something like supersonic speed. The crash occurred some way from the airfield but the noise was such that people rushed out to see what it was, for the aircraft was making a sound that I had never heard before and have never heard again.

The flying was not all grim though. Together with Bill Sheehan and Peter Richmond, a naval pilot, I took a Valetta to Khartoum for some warm-weather work, and later took a York to Nairobi in support of some "hot and high" trials on the Avro Athena trainer.

Some strange and unusual aeroplanes came our way too. A little thing called the Ercoupe was the solution to flying for the masses, having a steering wheel attached to the nosewheel for ground handling and to the inter-connected ailerons and rudders for control in the air. Although ingenious, it made landing in a cross-wind very sporting. A Westland Welkin, built along the lines of a Mosquito, was around for a while and was offered to me to deliver to Farnborough. It had a bubble canopy, not dissimilar to a Vampire, which was closed by cranking a handle on the port side of the cockpit, and locked by pushing the handle outboard to engage a spigot in one of a series of holes drilled in a circular plate. This allowed the canopy to be secured in any position on the ground or in flight – or it should have. I closed the canopy for take-off and opened the throttles in the quadrant immediately below the canopy handle. As the aircraft accelerated towards take-off speed, the canopy slid back, the handle giving me a sharp rap with each rotation. It was no time to be taking my hand off the throttles, so my hand was black and blue by the time the canopy was fully open. The locking mechanism was probably worn but that sort of trap should not lie in wait for the young player.

In the summer of 1949, the first two-seat Meteor arrived and was given to 'B' Squadron, theoretically to provide jet experience to our navigators before the arrival of the Canberra. It is difficult now to recall that at the time, only military *pilots* had flown in a jet-propelled aircraft since there was no accommodation for anyone else. The Meteor 7 changed all that and there was an immediate queue of IPs and VIPs claiming a ride. It also gave us the chance for a modicum of revenge on the boffins who had asked for some way-out activity which we tried and found impossible. One of them, for example, was convinced that the Meteor was capable of supersonic flight if only we would try harder. It was a great pleasure to get him into the air, show him what we had been doing (climb to 35,000 feet, half-roll at full power and pull through), and ask if he had any other good ideas. The strangled noises from the back were taken to mean "no."

The Meteor squadrons had not yet received their two-seat aircraft and it was felt that a short stay with No. 1 (Fighter) Squadron to establish the

Americus, Georgia. The Stearman PT-17 and my introduction to flying.

Cochran Field, Macon, Georgia. The Vultee BT-13 prepares to land.

Still in the South. The North American AT-6A Harvard. Tricky to land tidily for the novice.

Return to England and not quite the work I had expected: Tiger Moth.

A Miles Master I. The Kestrel engine coughed from time to time.

Introduction to big aircraft. The Armstrong Whitworth Whitley, always going downhill.

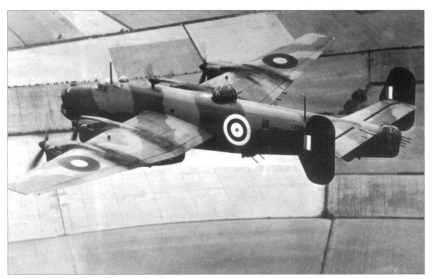

A Halifax V with Merlin engines. Tough, dependable and very hard work.

The Halifax III. The Lissett Squadron No. 158 was the first to equip with the radial-engined variant.

A Lancaster turning finals. Super aeroplane that brought a whole new meaning to "maximum bomb load."

B-24 Liberator of the RAAF. The conversion-to-type was painless and the comfort above average.

compatibility of the Meteor 7 with the single-seat Meteor 4s that they were flying would have some merit. Accordingly I took the aircraft to Tangmere, where they were based, and joined in their activities for a couple of weeks. They were commanded by a USAF exchange officer, Robin Olds, who was a very good fighter pilot and an absolute charmer to boot. He was married to Ella Raines, the film star, and lived off the station in a baronial mansion paid for, he said, by his wife's income from a film that she made whilst they were in England.

Back to Boscombe and within days occurred one of those things that you see, but do not quite believe. I was returning to the circuit and heard one of my close chums, Pinky Stark, calling the tower to say that something had fallen off his aircraft, a very early night-fighter Venom. He was flying with a lady boffin, Mary Boulter, just out of University and, until that point, thoroughly excited about development aircraft. Her presence also inhibited Pinky's description of the difficulties he was having. The radar nose had dropped off, leaving a very blunt bulkhead and not much else ahead of the crew. Seeing this in the air was startling, but the emergency was handled with great skill and the aeroplane was landed without further drama. Mary stayed in the business for a long time, married Mr Willcocks and became a technical instructor at ETPS.

There was some light relief when a Ghost-engined Vampire was to be delivered to the reviving aviation industry in France, the start of a revival that was to cause our industry some headaches in the future. The same Pinky Stark flew the Vampire and I followed in the two-seat Meteor to bring him back. The delivery was made to Albert/Meulte near Amiens, and our reward was to be a night in Paris as the guests of the French Air Force. Before departing in a small Nord 1101 passenger aeroplane, I watched my Meteor being taken to the hangar to await our return the following morning. To my horror, the man in the cockpit, giving directions to the tractor driver at the other end of the towing arm, was smoking a cigarette. I was to learn then and subsequently that many of the other things done in aviation by the French were strange to our eyes. Our host for the night was Capt. Jean Rigaud and, after a quick shower, we were guests for dinner at his flat. This was charming, but not quite what we had in mind for our first postwar night in Paris. Time went on and we were stealing glances at the time, wondering if we should see the city at all when at about 11.30 Jean said: "OK, now we go out." He and his wife took us to a jazz club where black American musicians were blowing up a storm, and where one beer lasted all night. It was splendid.

In the middle of 1950, the Institute of Aviation Medicine at Farnborough had developed a cockpit supercooling system which they had installed in a Vampire 5 and which they wanted to test in 'real' conditions. They had also designed and produced the first air-ventilated suit and were keen to see if that worked. It bore a remarkable resemblance to the piece of kit that eventually became standard issue, and was very effective. John Howitt, one of their doctor-pilots, would fly the aeroplane and they borrowed another Vampire and pilot from Boscombe so that they could travel as a pair. I flew the supporting York to become the third Vampire trials pilot when we arrived in Khartoum. The route was dictated by the range of the Vampires since they were dependent upon the support crew to refuel them and see them off. After trailing across North Africa we eventually arrived in Khartoum for the trial to start. The aim was quite simply to fly the aircraft under identical circumstances, first without the additional cold air and then with it 'on,' measuring cockpit temperatures in both cases. The extra cooling was obtained by passing the 'normal' cold air through a biscuit tin full of ice, and the difference, particularly at low level, could easily be felt. The standard cockpit temperature control, a small wheel on the starboard wall by the seat, was used to allow more or less cold or hot air into the cockpit. Before flight we stripped and were weighed and this was repeated after landing so that weight loss could be recorded and referenced to the cockpit conditions. We flew fairly intensively for a week covering all times of the day and night to provide enough data to prove what was manifestly clear from using the device, that is, it was cooler.

I drew the short straw for the trip in which all cooling was to be turned off briefly to provide another point on the graph. The first part of the flight went as planned, recording temperatures against cool air or super-cool air, and then came the cool air 'off' bit. The change from cold to hot was not shown in the cockpit for the good reason that it was easily felt on the face as the air came out of the gallery under the windscreen and through louvres scattered around the cockpit: no other indication was necessary. I turned the air control wheel and felt the blast of cool air fade and, although I stopped turning, hot air began to flow and got hotter and faster without any action on my part. Furthermore, no action that I did take seemed to make the slightest difference, I was stuck with hot air and at low level in the Sudan it took but a short time for me to start feeling very distressed. I declared an emergency, rushed into the circuit and flung the aircraft on to the runway, wrestling with the canopy handle to try and get some breathable air. I had told them my problem and, having got back to the flight line saw the doctors lined up, clearly anxious for my well-being. Or so I thought. I dragged myself out of the cockpit, still gasping, to be assisted into the Flight Office, stripped and weighed, and only then given a glass of water. The mishap had been too good for the doctors to miss and another point was added to the graph, albeit an eccentric one. In 30 minutes I had lost nearly 6 lb and felt distinctly seedy for the next couple of days; more than that I was fed up that my medical companions refused me medical help on the ethical grounds that I was being treated by the station doctor. Nice to have friends.

In July 1950 I took part in a double event. Jimmy Orrell, Avro's chief test pilot, brought the Shackleton to Boscombe for first flight outside the company, and we took off from the new north-south runway, the first aircraft to do so. Neil Macdonald and I shared the flying and I remember as though it were yesterday a rather apprehensive Jimmy Orrell standing in the well between the seats, puffing furiously on one cigarette after another for the 40 minutes he was with us. Having seen us safely launched he very sensibly returned to Woodford. That had to be the noisiest aircraft ever when first offered to us. Sitting in line with those contra-rotating propellers was painful and we resorted to all sorts of palliatives to try to improve things, even going back to that helmet with "Sorbo" pads in the ear pieces which had been out of service for years. Poor old Jimmy, I think his hearing was permanently affected.

The end of my three-year tour at Boscombe was now uncomfortably close and I was clearly excluded from any new projects which time would not allow me to complete. It was a difficulty of the system that, on joining the establishment, projects were already manned and newcomers could not immediately be slotted in. Towards the end of the first year the chances were good as long as there were new projects in the offing but any delay could be fatal if completion was threatened by end-of-tour posting. My final fling, outside of the routine work, was a proving flight in the Hastings before the release to service was finalised. Together with Teddy Tennant, who soon afterwards retired and joined Follands, I took the aircraft to Gibraltar and back, completely uneventfully. On completion of this tour at A&AEE my total hours had crept up to 3,000 but these hours were now distributed over 48 types, and I felt that I was beginning to get to grips with my profession.

Writing about the flying side of the job does not capture the spirit of the establishment nor the characters that made it the odd place that in many respects it was. I mentioned earlier the mixed military/civilian organisation in which we worked, which led to an almost academic atmosphere, with some of the boffins, if not barking mad, decidedly odd by RAF standards. One of them who by chance always seemed to be at my table at breakfast time was always friendly although detached in an odd sort of way. It was years later that I realised that the strange, although not offensive, air that surrounded him was gin!

The mess was run along the lines of a London Club with a butler who appeared in morning suit at breakfast and white tie at dinner. There was no bar, but drinks were brought to the anteroom in response to a bell. The major-domo was a Mr Noble (called Mr Scrotum, the wrinkled old retainer, by Paddy Barthropp), and he had the most expensive complexion I have ever seen. Drinks were recorded in a personal bar book and signed for on delivery. Mr Noble, his brain long addled with booze, could remember nobody's name and would stand hand to head, saying to himself but audible to everyone else: "Now what's this officer's name?" this occurred without fail, even if he was bringing drinks for the tenth time that night, and frequently he was. When Sam Patch took over the place from Claude Pelly, he threw a small party in the Ladies' Room for each squadron in turn at which, of course, Mr Noble presided. At the end of ours, when the air commodore asked for the account, Mr Noble could be seen, hand to head, with the eternal question on his lips. Sam Patch (who became Sir Hubert) was a great sporting figure and featured in all his addresses to the troops his story of stepping off the boat in Suez in 1936, and half an hour later being unconscious on the rugby field. He was tempting fate when he told this story to the officers when he was seeking recruits for his boxing team to win the Wakefield Trophy. Inevitably a voice from the back asked if he had ever recovered.

The Flying Wing was commanded by a group captain, the first in my time, a man named Dawkins who seemed to take no part in our affairs. He was a fatherly figure who was most kind, and had I think, settled for the quiet life. Appointing senior officers at Boscombe and Farnborough was difficult because ETPS had its first course only in 1943 and no graduates had reached the sort of seniority necessary for high rank. In consequence, positions of authority were given to some most unsuitable people, probably because it took them out of RAF circulation for a while by seconding them to the Ministry of Supply.

One who fell well short of our critical standards was H.P. Broad who was, frankly, a clown. With the connivance of his adjutant, he received a phone call which went something like this: "Post Office 'ere sir, we are 'aving trouble with your haspirants on the phone. Would you please repeat after me: 'I cannot hold a hot potato in the hollow of my hand.'" The mug duly said it and was told what to do with the potato. He also gained the impression that we were not sufficiently military and ordered that we should parade every Thursday morning. In anticipation of the annual inspection by the Air Officer Commanding, he ordered best uniforms and greatcoats. This rather embarrassed Bill Sheehan who, since he had married and was being properly fed, had put on a few pounds so that he could wear a tunic or a greatcoat, but not both. After inspecting us in greatcoats, the group captain ordered "coats off" to inspect us in best uniform. Bill had no tunic on, so that when we trooped into Station Headquarters to dump our topcoats, he kept on walking and was never missed. As the day of the inspection drew near, more and more flying was left undone as we paraded with the airmen on the tarmac in front of the hangars, trying without much success to look like a disciplined organisation. We all had to learn the commands, and what to do when orders were given and it was some time before we achieved any resemblance to a fighting formation.

Red Evans was always slightly individualistic in the matter of uniform, never in a big way, but enough to be different. At this time he was favouring crêpe-soled suede desert boots, dyed black almost to conform. As officers took posts I was immediately behind him and as we marched off, the crêpe sole of his right boot stuck in the melting tarmac and separated from the upper. With every pace he took, the upper went further up his shin and started to turn to the right, whilst his sock accumulated more and more tarmac. I am easily amused and this was hysterically funny to watch and the only surprise to me was that I could continue to walk, never mind march. Red too was laughing and this did not go unnoticed. The group captain was apoplectic and, when he was excited (and he frequently was), he stuttered badly. The gist of his message was that we were dismissed from his parade and furthermore would not take part in the real parade for the AOC. This was like winning the spring double and on the great day Red and I were in the Flight Office drinking coffee while the others marched up and down in the hot sunshine.

It was during the endless rehearsals for this major event that an unforgettable notice appeared under the signature of the Station Warrant Officer, whose great moment of the year was the AOC's Parade. It read: "Following the cancellation of Tuesday's practice, all airmen will parade on the apron of 'B' Squadron hangar at 08.30 on Friday, irrespective of adverse weather conditions or not." As with most Station Warrant Officers that I met, his colourful language, audible at a range of 100 yards, did not translate easily to print.

The Wing Commander Engineering started a farm at the eastern end of the airfield to grow things for the mess to augment the rather sparse diet of the time. Sam Barnard was a countryman and I think that secretly he enjoyed the farm more than the engineering. On one market day in Salisbury the NCO who did most of the work on the farm was sent in to buy a couple of pigs, the reasoning being that there was enough swill from the mess to raise the beasts, after which – bacon and roast pork for all. On market days in Salisbury the pubs were open all day and were the main centres for business. Our NCO finally arrived back at the airfield astride a horse which, he had been persuaded, made much more sense than pigs. The horse not infrequently appeared in the mess on dining-in nights (not on the menu, I hasten to add), but being ridden by an officer who felt that the horse had every right to a party once in a while.

'A' Squadron had lost their CO, Johnny Baldwin, who had gone to Korea to operate with the Sabres, and was never seen again after entering cloud. His replacement, in due course, was Peter Wykeham-Barnes who had been an air commodore in the Desert Air Force but was again, for the time being, a wing commander. He was the first officer I met who struck me with some force as a future Chief of Air Staff, and who in the event only missed it by one. He was not a graduate of ETPS but he was a kindred spirit and ran the squadron extremely well, as might be expected from an officer with so much command experience. The North Koreans were causing the UN forces some grief at the time by infiltrating troops under cover of darkness. The USAF asked if anyone had any good ideas, and the Air Ministry sent PW-B to Korea to help, since he was an ace on interdiction. He sent for some illuminating flares, got checked out on the Mitchell, and lit up the infiltration routes so that the air force and the army could take effective countermeasures. The Americans gave him a medal and on his return he was asked by the Air Ministry to travel around the Commands and Stations telling the aircrews what it was all about. The only RAF participation in the Korean war was by an exchange of officers with the Americans and Australians so that there was no widespread knowledge of operational developments, for example, in jet fighter combat. The Boscombe aircrew were the trial audience for PW-B's presentation which was informative and amusing, and he then set out to preach to wider gatherings. One of his last targets was Gibraltar, then a quite significant maritime base. He chose to go by Meteor 8 and, in the process, established a new UK–Gibraltar record. He is a class act.

I have never been a political animal, and indeed I find the whole racket tedious in the extreme, but one or two actions of the socialist government of the day caused me to pay more attention. The first was a declaration that all branches of the RAF would have the same rates of pay, which is a good principle, but overlooks some practicalities. For example, aircrew were not the favourite clients of the life insurance companies, and those that called at the Boscombe mess could prove that our premiums had to be twice as high as everyone else's, if we were acceptable at all. Doctors began to leave in droves when the rewards of the newly-founded NHS became clear. That was close to home, but I recall hearing or reading about the miners' leader who had convinced the caring politicians that it was unjust that a miner should lose a day's wages because he was ill. My sentiments exactly. The outcome was that Monday became a non-working day in the mining industry and this started the decline that today is almost total.

At the end of a tour at Boscombe or Farnborough the postings branch used to open the interview by saying that it was time to return to the RAF after that swanning around, and then search out the job that would contrast most vividly with their view of life at an experimental establishment. The Royal Navy were much more intelligent and usually appointed the project pilot of a new type to command the first operational squadron. In my case, my punishment for 10 years of continuous flying jobs was a posting to the Organisation Branch of a Group in Home Command, at RAF Kenley.

CHAPTER VIII
LIFE GETS TEDIOUS, DON'T IT?

Being on the organisation staff of a headquarters presented a new challenge and one for which I was ill-prepared. Writing was not a problem because an essential part of test-flying is the ability to report accurately what has happened. Nor was I fearful of something new. But I was deeply concerned that the change of pace would be frustrating and that I would be driven to distraction by the tedium of it all. There was a glimmer of light in that a communications flight was based at Kenley and they were always looking for a spare pilot to help out at weekends.

I worked for a good boss, Bill Dixon, who taught me a valuable lesson about pacing my effort and not trying to do everything by close of play, a habit formed by experience I suppose. At the end of the working day he stopped, even in the middle of a sentence, for the good reason that the work would be there in the morning. He never stayed on and never took anything home with him, arguing that to do so was a sign of poor organisation or pointed to the need for more staff. It was a philosophy that I admired but could not follow. I never rested easy if a task was outstanding and could not relax until the 'in' tray was empty. Kenley certainly broadened my experience and I learned some administrative skills which later stood me in good stead.

The flight embraced Oxford, Anson, Auster, Proctor and Tiger Moth aircraft and, at the back of the hangar, a Spitfire 16, personal property of the Air Officer Commanding, which never seemed to move. I flew people from A to B, gave experience flights to ATC cadets and joyrides to staff officers who were not pilots. Occasionally I flew to the gliding school at Detling and spent the day towing gliders. Breathtaking stuff.

My attention was caught by an influx of officers to the mess and even more, by the arrival of some Hurricanes, flown by some obviously foreign gentlemen, heavily perfumed. The officers were extras for the film "Angels One Five," and the Hurricanes were Portuguese which, augmented by every flying Hurricane that could be rounded up, provided the flying action for the movie. From my office window I had a good view of the signals centre which, for the film, became the wartime operations room, heavily sand-bagged. One morning I watched fascinated as Jack Hawkins, playing the Station Commander, approached the sentry and was stopped and asked for his identity card. He attempted to bluster, telling the sentry that he must know who he was and so on, but without gaining entrance before he produced the required document. "Good lad!" he said to the sentry who, after the Station Commander had passed inside, made the comment: "Won't catch me with that one." I may have the dialogue slightly wrong but

68

it was on that sort of elevated plane. I saw the film subsequently and the scene lasted perhaps 30 seconds, but I knew that some 20 people had spent an entire morning and heaven knows how much film to capture those magic moments of drama. The real highlight of the filming for me occurred when two of the Portugese, who had probably never scrambled anything in their lives, except perhaps a few eggs, collided on the perimeter track in staging an emergency take-off for the cameras as the airfield came under attack.

On a sunny Sunday morning I turned up to fly some air cadets in the Anson, a job I quite enjoyed because they were all so enthusiastic. The routine was to ask where they lived and went to school, and sketch out a short cross-country on the map to show them where we were going so that they could identify familiar spots. On this day the Anson had come off inspection and my trip was to serve also as an air test. After take-off the boys took it in turns to sit in the front right-hand seat and have a bit of a drive whilst I stayed on the controls from the captain's seat. After half an hour I headed back to Kenley to pick up another lot but, on selecting wheels down, nothing happened. I tried everything that I could think of, applying 'g' to try and jolt them loose, stalling the aircraft to try and suck them out, all to no avail. The tower had finally located the duty foreman from the hangar, who offered the opinion that a valve must have been installed the wrong way around and that the only solution was to hack up the floor boards and release the up-locks manually. There were already some rather green and round-eyed boys in the back and what they felt when the maniac in charge took the fire axe and started chopping the aircraft to pieces I can only conjecture. Needless to say I achieved nothing and prepared the passengers for a wheels-up landing. The wheels in the Anson did not retract completely and even when locked up, about half of the wheel was in the airstream, so that a no-wheels landing was not likely to be too damaging. In the event I had to use some brake to stop it and no one was hurt. The boys of course thought it was marvellous fun when they were safely back on the ground, but I wonder how many opted for another career as a result?

The word came to me from the hangar that the AOC's Spitfire was to be delivered to the Maintenance Unit at Llandow so I went and sat in it, assuming it would be my last chance. I guessed that the AOC himself, T.M. McEvoy, would fly it to Wales or that Al Deere, the New Zealand ace who was on his staff, would take it. As with the posting from Tern Hill, I have no idea how many others turned it down, but eventually it was offered to me. The runways at Kenley all appeared short after the 10,000 ft of Boscombe and, lining up in the Spitfire, the far hedge looked very close. However it was no problem and, after all, Spitfires had operated from there throughout the Battle of Britain; nevertheless it *was* exhilarating.

Kenley was the first station on which I served that operated a peacetime routine in that on Wednesday everything stopped at lunch-time and the troops played whatever team game was in season. I was roped in for the station rugby team and enjoyed some very good games against other stations and local clubs. One day we were playing the Medical Rehabilitation Unit at Chessington and winning so comfortably that anyone who scored took his own conversion. Almost at full-time I kicked from in front of the posts and felt a twinge in my right knee which I ignored until the evening, when the joint was so swollen and so painful that I could hardly move. The station doctor said that I had a cartilage problem and to take it easy for a day or so, which I did. Recovery was slow and he arranged for me to go to the aircrew rehabilitation centre at Headley Court for treatment or preparation for surgery, whichever seemed the more appropriate. I arrived, limping and leaning heavily on a walking stick, to be met by a well-muscled corporal PTI who took the stick and advised me to put my kit into a room at the head of the stairs. He made no offer to help so I struggled up on my own clutching the banister for support. Halfway up he called: "See you in ten minutes, sir, PT kit please." He had set the tone for my stay, which was gruelling but therapeutic to the point that I was released with a warning not to return, but with a serviceable leg. They had some very clever tricks; for example, my right leg was damaged so the bicycle that I was required to ride had only one pedal, on the right side. We played five-a-side soccer with a boot only on the defective leg. Of the 30-odd inmates, three had actually been in flying accidents, and one of those was an Argentinian. Another was Malcolm Smith who was doing some fighter affiliation in his Meteor with a Bomber Command Lincoln and unfortunately hit it. He banged out but, not unusually with the early seats, damaged himself quite badly in the process. Quite aside from a broken neck his right ankle had been smashed with serious nerve damage. He was in a cast from his head to his waist and could walk only with the greatest difficulty. We became chummy during my time there and none of his injuries had taken away his capacity for a pint.

After about a year at Kenley I again began studying the "sits. vac." in Air Ministry Orders and came across one for a test pilot required for an exchange posting to the Royal Canadian Air Force for which I applied, thinking that there would not be many applicants who were properly qualified, in fact I might be the only one! This could well have been the case because my administrative tour was declared at an end and I was off to Canada.

By way of celebration, I went to see Mary Martin in *"South Pacific"* at the Drury Lane theatre. Even the magic of the show could not divert my attention from the fact that my right knee was again assuming balloon-like proportions. It was back to Headley Court and, once again, their tender ministrations had me back on my feet but this time with a stern warning to stop playing rough games or prejudice my flying career. My rugby days were over.

I went to the Air Ministry and Ministry of Supply to establish precisely where I was to go and what I was to do. I was to join the Winter Experimental Flight at Namao, Alberta and before departure I should try and fly an Attacker and a Sea Hawk. There would also be a Venom in the first season's programme but its similarity to the Vampire made a familiarisation flight unnecessary. I arranged to go to Aero Flight at Farnborough to fly the Attacker and to Hawkers at Dunsfold to have a whirl in the Sea Hawk. The Attacker was pretty straightforward if you could get it out of dispersal. The tailwheel seemed to take up a position from which it was reluctant to move so that, if it was not straight when it was parked, it tended to go round in circles. As always with a new type, the first reaction is: "I must be doing something wrong," but that was not the case, it just had to be beaten into submission. I spent quite a lot of time at Dunsfold on the promise of a serviceable aircraft becoming available but achieved nothing other than seeing some old friends like Neville Duke and Bill Bedford.

CHAPTER IX
BABY, IT'S COLD OUTSIDE

The Atlantic crossing this time was quite different from those during the war and I began to appreciate why cruising was such a popular pastime. The Cunarder "Franconia" steamed sedately along, a first-class floating hotel, finally entering the St. Lawrence and berthing at Quebec. From there to Ottawa to the High Commission to collect tickets for the rest of the journey west, with a couple of days to look around the capital hosted by the staff of the Commission. The Bytown Inn (Ottawa was originally called Bytown after an early British town major) was the hotel used by the High Commission for transients – sadly in need of refurbishment and, in that steamy Ottawa July, air conditioning.

Crossing Canada by train is the way to get a full appreciation of the size of the place. Waking each morning for three successive days to apparently the same scene outside the train windows is both sobering and instructive. With the break up of the Soviet Union Canada is now the biggest country in the world, and it is the train traveller who best appreciates that fact, at the same time perhaps finding the scenery on the dull side.

Winter Experimental Establishment (WEE) Flight as we were known, more properly the Climatic Detachment of the Central Experimental and Proving Establishment, was set up to test and develop aircraft and associated equipment under arctic conditions. All British aircraft were required to be pan-climatic and Namao, about 10 miles north of Edmonton, was at the other end of the scale from the Tropical Experimental Unit. It had a small complement of Ministry of Supply boffins, one of whom, Bill Barnes, had welcomed me on my first arrival in Khartoum. An RAF exchange post had been established to look after British interests, which were not necessarily shared by the Canadians, but also to help with the other odd jobs that came along.

I arrived to find that the flying wing comprised five pilots, of whom I was the only one jet-qualified, and three navigators. There were 11 different types of aircraft on strength, with more expected in the autumn, and nobody else with any research and development training or background. The shortage of jet experience was not immediately significant with only a Sabre and Vampire in the hangar but, with the build-up that was expected, I could see busy days ahead. This dilemma was solved when, after a very few weeks, I was joined by Russell Janzen RCAF, just graduated from the USAF Test Pilots' School at Edwards AFB.

The Sabre presented my first opportunity to fly supersonic, although patience and determination were needed to achieve this fairly meaningless milestone. Starting British jet engines, the only ones of which I had any experience, required care and attention with the high-pressure fuel cock if a rumble started which, if ignored, could lead to excessive engine temperatures, but was child's play compared with the J47 in the F-86 Sabre. I was warned to keep an eagle eye on the jet pipe temperature gauge during light-up because if it began to rise too quickly, melt-down was almost guaranteed. Whilst this was an exaggeration, it certainly required great care to keep within the limits, and must have been most trying under operational conditions with the adrenalin flowing. The other needlessly complicated piece of kit was the ejection seat; this had no built-in parachute, so it was necessary to carry one from safety equipment for each flight and, furthermore, it had to be put on before entering the cockpit because it was a backpack, impossible to get into when seated. The seat was fired by three quite separate actions, two with the right hand and one with the left, or it could have been the other way around. I used to quiz myself in flight and figured I had a 50:50 chance of getting the sequence right. Fortunately, I was never put to the test.

With the passing of the brief Alberta summer work began in earnest. The test conditions required operations down to -45°C, perhaps not as bad as it sounds since the Fahrenheit and Celsius scales are coincident at -40, but it is still 75 degrees of frost in old money. If Edmonton did not produce the right temperatures the aircraft were flown to, and operated from, Watson Lake in the Yukon or Fort Churchill, Manitoba on Hudson Bay, where the required temperatures were guaranteed.

The British aircraft arrived in crates and were assembled under the watchful eyes of the technical representatives of the manufacturing company concerned. The Venom was the first to be completed and I flew it in October. In November, the Attacker was ready for flight but the Sea Hawk only just made it into the air on the last day of 1952. There was other flying to be done too and, in a typical month, I was flying between 20 and 30 hours on five or six types. Russ Janzen assumed prime responsibility for the Sabre and Venom and I took the rest although I flew occasional checks on all the aircraft. I shall never forget putting my head round Russ's door to ask if he could take one of the two aircraft that had come up, to be told that he was busier than a "one-legged man at an ass-kicking contest," which was both accurate and graphic.

Like all test-flying, the exciting bits occurred amongst otherwise monotonous spells of flying with extreme accuracy to produce data to give the complete picture of the aircraft's performance. In the British aircraft there was always a good chance of becoming lost since they had no navigation aids except for the voice radio connection to the tower which allowed the controller to give homing bearings. The work usually required the aircraft to be cold-soaked at or above 30,000 feet for half an hour to ensure that the temperatures were stable before starting to record the eight or ten parameters being measured. Often this meant being above cloud most of the time, maintaining a mental-dead reckoning plot of position, and at the end of the test descending and waiting for things to warm up sufficiently for the radio to start working again. Below cloud, one patch of snow looks very like every other and only the lights of Edmonton or the flares from the oil wells offered a clue as to which way to turn for Namao.

On one occasion in the Attacker, my relief at finding the airfield in the gathering gloom was such that I ran in and broke with more than usual vigour. As I pulled up the aircraft yawed and an undercarriage light flickered, which caused me no concern since one-off and inexplicable electrical incidents were common in all the aircraft in the extreme cold. However, on selecting gear down the red light stayed on on the port leg indicating that the wheel was not locked down, but I found that I could get a green gear safe light by yawing the aircraft. The only solution that made sense was that the leg was dangling with some sort of failure in the locking system. I considered retracting the other wheels since landing on the snow-bound runway was always tricky even with a complete undercarriage. Second thoughts were that landing with a bit of drift to force the leg to stay vertical until the weight was on the wheels might work as long as it rolled straight and I remembered not to touch the brakes. I approached as slowly as I dared and flamed-out the engine as I crossed the approach lights. It worked like a charm and in no time the naval servicing crew had fixed a 4" x 2" timber jury strut to the leg and towed the aeroplane into the hangar.

At about the same time I gave a Vampire demonstration at an airshow in Wetaskiwin, a small town not far from Namao, with no suitable airfield on which to land so that the planning and briefing were done by telephone with the show organiser. This was a departure from the meticulous planning that had gone into all previous demonstrations that I had been concerned with; still, when in Rome . . . My five-minute slot was defined and, after a cursory rehearsal to make sure that there were no loose articles in the cockpit, I set course for Wetaskiwin. At the advertised time I rushed in and did my loops, rolls, Derry turns and then flew past inverted but with the wheels extended (which usually amused the crowd), before the high-speed flypast which was to be the finale. During the inverted bit I became aware of a box-four formation of RCAF Mitchells below me. I flew slowly and thoughtfully back to Namao. The subsequent inquiry showed that the Mitchells were a minute early for their slot but pressed on because they could see that the area was clear. Sometimes, even now as a spectator, knowing that the show is properly run, I have moments of unease when I see the amateur approach of some of the enthusiasts.

The winter of 1952/3 was cold in Edmonton and we had all our target temperatures without leaving base except to take the Sabre to Watson Lake for one night. Watson was an interesting place for a masochist with a taste for venison and bear meat. There was very little comfort but for a $1 licence, purchased from the resident Mountie, you were allowed to shoot unlimited deer but only one bear and one moose. The lake was full of trout which could be fished through the ice in winter or caught by trolling from the rescue boat in summer.

In the new year we received our CF-100 Canuck and it turned out to be a trainer version which we used for gathering data and for conversion-flying for some of our pilots. It also allowed us to give our other aircrew and some of the engineers some jet experience. It flew like a big Meteor and the main interest for the pilot was to find an engine setting on the Orendas which gave the speed that he wanted without infringing the prohibited RPM bands. After about a month of this we were informed that the operational version that we should have had in the first place was ready for collection at the Operational Conversion Unit at North Bay, Ontario. Accordingly, in late February I departed Namao in the CF-100 *en route* Winnipeg and North Bay. I was accompanied by a most excellent Canadian navigator named Joe Kueber who rarely smiled but was one of the most amusing men that I have ever met. As always the aircraft was late out of the hangar and instead of getting to North Bay for our night stop we held over in Winnipeg where it was both dark and snowing heavily. The next morning it was still snowing but the forecaster said that it was very local and that we would soon climb out of it.

To understand what follows it is necessary to explain that in most trainer versions of operational aircraft, the fuselage is stretched to accommodate another seat for the instructor behind the student. In the CF-100, which already had a navigator's station behind the pilot, they simply duplicated the controls and as usual, gave the rear seat overriding authority for services like undercarriage and flaps. This allowed the instructor to forestall most of the disasters that students sought to inflict upon him, for example raising the wheels at the wrong time.

On this delivery trip I took the front seat so that I had the best view when manoeuvring on the ground or in the air, and Joe was in the rear seat. We filed our flight plan, strapped in and took off into the snowstorm still raging and with cloud almost down to the ground. After entering cloud, cleaning up the aircraft and turning on to the first heading, it was clear that we were not accelerating as we should. The instruments were working but we were more than 100 knots slower than we should have been. This was a good problem to resolve on the ground but I was not crazy about the idea of trying to get back into Winnipeg and instead concentrated on the possible causes of our misfortune. The wheels and flaps were up and the pitot head heater was on and working. The speed was stable and the flight instruments responded to attitude changes. I asked Joe to check the airbrakes, which could not be seen from the front cockpit, and he reported nothing amiss except "those spiky things sticking up on the wing." My own airbrake selector was 'in' but either accidentally or because he had been fooling around with the throttles and had tripped the selector, he had overridden my selection and extended the airbrakes. The indifferent performance of the CF-100 was not improved by this additional aerodynamic impediment.

Flying across Canada was controlled by a string of radio beacon stations, each with a duty operator. Aircraft in transit flew on the right-hand side of the beam approaching the transmitter. In the early fifties, the traffic was generally at something less than 200 knots and below 10,000 feet, with a flight plan that showed estimated time over the station. When passing overhead, indicated by a break in the signal, the pilot gave his identification and time overhead with his estimated time at the next check-in station. This was a fairly leisurely procedure and not infrequently the ground operator would maintain a brief conversation or pass the latest weather before signing off. In the aircraft, the frequency of the next station was selected on the radio compass, the call sign verified to confirm proper selection, and the aircraft turned to the heading demanded by the compass needle. Anything from 20 to 40 minutes later the procedure was repeated as another beacon was overflown. There was an elegant simplicity to the system since opposing traffic was separated by at least the width of the beam and the ground stations knew the whereabouts of the traffic arriving or departing. I found that the mid-Atlantic accent learned during my American training helped in my transmission being understood first time, and I quickly adapted.

When the military jets began operating, the frailty of the system was exposed. The ground stations were spaced at 75-100 miles on average, about 25 minutes flying time in the old aircraft, but only 6 or 7 minutes at 500 knots. It required some slick handiwork in the cockpit to report position, say it again because the ground operator was not very good at my modified English, confirm estimate to next reporting point, confirm 35,000 feet, tell him no, you were not kidding, and identify the aircraft type. By this time he was well behind the aeroplane and the next reporting point, where the same comic patter would be repeated, was coming up fast.

The countryside, seen from the air, was spectacular and the visibility, especially in winter, was almost unbelievable. There was usually a thin layer of smoke where the gases from the oil wells were flared, which became much worse when a temperature inversion occurred, causing the smoke to thicken because it could not disperse. From September/October onwards though, map-reading was a nightmare since the few distinctive features on the ground were buried under snow, and even lakes which were frozen and snow-covered were indistinguishable from the surrounding land. After the first fall of snow the temperature normally fell sharply and the runways were not cleared, neither were the roads, so that having found an airfield it was still necessary to find the runway in use, marked by short pine trees down its length. This was daunting initially since in the early stages of a landing the aircraft was free to wander at will and normal braking action was just not available. The jets did not help since the exhaust temperature at take-off was enough to melt the snow at the runway threshold. As soon as the take-off run started the thawed patch froze again leading to some interesting activity by the next aircraft trying to line up. The Attacker, which sat on a tailwheel, was a particular offender and, as reported previously, was not the easiest aircraft to manoeuvre on the ground. Watching Al Woods, our RCN pilot, making his first trip in the aircraft, I really thought that he might need to refuel by the time that he finally made the runway. He took the Attacker back to Halifax, Nova Scotia at the end of the season where it was lifted aboard a carrier and returned to England.

During the closed season we were effectively kept occupied with the production testing of aircraft overhauled by the North West Industries factory at the Edmonton civil airport. These aircraft were Mitchells, Dakotas, Expeditors, Harvards and the occasional Bristol Freighter. Our unit aircraft also had to be flown and I initiated a training programme to get every pilot qualified at least on the Vampire in the hope that the workload could in future be more evenly spread during the winter. It was a matter of some concern that an accident, or even a bad head cold, could bring all the programmes to a halt because only two pilots were qualified to undertake the experimental flying.

There was no mess at Namao, although there was a canteen which provided us with lunch, and in consequence we were full members of the Edmonton mess, which housed a Command Headquarters and a transport squadron. I was surprised to be slapped on the back in the bar one evening by a chap that I had last seen on Manus Island – "overlooking the calm blue waters of the Bismarck Sea," as the radio station had it. He was Val Hemming, an RAF navigator on exchange with 435, the transport outfit. Apart from seeing him, the other good news was that there was a cricket league in Edmonton, and I began to play for the RCAF against nine other clubs over the summer weekends.

During leave I visited Banff and Jasper, saw Lake Louise which really qualifies as breathtaking, and drove down as far as Spokane in the State of Washington on the Pacific coast. I had bought a Vauxhall Velox with the intention of taking it home, since new cars were still hard to come by in England, and it proved to be the key to conversation wherever I stayed. The

Alberta number plates aroused interest south of the border and the "cute little car" attracted lots of attention, greatly to my surprise. At filling stations it was regarded with suspicion until I asked for the oil to be checked, when the attendant would look at the engine and usually say: "Why! It's a little Chevvy!"

The Unit ran a series of lectures for the troops during the summer to increase civic awareness and generally to educate. Whilst officially I was excused these little chats on the basis of being a visitor, I asked if I could attend one to be given by Darryl Royal, the American coach of the Edmonton Oilers football team. Mr Royal was an all-American quarterback who had been lured to Edmonton with the promise of rich rewards and I was keen to hear him philosophise on his game, which came a poor third in popularity amongst Edmontonians after ice-hockey and baseball. His talk was thoroughly entertaining and at question time he was asked how he set about scouting talent for his team. He gave an example of checking a strong young prospect working on a farm. He would call when the young man was out ploughing and ask him the way to town. If he pointed he lost interest, but if he picked up the plough and used that to point, Mr Royal would inquire further. As so often with Americans, he found the perfect descriptive phrase.

In the autumn of 1953 we took delivery of a T-33, the Canadian version with a Rolls-Royce Nene engine, which was to occupy some of my time during the winter, and the Sea Hawk had been retained after a disappointing first season in which it was mostly unserviceable. Russ had already flown a T-33 so that we flew it together for my first trip. The aeroplane had a history of fire in the engine plenum chamber and a small spot of mauve paint was introduced on to the instrument panel and was meant to give early warning that something was wrong by changing colour. Russ pointed out that if this should happen he would shout "Eject!" three times and added: "If you say 'huh?,' you'll be talking to yourself." The Ministry had sent out a piston Provost, together with a Meteor 8 with a 30 mm Aden gun, for firing trials under arctic conditions. All the other aircraft were still with us so there was a wide variety of flying to be had.

The hazards of winter flying were underlined when we were asked to join the search for a light aircraft which had gone missing in a snowstorm, having told the radio range station that he was within five minutes of his destination. Using our Mitchell we searched for three successive days but neither we, nor any of the other search aircraft, saw any sign of survivors or wreckage. The aircraft and occupants were found in the following spring, three miles short of the runway. It seemed likely that the engine had failed and that the aircraft had crashed through the snow-covered trees, which had then closed over it making it invisible from the air.

By early December, temperatures at Namao had failed to reach the required low values and so the T-33 and the Provost were positioned at Fort Churchill. The T-33 was straightforward with a direct flight of a little over two hours, but the limited range of the Provost forced us into a series of short cross-countries to places with unlikely names like The Pas and Flin Flon. After landing at the last-named it required full throttle to persuade the poor little Provost to taxi in the deep, deep snow for which it had never been designed.

At Churchill, the aircraft were kept in the heated hangar until the last possible moment before flight because conditions were so harsh. With most aircraft, the crew could climb aboard inside the hangar and be towed out in relative comfort, with the canopy closed. The T-33 however required the clam-shell canopy to be open so that the ground starter battery lead could be fed in over the cockpit sill to the terminal inside the aircraft. Even in full winter clothing, helmet on, visor down and oxygen mask on, there was a real danger of frostbite and one of the ground crew had the sole duty of looking out for the tell-tale white spots appearing on what little of my face was still visible. The original A13 American oxygen mask had a rubber bar joining the two sides of the mask which fitted under the nose across the upper lip. When the Nene engine was reluctant to start my mask froze to my moustache and for a while it looked as though surgery might be needed. Since Churchill I have never complained about the cold – not ever.

The mess and living quarters were connected to the hangars by covered passageways so that living was not too uncomfortable until it became necessary to go into the open. Snow was frequently higher than the windows so that things were pretty gloomy even during the short hours of winter daylight. Sleeping was another problem. When Hudson Bay freezes, it freezes hard and there is nothing to define the shore line since the earth is similarly frozen and snow-covered. The polar bears come in off the ice to scavenge amongst the garbage and, although it sounds like a tall story, they made so much noise and disturbed so many people by scampering over the roof that eventually one family of them was shot. They are fearsome creatures and another very good reason for not straying outside the building.

In winter, the maps of the area are pretty useless since the whole of it is under snow but, interestingly, trappers' shacks are marked and are kept stocked with emergency rations, offering a haven for the distressed aviator. The prospects for survival after ejecting seemed to me minimal unless the searchers had a precise fix on the aircraft's position, although the case would be better today with personal locator beacons. I insisted that the emergency water bottle be removed from the survival kit in the seat-pack and replaced with spare socks since the last item likely to be in short supply was drinking water. Furthermore, it generally froze when the aircraft was in the open, even for a short time, and became a most uncomfortable seat.

In the depths of winter, Namao and, even more so, Watson Lake were cold but absolutely still. This could be deceptive since there was no immediate penetration of the cold although it quickly made itself felt. It introduced another problem for the aviator too because hot air from the engine at take-off would raise the temperature sufficiently for fog to form and effectively close the airfield for up to 10 or 15 minutes. With no other airfield for at least 200 miles the hope always was that no sudden failure would occur to force an emergency landing. Churchill was the complete contrast with a 50-knot wind blowing most of the time combined with a temperature of -40 or so to give a chill factor that could quickly kill. The RCAF ran a broadcasting station at Churchill which gave the chill factor at regular intervals during the day and the further warning "no lone walking," which meant that those outside must be in pairs. Rather like Bavarian dancers, the walkers would look at each other and start face slapping, not for entertainment but to stop frostbite, which can be seen but which the victim cannot feel.

On another occasion, returning to Namao from Churchill in the spring, movement on the ground caught my eye and I circled to have a closer look. My Canadian companion, Bert Meade RCN, explained to me that we were seeing the migration of the caribou which trek north of the tree line for 400 miles in numbers of up to 100,000. It was a most impressive sight, with more wildlife in one place than I had ever seen, even in Africa.

Canada is probably richer in natural resources than any other country in the world, and if another 200 million people could be persuaded to live there and develop the place, it would make the United States look like a poor relation. Minor evidence of the abundance of mineral wealth came with every flight over the western provinces; magnetic compasses behaved strangely for brief periods and then resumed normal functioning. In summer when the snow had gone, looking down while the compass needle was wandering, frequently revealed a small lake in which the water was emerald green, presumably full of copper. In northern Quebec, an airline crew who repeatedly noted this phenomenon at the same spot on one of their routes decided to investigate on foot during a leave period and discovered uranium. It's all there.

In the spring of 1954 my two-year exchange was coming to an end and one of my final tasks was to take the gun-firing Meteor back to Halifax, Nova Scotia, where it was to become deck cargo on a carrier going to England. Two 100-gallon drop-tanks were fitted which gave a comfortable 1 hr 20 min duration at high-level optimum cruise. A lash-up radio compass was fitted and the unit Dakota was to act as the support aircraft bringing the ground equipment and ground staff. On a shake-down flight the day before departure, the radio compass did not work at all but the ground crew found a fault and had it working by the morning. Progress was obviously dictated by the need to await the Dakota at every stop and so the first day was to be Saskatoon, refuel and then night-stop Winnipeg. Departure from Winnipeg the next morning was in heavy snow – shades of the CF-100 – with a stop planned at Lakehead before finishing the day in Ottawa. One section of the Winnipeg to Lakehead leg was going to be silent because the radio range stations were so separated that contact with one was lost before the next one came within range. I had flown the route several times by now and knew what to expect, so that having given my next ETA I was not disturbed when silence descended. I was in cloud at 35,000 feet and simply held my heading, tuned to the next station and waited for it to come within range to get a heading correction. On ETA there was still no signal so I called and gave my time overhead, which went unanswered, then took up the new heading for the next check-in point, beginning to take rather more interest in this dull ferry flight. The area north of my track was wilderness and I turned south a few degrees to make sure that I was heading towards the Great Lakes and not away from them. The aircraft remained very quiet and I was well past my ETA Lakehead with some concern for the fuel state and even more for the continuous cloud in which I found myself. Distrusting everything by now I elected to steer by the emergency magnetic compass, the sort that enthusiasts fit to their motor cars, crude and difficult to read but reliable. I closed down one engine to conserve the dwindling fuel supply and soon after, to my enormous relief, broke out into clear sky with no cloud below. With no idea of my whereabouts by this time, and well off the strip map that I had prepared but never expected to use, I scanned the terrain and could see what appeared to be a small town, and on one edge of it an open area that could be an airfield with a short runway. I started my descent from 35,000 feet committed to landing fairly soon, come what might, hoping that what I had seen was an airfield and not a mirage like the oasis that men dying of thirst see in the desert. I had arrived at Wasau, Wisconsin on a 3,000 ft strip built by the civic fathers the year before and until this time considered too short for any jet aircraft, never mind a British fighter. The aeroplane was empty and stopped easily in the space available. Just before touchdown I had seen the Stars and Stripes flying from a mast outside a school and deduced that I was quite far off track but I was never happier to be on the ground: I had been airborne for 1 hr 40 min.

The Meteor became the centre of attention for the local people while we contacted Lakehead to tell them that I had landed and to send the Dakota to join me. The local air defence radar station had picked me up but had no frequency on which to call and ask what I was up to, but had refrained from launching interceptors to shoot me down. The CO came into town in the evening and bought me a beer, saying it was the only exciting moment he had had in his three-year tour of duty. The support crew caught up with me and we took on board some 87 octane aviation fuel, the only thing available and which Pilots' Notes said was usable in emergency, and I darted over to the USAF base at Kinross to get some proper fuel before proceeding to Ottawa as planned.

I guessed that I had become mixed up with a jet stream (in those days, a newly recognised phenomenon and not well understood), which had carried me miles south of track. In clear weather this would have been obvious to me and I considered myself fortunate that the overcast broke when it did and that Wasau had decided on its modest airfield development programme the year before.

After a series of farewell parties in Edmonton I drove across the continent to board the ship in Quebec, pausing in Ottawa to meet and brief my replacement, Pinky Stark, he of the short, stubby night-fighter Venom at Boscombe.

CHAPTER X
I GUESS I'LL HAVE TO CHANGE MY PLAN

My instructions were to report to the Air Ministry on my return in order to discover what little treat they had in store for me by way of my next appointment. In due course I presented myself for interview by a wing commander of the personnel branch, who seemed prepared to devote some time to advising me that constantly asking for postings to Boscombe Down or Farnborough was not a good career move and that I must get back into the air force, a phrase that had a familiar ring. I tried to point out politely that it seemed to be the kind of work that I was good at, and that it must surely be the case that the service needed the very best-quality aircraft that were available. He did not disagree but insisted that a return to normal duty was essential if the time spent with the Ministry of Supply was ever to be expunged from my record. Faced with this immovable object there seemed little point in attempting to become an irresistible force and so I stated that, with the Canberra just entering service, I might use my limited talents in commanding one of the new squadrons. He rather surprised me by disappearing into another room briefly and on his return stating that that indeed was what I should do. He outlined the need to re-indoctrinate me into Bomber Command which would have changed in the 10 years since I had last been a member, and that the process would start a month later, at Dishforth. I would be hearing from him.

I continued my leave and, returning to my home one evening having been out all day, found a small, buff OHMS envelope on the mat. I guessed that it was my posting notice, slit it open, saw the green railway warrant inside and tossed it on to the dressing table. The next morning I began to read it to find out on which day I was to travel to Yorkshire and saw to my surprise that I was to report to the Empire Test Pilots' School, Farnborough, for tutorial duties. So much for planned careers and the persuasive tongue of the postings wing commander. The facts were that, even as we were talking in his London office, one of the test-flying tutors, Spud Murphy, was involved in a fatal accident in a Sea Fury at Farnborough. With a course in progress at the School the need for a replacement was urgent and guess who was available! It's not called planned careers, it's called expediency. I was delighted at this turn of events, although not by what had brought it about, and made immediate preparations to get to Farnborough.

The School was under the command of Sammy Wroath, a famous name in the business from Martlesham Heath days, who had been the first Commandant when the School started in 1943. It is difficult to imagine anyone more relaxed or more popular than Sammy, who let the staff get on with running the course while he looked after the politics of acquiring new

83

aircraft for the fleet and improving the facilities generally. The Chief Test Flying Instructor was Pop Sewell who had been my tutor when I was a student, and the other tutors were Tich Crozier and Al Marriott. It was like going home and I quickly settled in. The students were the usual interesting international mix and included, uniquely, an officer of the Royal Thai Air Force. He was in the syndicate that I took over and I tried once or twice to call him by his proper name, Bancha Sukhanusasna, but gave up and asked if he had a shorter name that he would allow me to use. He assured me that he answered to "Victor" and I had to ask why. He had previously completed the course at the Central Flying School where his instructors had the same difficulty as me and referred to him by his call-sign. Also in the group was Reg Kersey, who had been with me at Namao, and whom I had recommended for the course. There were some new aircraft in the fleet which I had not flown, but the high spot of the flying year for me was collecting the School's first Hunter from the Hawker airfield at Dunsfold. It is easy now to forget what a handsome aircraft it was before they started hanging drop-tanks all over it, and I was captivated by its appearance. I was also taken with its performance. By the time that I had settled down after take-off from Dunsfold, Farnborough, my destination, was miles astern, and the Hunter really felt like the thoroughbred that it was. We also acquired our first Canberra, which was pleasant enough but caused me to reflect that a whole tour on the type might have become a bit tedious.

I was tasked with arranging the course visit to Boscombe Down and accordingly took myself over there, parked my aeroplane, and headed for the headquarters building to see the Chief Superintendent. On my way to his office I passed a man in the corridor whom I recognised as the resident engineer, the chap responsible for the maintenance of buildings, and gave him a cheery greeting. He replied equally cheerily and added: "Have you been on leave?" Bearing in mind that I had not set foot in the place for nearly four years this seemed like a fair measure of the pace of his life.

The USAF student was Ivan Kincheloe who contrived somehow to break not only a Devon but also one of the gliders, which he put into a hedge. After the course he was posted to Edwards AFB where he joined the Bell X-2 rocket-propelled, stainless steel aircraft programme in which he set a new altitude record of 126,000 feet. The same aeroplane had already set a new speed record of 1,900 mph so that it must have been the speed of the Devon and the glider that fooled him. Kinch was killed in an F-104, the aircraft that the USAF did not want but which was sold in large numbers to the NATO air forces, causing particular grief to the Germans, and igniting the huge political row labelled the Lockheed Scandal. The aircraft originally had downward ejection and when the engine failed on take-off, Kinch rolled the aircraft to reverse the ejection mode and give himself a survival chance, but to no avail.

Our two Italians were masquerading as Air Force officers – which they were, in the Reserve – but in fact were more normally employed by FIAT. Indeed Ricardo Bignamini was the chief test pilot of the company, and this allowed him to invite us to visit the factories in Turin and Rome at the end of the course, which we did. Apart from a brief stop in Naples during my return trip by boat from Australia, I had seen nothing of Italy and I found the trip fascinating and Rome the most exciting city I had ever seen, a view which I still hold. We took a Varsity because it was fairly comfortable although it hardly moved with the speed of light, and we were royally entertained by the FIAT people. On the way back we were to clear customs at Blackbushe and as might be expected – after all, it was January – we needed a radar talkdown (GCA) to get in. Pop Sewell was flying the aircraft and I was in the right-hand seat. I never knew if what happened was meant to be some sort of test for me or if he had really lost the place. The controller was giving heights to fly and we were consistently below them until, on the glide path, he was telling us to maintain our height, also ignored by Pop. I stood it for as long as I could and then told him that I had control, opened the throttles, and climbed back to the proper height. Not a word was said, then or later, but I had a very good close up of the trees on the final approach.

The new year brought a new course and a change in tutorial staff as Tich Crozier went off to the embassy in Washington and we were joined by Stan Hubbard and Bill Sheehan as RAF members, with Pridham Price as the sailor. We were all old mates and the routine restarted without a hitch.

In February it was time for Annual Confidential Reports and, having completed the piece that I had to do, including choice of next appointment, (Boscombe Down, Central Fighter Establishment or any other flying job – I was already at Farnborough), I was expecting Pop Sewell to send for me because he had to complete the next bit. He was a blunt Yorkshireman (i.e. usually rude!) and he opened his address by saying that he thought that I had matured well (that was his exact phrase, which made me feel like a Wensleydale cheese) but that he had changed my first choice for next posting if I would care to initial it. He said that I needed to go to the Staff College and, seeking to stifle the idea at birth, I told him that I had not taken the entrance examination and therefore was ineligible. He then told me that my name had gone forward for the next examination to be held in August. I thought that this was a bit cool and that he was getting his own back for my taking over the landing at Blackbushe. However that was not the case and in his peculiarly gruff manner he was doing what he knew to be best for my career.

The next month he was killed in, of all things, a Pembroke, a gentleman's carriage that he rather favoured as a mode of transport. He was returning from Boscombe when a fire started in one engine. He overflew Andover which was quite big enough for him to land and where, by sheer chance, they were having a fire practice on the airfield. Soon afterwards he called to say that he was going to force-land in a farmer's field, but in trying to do so he clipped a tree with the wing that was by then on fire and turned it into the fuselage, cutting off their escape. I often wondered later if that aberration during the landing at Blackbushe was the first warning sign that he was not quite with the programme and if I should have told someone.

The student mixture was as before but with an Egyptian, Fikry Zaher. It was customary to have a welcoming party for the new syndicate and Fikry was offered the usual snacks, including prunes wrapped in bacon, which he ate with relish, having established by vigorous nodding that it was beef bacon. He wore several medal ribbons and, recalling the air battle between his Air Force and mine when I was in transit through Luxor, I asked what they were for. One was for being an A2 Flying Instructor, another for winning an aerobatic competition and another was for being a friend of the President and so it went on. Poor Fikry. I think that he was never quite up to speed although he seemed to fly well enough in those aircraft where he could have some dual. There was no two-seat Hunter and he seemed happy enough on his own but something happened (we guessed that he had not selected cabin demist during the descent), and he crashed just off the airfield when trying to land. By coincidence, Stan Hubbard had joined a de Havilland team delivering some Vampires to Cairo and was in the city at the time of Fikry's funeral. The chief mourner was President Nasser, which led us to think that Fikry was perhaps more than just a run-of-the-mill air force officer.

Another of my favourite students was on the 1955 course, an Italian, Michele Colagiovanni, who was a genuine Italian Air Force officer. When he arrived his command of English was uncertain, although it improved rapidly when he began to use it every day. I remember the change that came over him when Jimmy Lang, the chief technical instructor, stopped talking and began to write formulae on the board. Everyone else looked blank but Mike's face lit up, he was finally seeing something that he understood. Quite early on in the course his flying was being held up because we had no serviceable dual-control Meteor and, since he had never flown a twin-jet, it was considered prudent to give him a quick whirl before launching him on his own. After losing a couple of days, I briefed him carefully and climbed into the back of a Meteor NF.11 which had two seats but only one set of controls. We had absolutely no trouble and he flew beautifully until I tried to talk him through a re-light. He had closed down the engine without any difficulty but his English deserted him as I tried to remind him to press the re-light button as he opened the high pressure cock. He made a perfect single-engined landing and we went to the end of the runway, out of sight, where I hopped out, stood on the wing while we fired up the other engine and then taxied back to dispersal. All the pilots on the course were required to be experienced on a variety of aircraft and to be assessed by their own authorities as at least "above the average," so that flying with them was usually a pleasure. I add the qualification because two RAF former QFIs who were on the courses during my tutorial years talked to themselves – and therefore to me – continuously, as though giving the patter to a student. I had to remind them forcibly that they were now meant to be looking at aviation from a quite different perspective.

During those years there were several good Americans, navy and air Force, and in 1955 it was Captain John E. Allavie, a warm-hearted extrovert who became great friends with everyone. At the time parts of the film *"Bhowani Junction"* were being shot in the Frensham Pond area where an old railway spur was standing in for the plains of India. Ava Gardner, who starred in the film, was staying at the hotel and, after one of those quiet evenings that gets slightly out of hand, Jack Allavie decided that Miss Gardner would enjoy the company of a "good ol' boy." The rest is hearsay but I believe it to be true. The hotel staff told him that Miss Gardner had retired but, undaunted by this, Jack went upstairs, knocked on the door of her room and announced that: "Handsome Jack Allavie, best-looking man in the USAF, had come a-calling." Miss Gardner replied with two short, single-syllable words.

An Australian ace from the Korean war where he had flown Meteors was in the class of '55 and kept us all amused. Ken (Black) Murray was so called because of his dark colouring and because he was on uneasy terms with authority. It was rumoured that the RAAF had sent him to Farnborough because it was as far away as they could send him but I believe this to be slanderous. He was endlessly entertaining with his "g'day, mate, you'll do me for a dinky die" and other pearls from the Australian vocabulary. He was also a very good pilot. On the annual visit to Fairey Aviation, subject of a crude Australian joke as you might have supposed, it was usual for them to take us to lunch at Monkey Island. This is a spot in the middle of the Thames with an excellent restaurant, run at that time by two elderly sisters, I remember. There were two memorable moments to this visit. The first was the arrival in a powder-blue Cadillac convertible of Miss Diana Dors to have lunch, quite separate from us unfortunately. The second was after the main course when Black passed me his copy of the menu on which he had written: "If that was agneau, I'm a Watteau, and I'm no oil painting!"

The helicopter was beginning to be taken fairly seriously at this time and a dual-control Hiller, complete with RN instructor, was sent to the School. Everyone was invited to try it and, although I put it off for as long as possible, I finally accepted that I should give it a fair chance. The concept has never held any attraction for me (although I appreciate its uses) but I had then, and retain, a strong feeling that wings were not meant to rotate and to force them to do so is unnatural. By this time I was a pretty experienced military pilot (3,600 hours on 85 types), and I have never before or since struggled so hard with a new aircraft. I found that I was pressing hard on both rudder pedals at the same time, and gripping the stick as though hanging on for dear life. I hated looking at the air speed indicator and seeing zero and I particularly disliked the way the wretched thing went forward when I pushed the stick forward, instead of just dropping the nose in a christian manner. After 20 minutes it was quite clear that I should either stop right there or begin to take it a bit more seriously. I chose the latter course and, after a few more rides, flew myself around Farnborough just for the satisfaction of having done so. I have never piloted a helicopter since. Because it is so much cheaper to operate fixed-wing aircraft, early air experience was given on an aircraft like the Chipmunk to pilots destined for helicopters. This was a mistake in my view since the student learns habits and acquires reactions which are wrong for helicopters. I am quite sure that I would have found it much easier if I had never flown a proper aeroplane.

Another form of aviation that has never really grabbed me is gliding. The School always had some gliders and sailplanes and some people loved them, but the attraction always eluded me, despite several attempts to become involved. As a student, I was flying in the Auster tug aircraft with David McCall and with Bill Scott, our Australian, in the glider. We struck a very well-concealed emergency runway light as we took off from the grass parallel to the main runway and it seemed prudent to stop and assess the damage, which we did, Mac very concerned that he might be held to blame. For a moment, Bill Scott, who had never been in a glider before, was of secondary interest. Then I became aware of a shadow overtaking us and realised that the glider was still attached, so began the search for the tennis ball-sized handle which allowed us to cast him free. Perhaps the incident caused a deeper trauma than I had realised, but I think that I reckoned the hard work involved for three or four minutes in the air was not cost-effective. We took our syndicates to Lasham for the day with a tug and a couple of gliders, intending always to land back at the airfield but with a Land Rover and trailer in case someone landed away. I was giving some dual to Fred Hefford in the Sedbergh two-seater, a real case of the myopic leading the visually handicapped, when we entered cloud in search of some

88

lift. Nearby, at Odiham, they were re-arming with Javelins and soon after entering the cloud we both heard the noise of jet engines. We realised at the same time that, even if their radars were working, they would not see a glider. Exiting cloud was the only glider record that I came close to breaking.

The School entered a team in the National Championships that year because we had some good home-grown gliding talent including Bill Bedford and Peter Bisgood, who could claim close connections with ETPS. John Waldie, a Canadian on the course, was very good, and Espion Staaf, a Swede, was the national champion of that country. They did not win but were highly placed and certainly did not disgrace themselves.

Neil Macdonald arrived direct from Fontainbleau, where he had been serving on the staff of the Supreme Headquarters, to replace Pop Sewell. We, and Bill Sheehan, had been on the same squadron at Boscombe and the rest of the staff knew him well so that there was minimum disruption. Brian Trubshaw invited us to dinner during the week of the Farnborough Show, at a restaurant called "The Mayflower," just outside Cobham, and a good halfway point for us all. Trubbie invited Neil, as the recently-qualified expert on French wines, to make the selection, which he did. He was asked by the wine waiter, with some ceremony, to approve the wine, and declared it to be corked. The waiter was visibly shaken and the rest of us were seriously embarrassed. However, the waiter took it away and produced another which Neil pronounced fit for human consumption. I thought the waiter looked pretty smug and even now I reckon it was the same bottle, which made it fifteen all.

In general, flight-test work was meant to be done in not more than half cloud cover, although with our climate this was more honoured in the breach than the observance. However, bearing in mind that some of our students did not have English as a first language, if the weather was marginal we would fly a quick check before launching the flying programme to try to avoid recoveries where pilots were wrestling with a new aircraft and a new language. The deputy chief controller at Farnborough at the time was Bill Pendry, a former RAF pilot who had lost a leg in an accident. If I called Farnborough Approach and Bill replied I relaxed immediately. Where most controllers answer your first call to them by identifying themselves and saying how well or badly they are reading you, Bill gave a course to steer for Farnborough so that if the radio failed immediately at least you knew which way to point. Landing off the weather check one morning, in really awful conditions, Bill asked if I wished to be right or left of the centre-line, and put me there. They do not get any better than that.

The bar was pretty informal at ETPS and at weekends it was quite usual for children, who should have been confined to the Ladies' Room, to wander in and out. A small boy watched Bill at the dartboard finish his throw and stick his darts into his artificial leg as he reached for his beer. Soon afterwards the small boy, copying Bill, stuck a dart into his own leg, which caused him some pain but may also have given him a valuable lesson in the traps that await the unwary.

Towards the end of the year we gained an interesting addition to the fleet, the Avro 707B, the slow model of the pure deltas that the firm had been investigating whilst researching the Vulcan. The fleet aircraft were allocated to tutors for general supervision and air testing so that we became familiar with any little foibles that they might have. I had the Sea Hawks and Hunters and was given the new addition. It was interesting to fly, not wildly exciting, but interesting. The canopy was metal with portholes left and right giving adequate visibility but inducing a certain claustrophobia. It had very little fuel but each student was given one flight to conduct a short evaluation. Because of its shape, the aircraft rounded out on its own as soon as it entered ground effect, a point that I emphasised heavily during the pre-flight briefing.

Hawkers at Dunsfold found themselves with a serious problem during the year. They were producing the Hunter Mark 4 in big numbers but had no Ministry clearance to deliver them to the Royal Air Force. In consequence there were Hunters backed up to the fence at Dunsfold and the company did the sensible thing in renting a hangar at Lyneham to store the aircraft until the Controller of Aircraft (CA) release was given. This left them with only one more problem – how to get them there since with no CA release they could not be flown by the RAF. Someone recalled that, since at ETPS we were on secondment to the Ministry of Supply, we could fly them, so we did. Stan Hubbard and I were dropped off at Dunsfold whenever aircraft were ready to move and we took them to their temporary home. When the CA release was finally granted we took them all back again to be prepared for collection by the Service.

The year rolled to a successful conclusion without further dramas. Bob Moore, the USN student, won the McKenna Trophy, going away as they say in racing circles, and we began the selection of students for the next course. However before they arrived we made the first of what was to become a regular series of exchange visits to our French counterparts at the Centre d'Essais en Vol at Bretigny. To nobody's surprise we found that they had much the same approach to the job and much the same problems.

Before the new course had even assembled there was a repeat of the Hunter story, this time with the Mark 6. Over the next four months we helped to move quite a lot of these aircraft, this time to St. Athan, where the company had rented hangar space. In due course they all had to be returned to Dunsfold and, having all the fuel in the world, Stan Hubbard and I worked up a bit of a pairs act. In rolling one of the aircraft, I collected an eyeful of swarf and called off, leaving Stan to amuse himself whilst I went in to land at Dunsfold. I was taxying to the hangars on the perimeter track parallel to the runway when I saw a Hunter, inverted, going below the trees at the eastern end of the airfield. As I watched in horror, the aircraft staggered up, still upside down, rolled, put the wheels down and came straight in to land. As it passed me there was clearly something different about it but it took a moment to see precisely what. A piece of the canopy was missing behind the pilot's head and something was trailing from it. The aeroplane came to a stop at the end of the runway and, having secured my own aircraft, I jumped into the Land Rover heading down there. A rather shattered Stan Hubbard was struggling out of his parachute harness, and the cause of his difficulty was suddenly clear. As he rolled, the ejection seat fired its first charge and the seat rode up enough to shatter the canopy. At the same time his seat harness released so that he found himself looking at the back of the instrument panel and, to add to his woes, the manoeuvre was so violent that the windscreen anti-icing fluid reservoir released its contents: all this at something below 100 feet. That he survived was a miracle of cool airmanship and that he recovered the aircraft without further damage was equally remarkable.

One of the pre-flight checks on the seat was to ensure that two nuts were in alignment on the drogue gun and on this occasion they were not although the difference between safe and unsafe was not easy to see. After this, all the seats had a white line painted on the gun, so that non-alignment was immediately apparent. The man more upset than Stan was the safety equipment worker who had checked and signed for the seat and I really felt for him. Thereafter, all our deliveries were made in a most circumspect manner! This extended liaison with Hawker Aircraft was my first inside brush with industry and the people who worked in it. The pilots were already well-known to me through visits or, in the case of Neville Duke and Bill Bedford, by our having served together. The others, Frank Murphy, Frank Bullen, Hugh Merewether, Duncan Simpson and David Lockspeiser became close friends and splendid companions.

The class of '56 had the usual blend of characters including Daniel Ely Farr III of the United States Air Force, a giant of a man who had come straight from a squadron flying F-100s, an aircraft that could have been built to accommodate him. He was really a throwback to an earlier age of aviators and lived life to the full. We were due to fly together after lunch one day and I invited him to join me in a glass of squash before eating. To my surprise he said that he had already eaten but he would take a soft drink and ordered a crème de menthe *frappé*!

One of his old buddies, Dick Immig, was on an exchange tour with the Hunter squadron at Odiham and was a regular visitor to Farnborough. He made one unplanned visit though. The American Forces' newspaper *"Stars and Stripes"* had sent a photographer to get pictures of an aerobatic four that Dick led and time was pressing since he was almost tour-expired. They climbed above cloud to take the pictures and, as always, it was "just one more" until their fuel states were low. On return to Odiham they were told that the approach radar was acting up because of the heavy rain but nevertheless they tried to get in. They had to overshoot when the controller lost them on their final approach so Dick said the equivalent of every man for himself and the members of the formation went their separate ways. Two went to Tangmere and landed safely while Dick and his wing-man tried Odiham again. When they were at 5 miles on finals the radar failed completely and the fuel state was so desperate that they accelerated in order to have enough speed for a safe ejection. The watchful Bill Pendry saw them overshoot Odiham, picked them up and fed them straight on to Farnborough runway. As they slowed after touchdown Dick was recorded saying: "Pete, repeat after me, 'Our Father.'" A copy of the tower tape was given to him as a farewell gift when he finished his tour.

We had our customary pair of Italian officers, one of whom, Mario Quarantelli, surprised me after the morning lecture by saying that he had just got married. In response to my bafflement he explained that his fiancée was in Rome and he had married her by proxy! He later went to work for Macchi and was sadly killed doing some development on their new fighter.

We had two particularly bright Indians that year, Sudhakaran and Kapel Bhargava, as different as it is possible for two men to be, but each quite brilliant in his own way. Sudha was a fine cricketer and must have been close to county standard: certainly none of our opponents could get him out. He perished demonstrating an Indian-built Gnat soon after he returned to Delhi.

The golfing standard improved with the arrival of Jack Hindle, a qualified flying instructor and a single-figure handicapper. David Kribs, the USN student, was also very good and Sammy Wroath had been scratch – claiming to be 4 – for years. In the summer at the time of the British Open, Bobby Locke, the great South African champion, would spend a week warming up at the Farnham Golf Club. He had flown Liberators during the war and was known to be an enthusiast so he was invited to visit us. Jack Hindle flew him in a two-seat Meteor which Bobby Locke claimed was the most exciting thing that had happened to him for years. In return, he invited Sammy and Jack Hindle to bring a third player and have a game with him at Farnham. David Kribs made up the party and some hangers-on acted as caddies. It was sobering to watch the great man, still more interested in the Meteor than the golf, asking how the starting system worked, pausing, hitting the ball 250 yards down the geometric centre of the fairway, and then taking up his questioning again. His was a very special talent although his style was criticised by the purists. One is said to have told him that his right hand was all wrong, to which he replied that was OK because he accepted the cheques with his left.

Another regular caller was Mike Hawthorn, who ran the TT Garage in Farnham, and was at the peak of his career in 1956. The reputation for arrogance and aloofness that the newspapers created for him seemed quite wrong to me. On the contrary he was modest about his achievements and very good company.

In the summer we had a large party before breaking for leave and, with the contacts established through our naval contingent, a training flight to RNAS Lossiemouth was arranged to collect seafood purchased on our behalf by the ward-room caterer. The salmon were dead, but the lobsters were alive, as was discovered when the box in which they were stored fell over and these anoxic creatures were seen staggering down the Canberra fuselage; their flavour seemed unaffected, though.

I marvel now at the informality that surrounded our flying from ETPS under Sammy Wroath's benevolent eye. Bill Dixon, for whom I had worked at Kenley, made contact saying that he was commanding a B-29 Washington squadron, and would I care for a ride? I should have suspected a trap, but it was only sprung after I had flown one of his aircraft. He told me how desperate he was to fly a Hunter and expressed confidence in my ability to arrange it on a School aircraft. To the best of my knowledge, the only single-engined aircraft that he had flown were trainers, since when he had become a confirmed 'heavy' pilot. There was no two-seat Hunter in which to fly him, all of which I explained, but left him promising to do my best. Sammy Wroath could see no problem and readily agreed to turn him loose in one of our Hunters. I briefed him carefully and spent an anxious half hour until he returned to the circuit for the planned overshoot followed by a full-stop landing. It went off without a hitch, and I felt a bit mean about those doubts that I had had, but I was never more relieved than when he was safely parked.

One of the things that I had dreaded and did my best to avert occurred with one of the non-stop-talking former QFIs when it was his turn to have his one-off trip in the 707. The briefing was thorough, there were no apparent problems and I alerted him to look out for my Land Rover as a reminder not to flare on landing. About 20 minutes after take-off he returned as planned for one overshoot and one landing. The overshoot was unremarkable but on his final approach for landing the nose went up as he checked, the aircraft ballooned and stalled, thumped the runway and bounced again, shedding bits all over the place. I had started my Land Rover as soon as he checked his descent and was first on the scene of the accident in which, unlike the aircraft, he suffered no damage but came very close to being seriously and permanently injured by me. The aircraft could not be repaired because there were no spares and a unique learning opportunity for the rest of the course was lost.

Taking a cup of coffee in the crew room one afternoon, Owen Lines, another of our QFIs, said: "Off to Bracknell, then," or something similar, and I congratulated him, assuming that he was pleased at the prospect. "Not me, you fool – *you!*" was his reply. I had taken the Staff College qualifying examination as ordered by Pop Sewell and, until this point, was totally unaware of the result. It seemed that I had passed and, in almost indecent haste, had been drafted on to the next course. This did not at all accord with my plans and I pointed out to Sammy that he was already losing three of his tutors in the new year and if I left as well he would have no experienced staff at all. He was on to it like a flash and my departure was deferred for a year. He was running out of time too and ugly rumours started concerning his replacement. There were still few, if any, graduates who had made it to group captain and as can be seen, the job called for a flexibility not commonly found in a thrusting career officer. Neil Macdonald heard from somewhere that the same H.P. Broad, under whom we had suffered at Boscombe, was in line for the job and a distinct panic spread through those of us that had served with him before. Neil, with more courage than sense, wrote to the Controller of Aircraft pointing out the disaster that would follow if this man was sent to the School. He received a pretty frosty reply from CA, but the appointment was never made. In saving the School, Neil Macdonald ruined whatever future he had in the RAF, and ETPS had a lot to thank him for. The new Commandant was named Paddy Burns, and we awaited his arrival with interest since he was known to none of us. He turned out to be a delightful man and a very good boss.

The changes in tutorial staff caused no such flurry since all were graduates: indeed, Newton Harrison and Mike Crossley were on my course. When last seen by me, Newton was in the South African Air Force, but he had transferred to the RAF since as a non-Afrikaans speaker his future was limited in his home country. He had no bitterness about this but saw it as one of life's hurdles to be overcome. Mike was a Royal Navy officer who had completed his Boscombe tour and then taken command of a Sea Hawk squadron, thus exploiting the experience of the aircraft that he had gained during its development. An immaculately turned-out officer, Mike came slightly adrift on one of our visits to a manufacturer. We had travelled by train in civilian clothes, taking uniforms for the following day's factory walkabout. Mike, wearing a tasteful grey suit with brown shoes, had failed

94

to pack any others: Royal Navy uniform loses something when worn with brown shoes! Peter Baker was fresh from a tour at Boscombe and much later was back-up to Brian Trubshaw on the Concorde programme.

The new boys were the customary mix of nations who settled quickly into the lecture/flying routine. The two Australians were on their first visit to the "old country" and clearly found it all very different. Doug Cameron persisted in calling the London railway station from which he travelled to visit relatives "St. Pancreas" in spite of my efforts to correct him. Russ Law, his companion, was excited by everything he saw and had tremendous enthusiasm for all our activities.

The two Indians, Chopra and Dey, had distinguished careers in their own country after the course. Chopie eventually became the boss of Hindustan Aircraft Industries and Bobby Dey was an Air Marshal when last heard of. He surprised me when we were flying together in a Canberra at night; he was making a handling assessment and I was just watching. Turning finals to land, an engine fire warning light came on which caught my attention, and I waited for Bobby to take some action. He did nothing so I pointed out that the light had now been on for five seconds or so. He told me not to worry, it was a spurious warning. This was said with such conviction that I closed down the engine but did not activate the fire extinguisher. The light went out and we landed without further incident. I asked him how he had been so sure that the warning was not genuine and he replied that it had done the same thing when he flew the aircraft that afternoon!

Mike Goodfellow had joined from a Hunter squadron and completed the course with considerable flair. He subsequently returned as a tutor and, on leaving the service, joined Hawker Siddeley at Hatfield to become the chief test pilot for the 146 programme. One of the sailors was Ted Anson, who kept reappearing as time went on, gradually in more senior positions, until he retired as a Vice-Admiral, and even that was not the end of our working together.

The only new aircraft to join the school fleet during the year was a Javelin. The aircraft had caused considerable grief during its development and may never have seen service had the DH.110 not been lost in such spectacular fashion at a Farnborough show with John Derry. By 1957 however, the snags had been sorted out by Dickie Martin and his team, and it was a most comfortable aircraft to fly and rock-steady when set up for landing in bad weather. It allowed no liberties though and required careful handling anywhere near the stall. Short Brothers brought over a Seamew for us to look at and, although I flew it for an hour, it made so little impression that I recall none of its characteristics.

As the year wore on an undertaking was given by Paddy Burns to provide a Canberra display at the Gibraltar Battle of Britain celebration on 15th September. I had a quick rehearsal, inspired by the stirring performances put on by Roly Beamont, and scared myself half to death when, on the first slow roll, there was a nasty crash from the rear of the fuselage. I returned carefully to Farnborough where it was discovered that the navigator's plotting table, normally strapped to the side of the fuselage, had fallen down. That's all it was but it sounded like the crack of doom. I set out for the Rock with John Neilson, a member of the course, and Norman Atkin, a flight engineer, to look after the servicing and refuelling. There were bits of Spain that we were not allowed to overfly at that time but, having checked the Spanish air defences, I figured that if we went high enough there was nothing in their inventory that could reach us and so flight-planned the most direct route. The trip was totally uneventful and, after sorting out the aircraft, I went to the show briefing to discover what was expected of me. The main performers were to be the locally-based Shackleton squadron, who were to open and close the show, whilst the other aircraft, which had assembled from all over the place and of which mine was one, slotted in later on. It all sounded pretty straightforward and we checked in on Saturday, the day of the show, in good time to look over the aircraft and stand by for our start-up time. We were therefore standing by the Canberra when the three local Shackletons approached to open the show in a majestic rather than thrilling manner. They flew down the runway and split, one left, one right, and the leader straight on. The leader continued his circuit and appeared off the end of the runway again with two engines feathered and the radar "dustbin" lowered. He was quite low and I remarked to John Neilson that here was a man who really knew his aircraft or, if he did not, we were about to witness a very dramatic incident. It turned out to be the latter. As he approached he was sinking and very significantly he raised the nose, which may have made him feel better but actually aggravated his difficulties. At almost the last moment he seemed to appreciate what was happening and tried to lower the wheels in order to turn the fly-by into a landing, but without success. The main wheels had just appeared when he struck the runway and bits of propeller flew in every direction. With eight propellers in total there was plenty of scope for damage and it seemed to me to be terminal. No one was hurt and the fire crew were quickly on the spot to suppress any hint of flame.

The spectators standing around all applauded politely as though it had been staged for their benefit and I truly believe that they had no idea just how wrong things had gone. From my point of view, my rehearsals had been in vain because with that great wreck stuck on the only runway there was bound to be a lengthy pause in the proceedings. In fact there was no more flying and the police dogs and their handlers became the stars of the show.

At year's end we made our pilgrimage to Bretigny where I had the chance to fly some of their aeroplanes, one of which I remember for all the wrong reasons. It was a Paris with four seats like a saloon car, two tiny jet engines and a butterfly tail very like the Magister trainer which was produced in some numbers. The company pilot, M Clicquot, flew with me and there was a communication gap. The aeroplane had tip-tanks which were full and I understood that, reasonably enough, it was not aerobatic until the tanks were empty. I established that the difference between stalling and flat-out was not very great and was considering what to do next when M Clicquot turned to me in the very confined space of the small cockpit, said something which I did not understand, grabbed the stick and began rolling merrily. I should say that I do not like garlic, particularly other peoples' garlic, and Mr Clicquot had clearly indulged at dinner the previous evening. That, the apparent rush of blood to the head and my having been told not to carry out any aerobatics until the tips were empty (and they were not), made me wonder if my constitution would stand it. When he pointed the other way I quite enjoyed myself with the little aeroplane although not to the point of craving ownership.

And so, 3½ very happy years came to an end, and with it, the end of my years of pulling on a flying suit for a living. The Royal Air Force Staff College, Bracknell, beckoned, and the best flying days were behind me with the near certainty of spending much more time behind a desk.

CHAPTER XI

SLEEPY TIME DOWN SOUTH

The Royal Air Force Staff College at Bracknell in Berkshire was based on an old mansion, the grounds of which had become overgrown with temporary buildings of singular ugliness. I know that a great deal of money has been spent on the place since I was last there, and I should like to think that its physical appearance has improved, but it would not be the biggest disappointment of my life to find that I was wrong.

At the time, there were two RAF Staff Colleges. The one at Andover drew half its students from the RAF and the balance from other services and countries. Bracknell was predominantly for the RAF with a leavening of what was called "Old Commonwealth," a phrase guaranteed to warm the hearts of the Americans on the course. The student body numbered about 100 and was divided into five or six groups headed by a group captain, and further divided into syndicates of half-a-dozen under the guidance of a wing commander. The deputy commandant was an air commodore and the supremo was an air vice marshal, in my time, Sam Elworthy. He was my second selection of an officer bound to make Chief of Air Staff if there was any justice at all and quite properly he did that and followed it by becoming the best Chief of Defence Staff that we have ever had.

One of the group directors was Al Deere with whom I had previously served at Kenley. He was a wartime graduate of the college course which, it was rumoured, had lasted six weeks, much of which he spent at Biggin Hill where you will remember he had many friends. It is my firm impression that at Kenley and Bracknell I did not see this gallant officer in his natural environment. Among the syndicate directing staff were Peter Parrott and Cyclops Brown, both test pilots that I had served with at Boscombe Down. Cyclops was on the test pilots' course when Dick Ubee joined as Commandant; they did not know each other when they met in the bar and the new Commandant was not amused by one of the students wearing a patch over his right eye in order, he thought, to give an impression of the new boss. The student in turn thought it was pretty poor taste, even if he *was* a group captain, for the visitor to adopt an eye-patch, and on the same eye too. Each had lost his right eye and, when they knew each other better, they would boast that they did not have a pair of eyes between them. The other one that I knew vaguely was Gerry Edwards, a Canadian, who had commanded the transport squadron at Edmonton while I was at Namao.

The course followed fairly predictable lines, starting with basic tests to establish literary skills, if any, and moving on to the study of air warfare and its application to real and imagined scenarios. Each section of study was rounded off by a written exercise in which all the necessary facts were provided to allow a reasoned and practical solution to be reached. These were for the most part individual exercises, with the occasional syndicate solution required for presentation to the rest of the staff and student body. A generous amount of time was allowed for the completion of each exercise based on the convoy principle i.e. timed to the slowest member. I followed a rigid system of working a normal day, starting at 8.30 and finishing at 5, until the task was completed and handed in. By this simple method I reckoned to complete a five-day exercise in three and, since Bracknell is not far from Farnborough, earned myself a couple of days back in the real world. My fellow students were impressed at the speed with which I completed my assignments until I asked them to describe their working days. It usually went: breakfast at 9.30, walked the dog, played 18 holes at Wentworth, started work on the exercise. The point that I am making is that I was not brighter than anyone else, just better motivated to finish.

Early on in the piece we were required to prepare a short talk lasting five minutes or so to entertain and inform the student body before the main lecture of the morning. Anyone with specialist knowledge of an establishment on our visit itinerary was allowed to give a briefing on the work and layout of the place; this permitted me to prepare my talk on the RAE Bedford which was on the visit programme.

Before the first of these short talks we were addressed by a member of the National Theatre on the way to project and to avoid those mannerisms familiar to anyone who has sat through a lecture by a poor presenter. I have forgotten the man's name but I do remember that he was very amusing in his demonstration of what not to do. He deliberately dropped his voice as he studied his notes until we were straining to hear what he was saying. He rattled the change in his pocket until we were concentrating on that and not on his address. It was very well done. My syndicate partner, Major Carl Weaver USAF, was especially taken with the need to relax, take a drink of water if the throat was dry and ensure that the audience was paying attention before launching into the talk. On his morning he waited until the Commandant and directing staff were seated, poured some water from the carafe into a glass, took a sip and threw the glass out of the window next to the lectern. He explained that he was simply following the good advice that we had been given and went on to make clear that the glass was not mess property.

Jock Calder, my CO on 158, was on the course looking exactly as he had when I had last served with him 14 years earlier, and Malcolm Smith, recovered from his broken neck but with a bad limp which even Headley Court could do nothing about. Nerves in his ankle had been severed in the accident and as a result the message from the brain to raise the toes before taking a step was never received. After a lot of surgery it was proposed that the nerves which allow the rotation of the foot in a horizontal plane, but which are rarely used, could be cross-grafted so that his brain would say "rotate the foot" but the toes would lift. Understandably, he was not game to try that and limped for the rest of his days. It spelt the end of his flying because toe-brakes were becoming increasingly common and he could not operate them.

It was the custom for a student to be detailed to open the questioning after the guest lecturer had finished, and after we had all taken coffee followed perhaps by a quick game of croquet. Honestly! During one term I sat next to George Bates, who had drawn the short straw to begin questioning Harry Broadhurst, Commander-in-Chief of Bomber Command – as it was still called. I watched him fasten on a point made early on in the lecture and begin framing his question. By coffee time he had gone through several drafts and, more importantly, missed the comprehensive elaboration of the point made by the Air Marshal later in his address. Everyone settled as the great man was conducted back to the platform by the Commandant and George Bates was on his feet. His question was beautifully crafted without being overlong, and he sat down, his pride at having got to the nub of the problem reflected in his face. Broady regarded George closely, reflected for a moment and then offered his opinion that one of them was an idiot (not the word he used) and that he, Broady, had been alright when he left High Wycombe that morning. I sometimes wondered if the C-in-C remembered the man when George was given command of a Canberra squadron at the end of the course.

In the Naval phase of the study year we were addressed by a selection of old sea dogs who, for some reason, all told the same whiskery old story of the sailor writing home to say that he had met another woman in Gibraltar/Malta/Ceylon: the location varied. His wife wrote back, asking what the new woman had that she didn't, to be told: "Nothing, but it's here." It was not very funny to hear once, but every possibility of raising a smile had gone after the second hearing. Our flying sailor, Ivor Brown, gave the briefing on our forthcoming visit to the combined operations centre at Londonderry. Full of information and witty to boot, he paused before the end to say: "And at this point of the visit, the Admiral will tell you the story about the sailor who wrote home etc. and my future depends upon everyone laughing heartily."

We were prepared for the Army phase of the year by the resident soldier, Colonel Pope, who gave an extensive briefing on army formations and how they work. Most of us badly needed this information since our acquaintance with the brutal and licentious was passing at best, and we were about to be flung together in exercises to decide the future of the world. The Colonel took most of the pain out of the learning process and I remember particularly, during the section on Middle East Command, his reference to the visiting staff officer who opened by giving his name and adding: "I am here to help you." The Colonel who had experienced this as a regimental officer was dismissive of headquarters personnel (bread is the staff of life but the life of a Staff is one long loaf), and referred to the people in Cairo as "the gaberdine swine." For this part of the course I had as a fellow syndicate member Pat Porteous VC and I made it clear to him that I should seek his protection when we began to mingle with the Camberley mob.

The highlight of Army Week was without any doubt the lecture to the massed Staff Colleges given by Field Marshal Montgomery. Even though he was a national hero I had never been impressed by newsreel pictures that I had seen of him and was quite prepared to be disappointed. There were, I suppose, 400 assembled in the vast auditorium at Camberley when this diminutive figure was led on to the stage and introduced. Behind him was a map, with Moscow as its centre, and he spoke without notes for more than an hour as the Director of War Plans of the Soviet Union. It was spell-binding and I became an instant convert. Just as at Bracknell, an army student was detailed to open the questioning and was interrogated by the Field Marshal as to number, rank, name and regiment. His response led to a pleasant exchange, with Monty reminiscing about a man of the same name who had served with him, a relative perhaps? Or, in the case of the Scot who posed a question, a short review of his regimental history and the outstanding soldiers that the regiment had produced. This was Montgomery amongst his own and removed from the cares of high office.

He told us about landing his 8th Army in Italy, to be met by the local Italian Commander, now an ally against the Germans, who as a Lieutenant General outranked Monty and would therefore assume command of the liberating forces. Monty asked him what he had been doing before the Italian army had changed sides and was told that he had fought in the desert. "I said to him: 'Oh! really, how did you get on?'" There was no further discussion of who was in charge.

The sad part of this phase for me was the realisation that the soldiers, generally speaking, had absolutely no idea of the capabilities (and limit-ations) of air power and furthermore, many took pride in not under-standing. In the joint paper exercises that we did, one sailor and one airman were attached to each syndicate of soldiers and we could well have been speaking different languages. Sailors and airmen seem to get along well with an instinctive sympathy for each others' jobs but there is an insurmountable barrier between them and the soldiers.

1958 was the year of the Brussels Exhibition and a visit to the forces in Germany allowed us to see it on the return trip. Allied Forces Europe was a vast organisation and we travelled around by coach seeing as much as possible. On the visit to the USAF at Bitburg, we were greeted by their aerobatic team flying F-100s, who gave a stirring performance. We had a look at their aircraft after landing and I noticed that the paint was missing from the tips of most of the fins, which is hardly surprising considering how well tucked-in they flew. They joined us in the Club for lunch, still in flying kit, and in the American manner, wearing their names on their flying suits. Some American names still seem strange to me and I was not too shocked to see "Slot" on the name tag of a young lieutenant whom I therefore greeted by name. He was not offended but pointed out that "Slot" was his position in the formation!

The time was approaching for us to hand in our major individual exercises, the subject of which we had to choose from a short list provided by the college. None of the subjects was particularly appealing to me but I realised that I could air an opinion strongly held by adding a subtitle to "SAGW," the then current acronym given to surface-to-air guided weapons, now universally called SAM. Mr Duncan Sandys had announced that the Lightning would be the last manned fighter aircraft in service with the RAF, a policy that even on superficial examination was clearly absurd. I therefore chose as my subject "SAGW – The Case for the Manned Aircraft," and I still have the thesis which I wrote. In it I emphasised all the things that even the smartest guided weapon could not do but which are essential tasks in peace and war. I chose as examples the most blindingly obvious: investigate, discriminate, identify, be recalled, be globally mobile and all the other things which are, or should be, clear to the meanest intelligence. I assumed that the Air Council had made these points to their political master and had been told to keep quiet or lose their jobs. I could think of no other reason for this extraordinary statement being allowed to pass. I think now that a deal of some sort had been struck and that the air marshals were simply biding their time in the knowledge that a policy revision was inevitable. I certainly hope that was the case although my confidence in the top echelons was slightly undermined when the CAS, at the ceremony to name the operational English Electric P.1 the "Lightning," was reported as saying that all previous interceptors had finished their service lives as ground-attack aircraft and that the Lightning would be no different. Whoever wrote his speech had a very limited grasp of the subject and the CAS should have been on his guard for such misjudgment.

My 10,000 words were finished and handed in to my directing staff, Gerry Edwards. It might be thought that, as a Canadian, he would have felt free to support what I suppose could be seen as a tilt at the accepted wisdom, or at least to have applauded a non-conformist view of a very serious subject. Not a hope. My painfully-typed paper was returned, heavily edited in DS red ink, with phrases like: "Have you not understood the new policy?"and similar expressions. Gerry said that he had been looking forward to reading my essay and was disappointed. I could only apologise. I wonder if in later years he ever thought about my essay when successive new fighter aircraft were introduced into service.

In the dying months of the year the appointments for the RAF graduates were published on the notice board for all to see. Against my name it said "TFIa Air Ministry," which sent me rushing to the Air Ministry Directory to establish if such a post existed and, if so, what it did. I discovered that it was a junior post in the Directorate of Flying Training and the job specification required that the incumbent be a flying instructor. Certain that a mistake had been made, I asked for a recount, to be told that it was no error and that there was a particular reason for my being sent there, although the reason was not disclosed. I wondered, somewhat fancifully, if I was to be given the task of closing all the flying schools since policy said there would soon be no need to train new pilots!

Almost the final fixture of the year was a meeting with the Commandant or his Deputy to go over the course syllabus and to give the students' eye view of the establishment. I was detailed to attend upon the Commandant and, as before, was immediately at ease with that splendid officer. He encouraged me to be frank and I told him that I felt that I had learned a lot and would have enjoyed it more if it had taken say 9 months rather than 12. He understood this point of view. I ventured that my posting seemed a touch "square peg in a round hole" but, after glancing at his notes, he advised me to wait before protesting too loudly. It turned out to be good advice.

I had managed to fly each month of the course, courtesy of my Farnborough chums, particularly the doctors at the Institute of Aviation Medicine who were always looking for a safety pilot for their instrument flying practice. This was not one of the more enjoyable ways of spending time in the air because most of them were frankly not very accurate on instruments. This is not to say that they were unsafe but to fly to the accuracy required for an instrument rating test needed constant vigilance and small corrections, whereas the doctors tended to get close to the limit and then give a great heave on the pole to recover. 360-degree turns were the worst because they would allow the nose to drop and heave on the stick to recover instead of taking off bank, so that to an outside observer, the Meteor would have looked like a dolphin, snatching at a fish held above the water as it circled the pool. A bonus came to me during the course visit to the Bristol Aircraft Company at Filton. I knew the pilots, who were all ETPS contemporaries, and was invited to join in the production test of a Britannia, which occupied the whole morning, and avoided the dreaded "factory foot."

I would not claim that my year at Staff College was undiluted joy but on the other hand I learned a lot about my service, the other services and life in Britain from the political and industrial views that I had never previously considered. That, of course, was precisely the point of the exercise.

CHAPTER XII

BUSY DOING NOTHING

In the beginning of 1959, the Directorate of Flying Training was housed in Richmond Terrace, opposite what is now the Ministry of Defence. The building was a warren, with once-noble rooms divided and partitioned into cupboards which served as offices. Only very senior officers had a window with natural light, the rest lived in perpetual gloom in conditions which would interest the Health Ministry who, I believe, now occupy the site. Fortunately we moved after a week or so to the ground floor, river side of the Air Ministry (now MoD).

The Training Directorate was a friendly place headed by Dougie Amlot, with a vertically challenged deputy, Don Peverill. The cell to which I was drafted had Sam Hoare in charge, and I was to take over from Joe Waddington, who was leaving for the Flying College course at Manby. It was at my arrival interview with the air commodore that I learned the purpose of my being there. In summary, Flying Training Command needed a new advanced trainer and had made a proposal which the Directorate felt it should examine before endorsing. There was no one in the place with evaluation experience and they had therefore asked for a test pilot to be added to the strength. I was given some fat files and told to get on with it.

The first enclosure was a letter from the C-in-C, Sir Richard (Batchy) Atcherley, to the CAS, Sir Dermot Boyle, tracing the history of new equipment for the advanced flying schools. It showed that the two-seat variants of the Meteor and Vampire had not been designed as trainers but for conversion, a vastly different thing. He ended by saying that Follands were offering to produce a two-seat version of the Gnat specifically for pilot training and could he please have it because he was sick of "Dad's old boots," a phrase I shall never forget. The only other contender was the two-seat Hunter which had been produced by Hawkers and was busy establishing point-to-point speed records all over Europe. Whilst this variant of the Hunter, the T.7, fell into the category of a conversion from single-seat fighter, to which he so strongly objected, so did the proposed version of the Gnat! The difference was that one was a huge success, selling to many of the major European air forces, the other was not and had been bought only by the Finns. I found myself puzzled by the facts as presented and when I sought guidance I was told that I had been sent there to get to the bottom of it all and make recommendations.

There were lengthy comparative flying reports on the two aircraft and I looked for the authors' names to see which of my test pilot chums at Boscombe Down had written them, and upon what the comparison was based since there was no two-seat Gnat. The fact was that a single-seat Gnat had been compared with a two-seat Hunter by some skilled instructors from the Central Flying School, the jewel in the flying training crown, and close to the C-in-C's heart. They had made the unanimous recommendation that the envisaged two-seat Gnat would be an infinitely better training machine, cheaper to operate and with better performance than the Hunter. Graduates from the jet training system (Jet Provost/Gnat) would be fully prepared for conversion to the front-line aircraft in service and foreseen. That was the background to my problem, and I was in no doubt as to the solution expected of me, although no attempt was made directly to influence my studies.

I spent a lot of time at Hamble finding out from the Folland design staff how they proposed to force another seat into the already tiny space available, and was impressed with their enthusiasm and confidence although concerned at some of the ruses they were looking at. There was never a Gnat available for me to fly because so much development was in progress on the small fleet. The company pilots were all old friends, and spoke to me freely, but with total loyalty to the company. If they had any doubts about the practicability of the scheme they certainly did not tell me.

I had less need to research the Hunter since I knew it quite well, although not the two-seater, of course. The aircraft had not yet been ordered for the RAF, but an order was expected on the usual basis of one per squadron for instrument and other checks, but until these aircraft were introduced graduates from the flying training system would continue to go from the Vampire T.11 to the single-seat Hunter.

The costings of the exercise were included in the file and made interesting reading for the novice staff officer. It had been assumed that graduates from either type would be capable of flying any front-line fighter without further training and neither aircraft gained points on that account. However, if the Hunter was chosen, the costs so far expended on the Gnat development would be added since Follands would have to be paid for work already undertaken. If the Gnat was chosen there would be no residual costs to be added for the Hunter since its development was funded by the company. In short, to get the aircraft you wanted you must pay for the cancellation of the one that you did not want! Further, it neatly got around the need for the person responsible for authorising the work to apologise for the waste. There were many factors not recorded in the files but which could be guessed, such as the effect upon employment in the area if the Gnat was cancelled, leading inevitably to the closure of the factory. Whichever aircraft received the RAF stamp of approval should benefit from sales abroad which would save Follands, but was not of critical importance to Hawkers.

I applied myself diligently to the task, examined it from every aspect and was driven to the conclusion that, from every possible point of view, from flight safety to maintenance man-hours per flying hour, the Hunter could be shown to be the only solution. Furthermore, I wrote, many of the claimed virtues of the proposed Gnat would prove to be handicaps, and a heavier aircraft with more inertia and with handling much more representative of front-line aircraft would need to be introduced between the Gnat advanced trainer and the operational type.

My paper, and all the supporting data, were approved by the Directorate and forwarded to the decision-makers. The order was given almost immediately, to proceed with the two-seat Gnat! The C-in-C Flying Training Command retired and became a Director of Follands. Hawker Aircraft bought Folland Aircraft and I received a telegram from Bill Bedford which read: "If you can't beat them, buy them!"

The Gnat became a popular and, I believe, efficient trainer although not with the performance predicted for it in my studies. It was found to have too little internal fuel for a full, safe training sortie, and external tanks were fitted. These made the aircraft heavier so that climb and absolute performance suffered. Moreover it was found that the transition from Gnat to, for example, Lightning was much too difficult and an interim Hunter course was introduced to give students more representative handling experience.

My disappointment at having apparently wasted six months was more than offset by the news that I was to leave almost immediately, on promotion, to join the staff of Fighter Command at Bentley Priory. This is what Sam Elworthy knew, and I did not, when he saw me for the final interview at Bracknell.

CHAPTER XIII

FINGS AIN'T WHAT THEY USED TO BE

Bentley Priory, in Stanmore. North London, is steeped in the history of this country, for it was from its Operations Room that the Battle of Britain was directed. By the time that I arrived, in the summer of 1959, the glory days were over although all the trappings of a major command still existed.

Defence organisations stem from the assessment of the threat posed by known and potential enemies and, like a supertanker, have to overcome enormous inertia to get started and take a long time to change course or stop. Thus, in 1959, all the evidence showed that the air threat to Europe was from ballistic missiles against which there was no defence, certainly not by manned aircraft, and yet this highly organised and effective fighter force continued to exist. Part of the justification for its retention was the need to preserve the integrity of our air space, to deny covert or overt reconnaissance to the enemy. A further concern was that if we had no air defence, an enemy would not need to launch missiles against us, inviting massive retaliation from our allies, but could attack in a more modest way using his vast air fleet, and perhaps achieve a victory without exciting the rest of the world. The short-term threat saw these possibilities but the longer term accepted that deterrence was our only hope and the air defence fighter had no role in that.

My appointment as Air Plans, charged *inter alia* with further reducing the Command to a level much below its 10 airfields and 20 or so squadrons, was not calculated to make me the most popular man in the place and may well have been the reason that a dedicated fighter chap had not been appointed executioner to conduct the death from a thousand cuts. My immediate chief was Denis Crowley-Milling, whom I had first met when he was commanding the Tempest squadron in Khartoum. He left shortly afterwards to take command of West Raynham and was replaced by Brian Morison, a thoughtful man and all-round good egg, who had just returned from a stint as Air Attaché in Oslo.

Tom Pike, of whom it was said (although not in his hearing): "Of course things were different when the C-in-C was alive," had just been succeeded by Hector MacGregor, a New Zealander. The planners worked directly for the Senior Air Staff Officer, Ronnie Lees, an Australian, who lived in a superior house in Stanmore village. Invited there for a drink one evening I was puzzling over its quaint name, "Sandy Saden," but all became clear when I learned that SASO had been promised the Gulf Command until Mr Duncan Sandys gave the job to a sailor.

My office partner was my deputy, Jim Walton, a navigator/radar operator with a vast night-fighter background, who was to become one of the first navigator squadron commanders when he took over No. 25, a Javelin squadron at Waterbeach. We worked in the servants' quarters of the fine house which is Bentley Priory shuffling the squadrons from their permanent bases to boltholes whilst runway improvements were in progress or other major works services like the very sophisticated air-conditioned, dehumidified weapon storage areas were undertaken.

The damage caused to the runway surfaces by high-pressure tyres led to the employment of consultants to find a longer lasting solution to surface wear. At Coltishall they did a marvellous civil engineering job with a hard top as smooth as a billiard table. Unfortunately the first landing, by a Vampire of modest landing speed, ended in disaster since there was no braking action at all and he ran off the end into the barrier. The solution was to cut grooves across the engineer's beautiful runway which would have broken a lesser man, and the final ignominy was that Germany was the only place having such a highly specialised machine.

Readiness shelters were all the rage then and, since they had to be built near the runway ends to be of any use, it was usual to stop flying when the contractors were working close to the aircraft operating area and to re-deploy the resident squadrons. Usually, a fighter station housed one day squadron, equipped with Hunters, and one night/all weather squadron flying Javelins. The Hunter squadrons were very flexible since they needed only fuel and ammunition to operate whereas the night-fighters carried Firestreak, an early infra-red air-to-air weapon, which was extremely temperamental, hence the air-conditioned storage. Each round cost about 100 times the price of a Sidewinder, which for some reason the Royal Navy was allowed to purchase from the United States, an option denied to the RAF. Indeed, Firestreak was so expensive that most Javelin crews had never fired one or even seen one fired. It was easy to complete a deployment with a flourish only to realise that a Javelin squadron had wound up on an airfield with no weapon storage for their Firestreak, rendering the whole exercise futile.

One of our "Secret" files was titled "Lincoln X" and had been around for some time judging from the dates of the enclosed correspondence. The background was that with attacking aircraft expected to approach from the east, the fighter airfields should be on or near, the east coast. With the Lightning about to enter service another airfield with a lot of runway was thought to be required near the Lincolnshire coast, since many further south could not be extended for one reason or another. A wartime airfield, built for the USAF and subsequently extended in order to accept strategic aircraft, was vacant and I was tasked with showing that without this airfield the entire national air defence plan would collapse. There were snags to the proposal. For example there was no accommodation, and the average fighter station had about 2,000 residents including families, and the advice that I obtained from "works and bricks" was that the domestic building programme would cost more than a new runway. Steering carefully around this and other problems, I produced a well-argued paper, full of cogent reasons why the airfield should become part of Fighter Command. Brian Morison made some slight amendments (he had been a staff college DS and recoiled from accepting anything without slight alterations), and the paper went forward to SASO. A day or so later the great man sent for me and rather embarrassed me with his fulsome praise of the staff paper which, he said, he had read with great interest. There was just one small thing however: could I please take it away and change it to show that the airfield in question was quite useless from the Command's point of view, and would Air Ministry kindly boot out the current tenants from Binbrook and give it to Fighter? Nothing if not flexible, the paper was rewritten and Binbrook passed to Fighter Command.

No. 74 Squadron was the first to rearm with the English Electric Lightning at Coltishall. The aircraft was a production version of the P.1 experimental supersonic interceptor, which had suffered a somewhat chequered career even in the hands of the company. This was hardly surprising since it took several steps into the unknown as far as British industry was concerned and was designed to be a research and development vehicle. Whilst many of the systems were changed in production, many more were not, and there were problems. The most dangerous operationally was the unreliability of the fire warning system which could be triggered by a slight escape of hot engine gas which might, or might not, be serious. When the warning lights came on the mandatory instructions were clear: eject. One or two people landed safely after spurious warnings, which sowed the seed of doubt in everyone's mind. When the C-in-C was watching a demonstration of his new aircraft at Coltishall, one landed and burned out at the end of the runway – that warning had clearly not been spurious. This, and the other incidents, led to a serious meeting at Stanmore to decide whether or not to ground the aircraft until a fix had been found. The danger of losing valuable aircraft, and even more valuable pilots, was so great that my vote was firmly in favour of grounding, a course of action that everyone was anxious to avoid. Alternatives were discussed, such as operating only in pairs, so that a wing man could check for signs of fire if warning lights came on. My suggestion, that if the instruction to eject was to be ignored or qualified in any way, it would be better to remove the bulbs from the warning lights and stop scaring people to death, brought a frown from Ronnie Lees until he realised that I was serious. Eventually the aircraft were grounded and extensive modifications were incorporated which greatly enhanced their safety record. It was interesting to observe that, after years of debate, we had finally convinced the USAF that serious night/all-weather work was a two-man task and that skilled nav/rads could read through enemy jamming and acquire targets that a pilot operating alone never could. This led them to the F-4 Phantom, an aircraft years ahead of its time. When the development cost of new aircraft dawned on our politicians it was decided that the single-seat Lightning should become the standard fighter for all air defence roles. Not for the first time, and almost certainly not for the last, the service adapted successfully to a bone-headed decision.

As part of my job specification I became a member of an air defence team trained to augment the professionals in case of emergency. This entailed a night duty every month or so, during which I sat at the control console, in touch with all the domestic and continental early warning stations and the flying stations at which aircraft were on ground alert. There was even a hot line to Strategic Air Command in Omaha. There were occasional alarms but each one was an incoming aircraft going about its legitimate business whose flight plan had gone astray.

During the annual 5-day air defence exercise the amateur control teams were employed full-time since the operations room was raised to full war status. I found it fascinating to read the intelligence being fed in as part of the exercise and to follow the threat assessment leading to declared readiness states on our airfields. It was difficult not to react too soon and to have crews at cockpit readiness which, for obvious reasons, could be maintained only for limited periods. Similarly, if they were launched too soon, for example against a spoof raid, they would all be on the ground refuelling when the real attack started. The time spent "down the hole" was extremely valuable to me although in the exercises it was usually clear when the action was about to start in earnest because the C-in-C arrived in operations, which removed some of the guesswork.

Command Headquarters had a communications flight based at Bovingdon and for reasons unknown, but unquestioned, the planners were on the very short list of staff officers allowed to use the flight aircraft. There were Meteors of various types and some Ansons, maintained under contract by Short Brothers. The flying sequences for a film called *"The Man Who Loved War"* were being shot at Bovingdon featuring at least one B-17 Flying Fortress. On this occasion the man strapping me into a Meteor suddenly flung himself off the wing, greatly to my surprise, until I looked up and, to my even greater surprise, saw a B-17 apparently trying to get into the cockpit with me. That aeroplane was low and, although I never saw the film, the cameraman, wherever he was, captured the sort of flying shot that is not often seen. I was able to fly two or three times a month on some pretext or other, usually to visit one of our far-flung stations, but sometimes just to have lunch with chums at Boscombe Down or Farnborough and catch up on developments. The fatuous Sandys White Paper declaring no further fighters had caused a promising Hunter replacement to be abandoned by Hawkers but there were whispers of a revolutionary design coming along nicely and about to be flown. When I was sent by the headquarters to attend a briefing at Dunsfold on this new aircraft, I listened spellbound as the design team outlined the potential of the aeroplane and Bill Bedford described the hovering and first transition to conventional flight of the P.1127. It was too much to take in at one gulp and raised so many questions that it would have taken at least a week to ask them all. However, the concept fired my imagination, always with the proviso that it could be made to work. My report when I returned to Bentley Priory created very little interest.

We had moved to fine new, airy offices, still in the Priory grounds, and life was proceeding at an even tempo. One morning Brian Morison popped in to ask if I had a current instrument rating, which I confirmed, hoping that he was not going to ask me to fly as safety pilot for him. I asked what he had in mind, to be told that a new CO was required for the Air Fighting Development Squadron at the Central Fighter Establishment. The incumbent, Jimmy Dell, was being released to join English Electric at rather short notice. This caused a flurry of excitement which quickly subsided when someone else was sent there. I could not be too disappointed about missing this one since I had been in my job for only a year and fully expected to be there for at least one more.

The CFE (Central Fighter Establishment) annual meeting at West Raynham was very good value and acted as a forum for the exchange of ideas, updating on new equipment and, at its most basic, gripes about every aspect of the job without fear or favour. One year the proceedings had been enlivened by the arrival of Batchy Atcherley, then Air Officer Commanding 12 Group, in a Meteor. Whilst still on the runway, the undercarriage had retracted, embarrassing for anyone, mortifying for an AOC. He completed the accident report (F765C), explaining that, in reaching for the flap lever, the cuff of his flying glove had snagged the undercarriage lever with the all-too-evident result. This was a design fault in the glove about which he had complained many times, and could we please have some sensible flying clothing, including gloves that did not flap around the wrist. After completion by Batchy (the pilot), the F765C went to the station commander for comment before being passed to Group Headquarters. The station commander noted the pilot's comments and added that he too had frequently criticised the design of the glove and was only surprised that accidents of the kind described were not more frequent: the pilot was clearly blameless. The F765C then passed to the AOC of the Group, Batchy, who wrote in the space reserved for his comments: "I have known this officer all my life and know him to be a consummate liar. I do not believe a word of his story and think that he simply selected the wrong lever." Difficult to imagine such an exchange today.

A diversion was about to occur in the form of a visit by a navigator on the administrative staff, Squadron Leader Wheeldon. He started by saying that he had bought an aeroplane, which he planned to fly as soon as he had overcome the slight handicap of not being a pilot. It was a Hornet Moth based at Elstree and, in a nutshell, would I care to fly it for him? It was summertime and the weather was good, so off we went to Elstree. G-ADKC was the genuine article and was great sport. I flew it for him twice and heard no more about it so that I guess he achieved his ambition.

The most demanding job to come my way was the production of the squadron seniority list which, in reverse order, would show how the run-down would be effected. Basically it was straightforward. Establish the precise date on which the squadron was formed; this was important since most dated from the Great War when units were being formed every week, if not every day. Define precisely any period of disbandment since the governing criterion of seniority was continuous service. The historical branch had all the data and it was heartening to see the meticulous care with which the records were kept. At the end of the research, a list was prepared for submission to the C-in-C and then the battle started in earnest. No. 74, the first Lightning squadron, was not very senior under the rules that we had been given, and would be amongst the first to go. How could I possibly have known that the C-in-C had commanded 74 as a young squadron leader and it would disband over his dead body! 74 was therefore declared exempt from consideration and the list passed to SASO. He had been a flight commander on No. 1(F) Squadron and he did not care about seniority, it would not be disbanded. (In case it sounds anomalous that No. 1 should not be the longest serving squadron, it *was* the first but had a lengthy period of disbandment.) When my list returned it was in ribbons and a lot of unhappy officers were crying foul. I could afford to be objective since I had served only briefly with one of them, but the hurt was genuine and I felt considerable sympathy for those affected. A great deal of effort went into preparing special cases for exemption from the chop list; these were all forwarded for consideration and some succeeded. It was easy to understand how loyalties to regiments with hundreds of years of service lead to such an outcry when disbandment is threatened.

It was customary for visiting VIPs to be given a briefing on the Command, its equipment and future, the latter being a commitment for Plans, and for which I became spokesman. A visitor whom I shall never forget because of his name, rather than any deep impression that he made on me, was General Odd-Bull, a Norwegian who commanded the northern region of NATO. Part of my briefing was required to cover the future air-defence radar installations then being planned under the code name Linesman and featuring a new radar, the Type 84. This search radar had been designed to be proof against jamming by employing a mass of small transmitters within the transmitter head, each on a different frequency. In effect even we would not know which frequency was in use at any instant so how could the enemy who, if he could not identify the frequency, could not jam it? In the presentation which I gave this feature was described as "pulse-to-pulse frequency switching in random fashion." This seemed to be slightly indigestible for a Norwegian visitor and I changed the piece to "rapidly changing frequency" which made the main point, but allowed him subsequently to ask how this was achieved, if he was particularly interested, which seemed unlikely. I moved quickly to the next part but had reckoned without the C-in-C who was in the audience and who had heard the presentation many times before. "Tell him about the pulse-to-pulse frequency changing," said the man, so I did, and the visitor's eyes glazed.

Security was strictly observed throughout the headquarters and in Plans, where we routinely handled Secret, Top Secret and Cosmic Top Secret documents, nothing was left on a desk even for a moment unless someone was there to keep a watch on it. Checks were made irregularly by the Provost Branch and it was properly regarded as letting the side down to be reported for not taking care of classified material. I was therefore surprised on returning from lunch to find a note on my desk saying that a file, prefix S/EX, had been found on my desk and could be reclaimed from security. I assumed that the prefix meant that the file related to a Secret Exercise that I was required to know or do something about, and could only wonder who had been stupid enough to leave it in my unattended office. I dashed down to Security, red with embarrassment, to reclaim the file. I was handed a large manila envelope containing the file and was forced to listen to a short lecture on the need to take better care of the country's secrets from a Provost Marshal who was enjoying every moment of my discomfiture. Humbled, and vowing vengeance on whoever had exposed me to such contempt, I returned to my office and opened the envelope. The file contained some *Playboy*-type magazines collected by Peter DuPlessis on his recent visit to SHAPE, in Paris, and which he had thoughtfully filed for circulation around the headquarters. S/EX was an accurate, but unfortunate title to have chosen. I went back to the security chief with the envelope and asked if he had looked at the secret file. With immense dignity he replied that he was not allowed to look at the material that he confiscated, only to impound it, and confront the guilty party. I saw no reason to enlighten him as to the true contents and was probably regarded from then on, by him anyway, as a grave security risk.

One aspect of life in a ground job close to London was our instant availability for those ancillary tasks that crop up from time to time like courts martial and appointments boards. The latter became fairly regular days out and made me aware, for the first time, of the postings system and put me in close touch with those involved. One of the workers was Hugh Tudor, who had been at Bracknell during my time there, and after one morning session I took him to lunch to explain that my time was running out at Bentley Priory and that I would appreciate a look at the situations vacant coming up. He gave me a review and I made clear that OC Flying at Changi(Singapore), would not upset me and indeed, a further lunch would be arranged in the event such a posting came about. He told me that I was as well qualified as anyone for the job and that he would put my name forward although, as I now knew, he could not influence the board. Weeks passed and I heard nothing until, fearing the worst, I called Hugh to say that the money for the promised lunch was burning a hole in my pocket and could I have a progress report? There was a problem was all that he could tell me, and my name had to be put forward again. This sounded ominous and I was on tenterhooks until the next board sat and he was able to tell me that I had the appointment that I wanted, but at Tengah, not Changi. To be frank, I was totally unaware of the existence of Tengah, which I thought had been closed after the fall of Singapore never to reopen. Closer investigation showed that it was the strike airfield of the Far East Air Force with Canberra, Javelin and Hunter squadrons. The delay in my appointment had been caused by the realisation that the number of candidates with experience of all three types was limited, and I might be better equipped to serve there than at Changi, a transport base.

Before departing HQ Fighter Command I completed a F1369 confidential report, as was normal on posting. Following my experience with the appointments people I had a new choice for next posting which was Air Secretary's Branch. My reasoning was that I was going to a flying job abroad and would certainly not have another on my return. My time to date in Air Ministry was six months and I must in consequence be a very short-odds favourite for another rather longer spell when I came home from Singapore. Finally, if I could not find myself a decent job when working at the hub of the postings empire, I did not deserve one. In my last days in office I had a call from Al Deere who was languishing in the Air Secretary's Branch, saying that he felt compelled to ask why I had offered my services in a job generally avoided by all right-minded officers, the first person in living memory to have done so. I explained my reasoning and he seemed relieved to learn that I had not gone barking mad.

CHAPTER XIV
ISLAND IN THE SUN

In 1962 Singapore was still a colony, recovered from the occupation and thriving. Arriving there in February in the middle of an English winter to go to a flying appointment was the RAF equivalent of winning the football pools. The journey out by Britannia, via Istanbul and Gan (in the Maldives), had seemed interminable but at each stop there had been a distinct increase in the ambient temperature. The aircraft landed finally in the middle of the night at Paya Lebar, then the main civil airport, and I was met by Joe Waddington, whose job I had inherited at Air Ministry and who was again about to hand over to me. This was a generous and much-appreciated gesture and was typical of the kindness that he showed to me during the hand-over/take-over phase of the switch. I met all the people that I should be working with, including the staff of my wing and the squadron commanders. Tom Pierce, commanding the station, happened to be on leave and we met rather more informally in the bar when he returned.

Tengah housed all the RAF combat aircraft of the Far East Air Force. At the time of my arrival this meant No. 20, a day-fighter/ground-attack squadron of Hunter GA.9s and No. 60, a night/all-weather squadron of Javelin 9s (with reheat) for defence. Strike was provided by No. 45 equipped with Canberra B.15s and No. 85(NZ) Squadron with Canberra B.2s. No. 81 PR Squadron with Canberra PR.7s completed the order of battle. A lodger unit on Tengah was the Royal Navy Aircraft Holding Unit, a sort of Maintenance Unit where replacement aircraft were repaired or serviced before being returned to their parent ships. The balance of our limited resources, based at Butterworth in Malaya, were two RAAF Squadrons, one of Canberras and one of Avon-engined F-86 Sabres, the latter having no radar and therefore confined to the same role as the Hunters. The fact that the sixteen Javelins of No. 60 were the only night-fighters in the whole of Malaya, North Borneo, Brunei and Singapore was to assume a significance that I did not dream of at the time.

Not long after my arrival, the New Zealand squadron was withdrawn, although I have no reason to believe that the two events were in any way connected. They remained in support of FEAF from their base in Ohakea, and joined in the war games and exercises that we used to while away the time.

All Royal Air Force units in the area had two commitments: to defend Singapore in the national interest, and, as members of the South East Asia Treaty Organisation, to react to any threat to a fellow member. To bring all this about there was a full Command Headquarters at Changi, but of more immediate concern to me was 224 Group, based at Seletar, and responsible for all the fighting aircraft in the command. The staff of the Command were mostly RAF with token representation from the other Commonwealth participants,whereas the very senior posts in the Group rotated between RAF, RAAF and RNZAF so that each service felt that it had a fair say in the proceedings. As in NATO, the United States were the dominant force of SEATO, but they stayed out of the immediate area except for exercises and the occasional exchange visit between squadrons.

Before departing Singapore, Joe Waddington took me to both headquarters to meet the staff officers with whom I should be in occasional, if not daily contact. The drive to Changi via the coast road took quite some time; the two stations were on opposite sides of the island, and not very far apart as the crow flies, but had no roads connecting them directly. As befits a Command Headquarters, Changi was very grand and with splendid domestic facilities; it was also home to a Hastings squadron and the terminus for trooping flights from the UK. Seletar was much less so and, in addition to the headquarters, had a Maintenance Unit, a squadron of Beverley tactical transports and a helicopter squadron based there. The drive to Seletar was through the remaining jungle of the island with a certain amount of wildlife to be seen, enough to allow a small survival school to operate there fairly realistically.

Our radar Control and Reporting station was at Bukit Gombak, the highest point of what is a very flat island, and it was under their control that we flew endless practice interceptions, usually against each other. The station launched the first pair of Javelins at 6 in the morning but came fully alive at 8 o'clock when everyone started flying. Activity continued until about 4.30 when there was a lull until the Javelins launched for night-flying at 6 in the evening, with last landing at about midnight. This 18-hour flying day was a bit of a grind until I learned that the squadrons ran perfectly well without any guidance from me and I began to relax. It was a paradox that, in the extremely debilitating conditions of the area, we still worked on Saturday mornings, sometimes flying, more often having a station parade on the runway. Parades were never my favourite occupation and I usually found some pressing reason to be elsewhere. Wednesday afternoons were given over to sports, and in the evening there was a film show in the mess, so that night-flying was suspended on Wednesdays. This was the basic routine around which everything else was designed, and in no time at all I felt as though I had been doing it all my life.

In my very early days in office I was startled by the hot line springing to life and a voice asking if I would get down to 60 Squadron immediately to resolve a serious problem that they had uncovered. It was not Peter Smith, the CO, whose voice I would have recognised, and wasting no time in asking silly questions I ran downstairs, jumped into my staff car and raced down to the Squadron. There was a large gathering in the locker-room led by Buster Unstead, one of the nav/rads. He informed me that they were sure there was a "queer" in the crew room. My immediate thought was that this had not been covered at Staff College, and I asked who it was. "Give us a kiss and I'll tell you!" said Buster, watching me closely. I almost collapsed with laughter and relief and I felt that I had been accepted into the night-fighter fold.

20 Squadron, under the command of Dick Calvert, was manned predominantly by younger men on their first tours, with a leavening of older hands on second or third tours. They were all extraordinarily enthusiastic and very knowledgeable about their aircraft, although with most other lessons still to be learned. I was invited to attend the solemn ceremonies which took place from time to time as new boys were declared operational and allowed to wear the squadron badge on their flying suits. As an adjunct, each was awarded his squadron pewter tankard, suitably engraved, filled with the most nauseating mixture of beer and sundry spirits which the novice was expected to drink. Most did so out of bravado and the wish not to be different, and I could only insist that each had the freedom to refuse this time-honoured custom, but none did. I wonder why we did things like that?

Because of their secondary role, to be in support of ground troops, preferably our own, the Squadron had a Ground Liaison Officer (GLO) supplied by the army. His job was to direct the air attack from any suitable spot that he could find on the ground, or in any aircraft that happened to be available. Modern avionics have almost certainly rendered the job redundant, but even then it seemed to me that the task had little appeal. When news came of a new GLO for 20 Squadron I therefore made the effort to be on hand for his arrival, even though it was to be on a Saturday afternoon. At the appointed time I positioned myself at the head of the steps leading to the mess to greet Captain Jeremy James of the Coldstream Guards. A small convoy of vehicles indicated his approach, with himself in the lead driving a Mercedes 190 convertible, followed by a Land Rover full of kit driven by his batman, followed in turn by another Land Rover packed with radio equipment driven by his wireless operator. The tall, languid young man that emerged from the Mercedes was everyone's idea of a Guards Officer and he seemed to me, even on brief acquaintance, to be well suited to the boisterous upper sixth that was 20 Sqn.

Michael Dawson, a navigator, was running No. 45 Squadron, and making a very good job of it too. His flight commanders were well experienced in the role but the majority of his crews were young, first tourists. Training consisted of low-level navigation sorties usually finishing with a practice bomb attack against a small, uninhabited island called China

Rock. Although the B.15 Canberras were new-build aircraft they were expected to last a long time and training was unrealistic to the extent that maximum speed and minimum heights were laid down to minimise the fatigue count on the airframes. In spite of the artificiality that these limitations imposed, training was undertaken enthusiastically and the crews attained an impressive state of readiness. The speed limitation sometimes worked in our favour in that at and below 250 knots the birds, including sea eagles of massive size, sensed the approach of the aircraft and took evasive action, so that bird strikes were a rarity.

The Photographic Reconnaissance Squadron came complete with its own mobile processing unit which gave it a deployment capability, never used in anger in my time. John West was in command of this highly-specialised outfit with mostly very steady, not to say, dour aircrew. The "life is grim, life is earnest" quotient of the squadron was greatly reduced by the arrival of Flying Officer The Marquess of Clydesdale and Hamilton, Canberra pilot, racing driver and all-round live wire. He pulled his full weight in the squadron and still found time to pursue his other interests, which included distance-measuring by a system which I had not encountered before. He drove a big Jaguar saloon, a Mark 7 or 8, which acted as support vehicle for his racing "team" and in the back of which was always to be found a crate or two of a famous Danish lager. The distance from A to B was measured in cans consumed between the first point and the second.

I was told after my arrival that a new post had been approved, that of OC Offensive Support Wing, which would allow the mobile squadrons (20 and 45) to operate under a recognised Wing structure when deployed away from Tengah. In due course, Ian Pedder (the offensive wing commander!), arrived, and in the nick of time. The Thai people, always concerned by the hostile activity on their borders, called upon SEATO to do something about it and, as a result, a detachment of 20 Squadron Hunters winged its way to Chieng Mai in northern Thailand. Ian Pedder found himself in the unenviable position of turning an airfield, with a control tower, a fuel farm and not much else, into an operational base. The perimeter was unfenced which gave a security problem but even more, allowed the tented domestic camp to act as a magnet for all kinds of wild life, from dogs to water buffalo. Unaware of what was ahead of them, there was keen competition amongst the squadron members to join the detachment.

The commitment dragged on and after three or four months, when the enthusiasm for Chieng Mai had subsided a little, I flew up to see how they were coping. Conditions were primitive; a tented camp is not the best place to be when it rains heavily every afternoon, and my abiding impression is of dampness. Pilots get hot flying fast jet military aircraft in which the personal comfort of the crew is not the principal design aim and, even when the cooling system is efficient, it does not start to function until the engine has fired up. Just strapping in when the temperature is in the high 80s in the shade (of which there is none) and the humidity is about 90% is wearing in itself, but then to sit at cockpit readiness for an hour is most trying. The first, usually unsuccessful, task of the day was therefore to find a dry flying suit and settling for the one that was least wet. Morale was extremely high throughout the camp and reminded me once again that, on detachment, even the barrack room lawyers pitch in to make the thing a success.

Naturally I called on Captain James, whose tent was better kept than the rest because his batman was extremely resourceful. Most soldiers seem to have the ability to make the best of their surroundings, no matter how unpromising, which I attribute to wisdom handed down by generations of army men skilled in the art of liberating those small comforts that can transform a wet and miserable camp. At the rear of the tent was a crude wooden cage which, on closer inspection, was seen to contain a bear cub. It was an orphan and not yet sufficiently tame to be handled. Moved by this concern for a dumb creature I asked Jeremy what he intended to do with it when he returned to England, or even Singapore. He answered in all seriousness that when it had grown it would be killed and made into a new regimental bearskin. I am in no doubt that that was his intention but it came to naught, and the bear was eventually found a home in the Singapore zoo.

I returned to Tengah in time to welcome a visit by a squadron of Okinawa-based F-100s. These exchange visits had a serious side, generally well concealed, but they were really social occasions which allowed friendships to be forged, usually over pints of Tiger beer. Tradition demanded that the host squadron flew as many as possible of the visitors in the two-seater, and that the visitors in turn flew us in their T-bird. The visitors had refuelled in flight from Okinawa to Tengah and, before setting out for the return, needed to make a contact with the tanker to check that the system was working. My trip in the F-100F had this check as part of its purpose and I launched with Colonel Rickett, the Squadron Commander, to rendezvous with the tanker. The take-off performance was not startling, even in reheat, but the generally dull business of tying into the tanker and taking on a token 100 gallons turned out to be quite exciting. In theory, the fighter approaches the tanker at a slight overtake speed, pushes its probe into the basket, which causes the hose to take up on its reel, and stays in formation whilst the fuel is transferred. On this occasion, the hose did not take up on the reel, and a great wave developed in the hose and banged on the canopy as though trying to get in. "Dump the board," said the Colonel from the rear seat, meaning extend the airbrake, which I did, and we uncoupled. I realised that I could no longer see the probe, which had been

Fairchild C-119 of the RCAF.

The Avro Canada CF-100 Canuck. Flew like a big Meteor.

In the F-86 Sabre, exercise great care on starting the engine! First chance to go supersonic.

Nice to fly but difficult to keep going. The Sea Hawk.

The Provost en-route Hudson Bay with Flag Officer Bob Crocker RCAF, the Project Engineer.

The Aden-firing Meteor 8 at Namao. Later seen at Wausau Wisconsin!

Return to ETPS. The first course as a tutor – 1954. The author is fourth from the right, front row.

A Dakota of the RCAF, but similar to the ones taken to Australia. Amazing workhorse and epitome of reliability.

The York, using lots of Lancaster parts and providing the same integrity.

bent or broken in this unplanned manoeuvre, but Colonel Rickett said that he could see it from the rear seat, took control, engaged the drogue and completed the flow check. My impression was that this near-disaster was not even an unusual occurrence in Tactical Air Command.

Soon after this we became involved in a SEATO war game in which all the FEAF squadrons participated, and with Ian Pedder still in Chieng Mai it fell to me to lead the Canberras, including those from Butterworth and Ohakea. We were based on Don Muang in Bangkok, with the air forces of the other nations based all over Thailand. The exercise followed the usual pattern with our ground forces being overrun until the air forces came to the rescue. We were tasked with taking out enemy targets designated by the army commander, and our reaction times and accuracy of attack were assessed by neutral observers. It was good fun and kept the squadrons sharp, although it has to be said that there are better aircraft than the Canberra for sitting in at cockpit readiness for lengthy periods under a hot sun. The ground crew, ever resourceful, manufactured canvas canopies which kept the direct rays off our heads but it was still desperately hot. Ideal ripening conditions for tomatoes.

The exercise finished without any of our blood being spilt, and the grand finale was to be a flypast for the King by all the participating aircraft. We were briefed by the wing leader of the Royal Thai Air Force who was to show us the way over the saluting base in the centre of Bangkok. His plan was to form up in national groups at designated rendezvous areas, then fly past the VIP stand in loose line astern, turn gently left in a racetrack pattern and fly past again. Our contingent consisted of Hunters, Javelins, Canberras, Hastings, Beverleys and Bristol Freighters so that there was absolutely no chance of matching speeds, which I ventured to point out. The plan was revised so that the fast jets would make the two passes originally planned with the transports tagging on at the back of the second pass. There would be no rehearsal, nor were all the participants necessarily represented at the briefing. We were to follow immediately behind the F-86 wing of the RThAF, which began to sound like the best place to be.

On the big day we took off, commending our souls to our various makers, and headed for our assigned rendezvous. All the Canberras formed up and we were soon joined by the Javelins and Hunters, in line astern of us. Exactly on time we fell in behind the Thai Sabres, and made our first flypast at a comfortable speed before starting the gentle turn to port for the downwind leg of the racetrack pattern before the second pass. To be absolutely fair, the wing leader had said that he would "step it up a bit" for the second pass, but I was not prepared for the throttle to the firewall that followed. Our aircraft were clean and, with a little coaxing, we were able to stay up although at speeds far in excess of those laid down in Command

Flying Orders. My wing men had ceased to exist as recognisable aircraft but were clearly still with me in a sort of ectoplasmic form. I had stopped looking at the airspeed indicator so that I could honestly say at the subsequent board of inquiry that I did not know how fast we were going. I glanced down and saw the main boulevard and the saluting base upon which the King of Thailand and the Commander-in-Chief of the Far East Air Force were standing.

The F-86 Sabre was a very good aircraft in its time, and one of its outstanding features was the air-brake which, for effectiveness, has probably never been bettered. Having passed the saluting base, the Thai colonel leading the Sabres closed the throttle and popped the air-brake with the almost immediate loss of about 150 knots. The Canberra, in sharp contrast, has no air-brake worth speaking of and this violent and unexpected change of speed left me no choice but to slide under the Sabres, striving desperately to keep them in sight. Somewhat shaken by these events, I led my troops back to our rendezvous to await our turn to be called in for landing. The day was rounded off by someone landing somewhat untidily and blocking the runway for nearly an hour which caused the Javelins and Hunters to divert to Chieng Mai; the Canberras, with plenty of fuel, simply waited for the debris to be cleared.

At the party in the evening, the C-in-C, Hector McGregor (my old boss from Fighter), remarked on the escape manoeuvre, not I suspect with the thought of making it a regular feature of future flypasts. I hoped that he had found some reasonable explanation for His Majesty.

Whenever our aircraft carriers were putting into Singapore, they flew off their aircraft at about 100 miles to land and become lodgers at Tengah. There was plenty of squadron office space since we were equipped to take a V-bomber squadron and all its personnel in the event of an emergency. Parking space was another matter and the place began to look pretty full with 12 Scimitars and 12 Sea Vixens on the pan in addition to the 16 Javelins of 60. At a later date, HMS "Victorious" put into the dockyard (HMS "Terror") having disembarked her aircraft to Tengah and I had the great pleasure of welcoming my ETPS old boy Ted Anson, now commanding the Royal Navy's first squadron of Buccaneers.

On the evening that Ark Royal tied up there was a monster cocktail party on the flight deck, beautifully organised for about 400, and rounded off by the Royal Marine band 'Beating Retreat.' It was a masterpiece of organisation, the sort of thing that the Royal Navy does so well. I was the guest of the Commander Flying, Ray Rawbone, who seemed to be tapering off as the evening wore on, hardly surprisingly since he had averaged about 3 hours rest in 24 for the previous week. I took him back to my house at

Tengah where he slept for a night and a day, and if he moved during that time it was not noticeable.

The generally even tenor of station life was disrupted when a series of engine problems with the Sapphires of the Javelins led to some near misses. The phenomenon, called "centre line closure" by the manufacturer, was new to me. The apparent cause was the engine casing cooling very rapidly, thus restricting the movement of the normally rotating parts. To misquote Oscar Wilde, to lose one engine may be regarded as a misfortune, to lose both looks like carelessness, and eventually it happened to the CO, Peter Smith, flying with his nav/rad leader Frank Jolliffe. The usual practice interceptions were proceeding as planned when, quite suddenly, the aircraft went very quiet. With fully-powered, irreversible controls, when the engines stop producing hydraulic pressure the aircraft becomes unflyable, and they ejected. Peter landed in the top of a tree, stayed there and was winched up by helicopter in fairly short order. Aside from a very sore back and a black eye he was undamaged. Frank was rather less lucky: during his descent he had seen a logging track cut through the jungle and decided to head for it when he reached the ground, assuming that he would meet someone there, or at worst be easily spotted from the air. On the way through the jungle canopy, where the trees are so close together that from high altitude they look like fields, his parachute rigging lines snagged and he found himself suspended, inverted, high above the ground. He cut himself free and landed with a terrible thump on the jungle floor. The aircraft searching for him were picking up strong signals from a rescue beacon, which we all carried in our Mae Wests. Unfortunately they were coming from Peter Smith's lifevest which he had left in his treetop to make it easier for him to climb into the halter lowered by the chopper. These signals either overpowered Frank's or quite simply his beacon was not working; whatever the case there was deep gloom when he had not been found by nightfall. The following day every available aircraft was searching, but without success, and a rescue team from the Gurkhas had gone in to see what they could do.

Only the survivor could relate the full story, but a synopsis was as follows. Like most of us, Frank was not too keen on the jungle and, having collected his scattered wits after his plunge to earth, he set out for the logging track leaving a page torn from his copy of Pilots' Notes indicating the direction that he had taken. He was not the first, and surely will not be the last, to underestimate the difficulties of jungle travel. He found lots of streams, all crossing his path and preventing him from holding his chosen heading, so that after a while he was no longer sure of which way he wanted to go. If this sounds odd, especially for a navigator, the jungle is dark and no sunlight penetrates the tree canopy so that it is very easy to lose all sense of direction. Night falls early and rapidly and he sensibly decided to make an overnight camp rather than blunder around in the gloom.

After a night of broken sleep, caused mainly by the mysterious rustlings and movements all around him, and still in some shock after the ejection, he awoke at dawn. Determined to effect his own rescue he again set out in what he assumed to be the right direction for the logging track. He was constantly aware of aircraft flying overhead and could identify many of them by sound, but had no way of attracting their attention. So the second weary day passed with a growing feeling that his survival scheme was not functioning as planned. At nightfall he again made a shelter as best he was able, and settled down to another anxious night, ears cocked for the sound of marauding animals. He was very tired by this time so that he did rest, and obviously slept, because it was a noise very close to him that awakened him at first light. The noise was caused deliberately by a Gurkha rifleman parting the bush beside him to ask if he was ready for morning tea. They had found him some time before but had let him sleep until the tea was brewed.

Following this heart-warming episode we invited the platoon concerned to visit us at Tengah and see us at work. I was enormously impressed by the charm which each Gurkha had in abundance, and by the obvious respect that the soldiers had for their NCOs and their officer, who could only just have left school. They were simple people interested in, but not overwhelmed by, the technology which we were able to show them, and who is to say if they were any the worse off for not being too impressed?

The Group had been taken over by a splendid Australian officer called Frank Headlam, with Neville Stack (RAF) as his Senior Air Staff Officer. They were much respected by the operators at Tengah since both demonstrated keen interest in what we were doing and dropped in whenever the mood took them. Each year, the Air Officer Commanding made his annual inspection, the signal for everything that did not move to be painted. The parade and inspection of the troops are immutable parts of such occasions, and all very well in their way; however they do not demonstrate the operational capability of the station, which is the only justification for its existence.

I proposed that we had two inspections. The first would be in working rig, with the AOC scrambling the air defence aircraft against the Canberras which would have been launched earlier. Bit of a fly-past before landing and everyone taking lunch together in the aircrew feeding centre. The second inspection would be the full treatment, honour guard on arrival, look at the airmen's barracks and so on, with all the aircraft on the ground in nice straight lines. The proposal was accepted and turned out to be a huge success. The PR boys picked up his car *en route* to Tengah and took pictures of him driving through the village, arriving at the main gate and moving down to the operational area. The little war went as planned except that Don Riches of 20 Squadron slid off the ORP (Operational Readiness Platform) and took no further part in the proceedings, and the lunch that followed was suitably spartan. Before the AOC left he was presented with an album of photographs taken by 81 Squadron from the air commemorating his visit. The second inspection was equally successful with the RAF Regiment squadron performing the ceremonial so well that the short-comings of the rest of us were disguised if not completely hidden.

By the middle of 1963 the Hunter detachment to Chieng Mai had finished and, isolated as we were from the war in Vietnam, a normal peace-time routine resumed. Changes were taking place as personnel became tour-expired and replacements arrived. No. 60 had a new CO in the form of John Fraser and, soon after, Dick Calvert was replaced by Max Bacon in 20 Squadron. Brian Carruthers took command of 45 and new faces appeared in the lower echelons of all the squadrons. There were more than 100 aircrew on the station and I had a rogues' gallery on the office wall with all their photographs, so that I could learn who they were and test myself on rapid identification. I reckoned to know them all by first name and enjoyed an informal relationship with them all off-duty, which was never abused on duty. This was a great help when the dreaded annual confidential reports had to be completed. I made a point of seeing them all, not to show them the report that I had written, but to advise them on how they might improve any aspect of their performance. It was useful to know the background, on and off duty, when acting as agony aunt.

In the station commander's absence I assumed the running of the station which entailed Orderly Room, at which defaulters were paraded for justice to be administered. My adjutant, WO Fred Peacock, a retired air gunner, was at his best on these occasions. After hearing the evidence, I would order the prisoner removed, whilst I considered all the facts. This meant asking Mr Peacock what sort of form the accused had, and he always had a pen picture prepared. "Thoroughly bad lot, sir," or "nice lad sir, had too much beer and he's not used to it" were typical summaries and dictated the punishment imposed. It may not have been the law but it was fair.

One of the saddest events of my tour at Tengah occurred with an aircraft of 60 Squadron. It was usual after a session of high-level practice interceptions to join up at low level for a tail-chase, to stay in touch with the old-fashioned art of visually tracking an enemy, a necessary art if he attacked at low level. Gordon Sykes, with Paul Burns as his nav/rad, was flying the middle aircraft of three so that he was both tracking and being tracked. It was therefore the man behind him who had the best view of the fin, rudder and tailplane breaking away from Gordon's aircraft with catastrophic consequences. He called for Paul to eject and he did so, safely and without serious injury. He then reached for his own face-blind, the preferred method of activating the Mark 10 Martin Baker seat, in order to escape himself. All this took far less time than I have taken to tell it and the sea was now coming up fast. The physical action of reaching up to pull the face-blind braced the body in an upright position, kept the arms close to the body and the blind protected the face from explosive or wind damage. The fast-approaching water convinced Gordon that the firing mechanism connected to the face-blind had failed. He leaned forward to pull the pan handle, the secondary firing system provided for those occasions when the aircraft was under so much 'g' that it would be impossible to reach up for the face-blind handle. The system had not failed, and as soon as he leaned forward, taking up the worst possible posture for ejection, the seat fired. It was a very low-level escape, and he survived, but at the appalling cost of being paralysed from the waist down. He was quickly flown home to the specialist unit at Stoke Mandeville, but he never walked again although, being Gordon Sykes, he drove a specially-adapted motor car, became secretary of the 60 Squadron Dinner Club and refused to feel sorry for himself.

Paul Burns lost an inch in height as a result of his spinal compression but was otherwise fit enough to return to flying duties. Whether from choice, or just one of those coincidences, he later found himself in Tengah again, flying with 45, the Canberra squadron. For a night-fighter, this was seen as a rest tour, but events showed otherwise when he was forced to eject again, and again survived. I think that he got the message.

In November 1963, what has now become known as the "Period of Confrontation" with Indonesia began, and Tengah was immediately deeply involved. When it started, communications between Singapore and Borneo failed to the point that nobody knew exactly what was going on. General Walker, C-in-C Land Forces, decided to see for himself and I took him to Brunei in a 45 Squadron Canberra. The General did not look at ease strapped into the navigator's seat, briefed on the function of the Martin Baker equipment and clearly apprehensive that he might have to use it. The trip was uneventful but led to a series of aircraft movements that transformed our routine and taxed our resources to the limit. There were rumours of landings on the Malayan and Singapore coasts by bands of infiltrators. However, if these events actually occurred, they did little seriously to disturb the calm of life in Singapore. More ominous, it was thought, was the threat to Brunei, Sarawak and Sabah, and sections of the Tengah squadrons were despatched to stabilise the situation and boost the morale of the locals. The only air activity that happened for sure was a leaflet raid on Kuching, it was thought by Mitchell aircraft. Army patrols reported meeting organised bands of Indonesians and there were skirmishes in which both sides sustained casualties.

Borneo was not well-known in those days and before our detachments were sent off I looked over the maps and charts of the area to see if we could get to Labuan and Kuching, the proposed detachment airfields. Apart from some fairly convincing mapping of the coastal region, the centre of Borneo was blank and overprinted "largely unknown, believed to be flat but with some peaks," or words to that effect. This was not a promising start for a Hunter F/GA squadron expected to operate down to 100 feet. The severity of the local weather was also a worry for the operation of short range jets with no diversion airfields. The Javelins particularly were in for a hard time if the airfields, which had no approach and landing aids, went out after they were committed to landing. The Hunters were better placed with their four external fuel tanks which gave them time to hold until the worst of the storms had passed.

It was easy to find the Indonesian Air Force order of battle intimidating with MiGs up to the 21 and some Badgers, the Soviet equivalent of the Canberra. Even worse in my judgement, on an airfield about 20 miles south of Singapore, there were Mitchell and Mustang aircraft which they had been flying for 20 years and which could have hit Tengah at low level before we had any warning. Our basic problem was that we were set up to fight an enemy approaching from the north. The new requirements, for the squadrons to be mobile and to face the other way, needed some adjustment to our plans. Our air-to-air weapons (Firestreak) had to be kept in dehumidified and temperature-controlled conditions to have a fighting chance of working when called upon to do so, conditions which did not exist on any deployment base. In consequence, the Javelins had to be recovered to Tengah every 28 days maximum, in order to remain an effective force.

The decision was taken at the beginning of these deployments that the airmen would be on the outstation for no more that 28 days in principle, and for sure if they were married with families in Singapore. There was a sound financial reason for this rigidity which, even now, is beyond my comprehension. Bear in mind that these men were on the strength of RAF Tengah where they reasonably enough expected to be with their families, transported with them from their former bases in the United Kingdom. Circumstances required that they be separated from their families in order to live in extreme discomfort and to fight the Queen's enemies. After 28 days, it was decreed, the "local allowance" would stop, since the head of the family was no longer living in Singapore. This silly and ill-considered ruling caused me more concern than the war because it was so obviously unjust. A plot was hatched therefore to ensure that each man was back on Tengah after 27 days away and not infrequently, when the transporters failed to provide the promised air lift, a Canberra found itself on a training flight to Borneo, returning with an airman passenger. I often thought back to Colonel Pope at Bracknell and his "Gaberdine Swine," and even coined a phrase to describe the treatment we received from some (but not all) of the headquarters staff: "every possible assistance short of actual help."

It soon became clear that we could not fulfil the new demands placed upon us without reinforcement. We were on 24-hour alert at Tengah, with four Javelins detached to Butterworth to give night cover there, aside from six Hunters in Labuan and four Javelins at Kuching. More Hunters and Javelins came from Cyprus and the United Kingdom to join us and, from time to time, a detachment of Victors pitched up as well. One such detachment was led by my famous namesake, J.E. Johnson, whom I met on the tarmac as he stepped out of his aircraft. I bade him welcome to Tengah and he studied my name tag briefly before saying: "Well, you've got the right name, anyway." That was the only time I have ever met or spoken to him, and I pondered the significance of his remark for weeks after. When Ark Royal disembarked her squadrons to Tengah we were full to overflowing. I counted 68 operational aircraft on the airfield, dispersed as best we were able, but still representing the ground-attack pilot's dream – straight lines of static aircraft waiting to be hit.

All this effort meant that the troops were working long hours to maintain and repair the aircraft required for continuous operations, and I made a point of visiting the hangars in the evenings to see how things were going. In 20 Squadron hangar quite late at night I watched an armourer fitting a gun-pack to a GA.9, a tricky job at the best of times, and he was lying on his back, "easing it into position" with a few well-timed kicks. The flight sergeant came up behind him, tut-tutted gently and advised him that he would "never do it that way, lad." The armourer, unable to see the "Chiefy" (or me), snarled: "What was that," as one does when offered useless advice in the middle of a difficult job that is not going well. "'What' to me!" said the Chief; "it'll be 'bollocks' to the CO next." I turned away quickly, satisfied that morale was not a problem there. As one flight commander finished his tour, the squadron acquired a new one, Peter Martin, who took on the individual demonstrator job in addition to his other duties. Before he went public I was required to check his performance and give it formal approval, largely from the safety point of view. It was very good, spirited and showing the Hunter in the very best light. My only concern was that the fuel available for inverted flight was being pushed to its limit and, after approving his show, I mentioned this to Peter when he landed.

There was great excitement when the readiness aircraft were scrambled by the GCI station at Bukit Gombak against an intruder approaching

Singapore down the Straits of Malacca. The Javelins went and were vectored on to a Badger, just on the Indonesian side of the international boundary which divides the Straits. On the face of it a singleton, in daylight, was unlikely to be intent on any serious mischief, and he was in his own air space. The crews that made the interception reported an apparent airborne Marie Celeste; there was no sign of life on board at all. Eventually they attracted the attention of the crew on the flight deck. Faces appeared everywhere and the aircraft turned violently away, deeper into Indonesian air space. They cannot have known how anxious we all were to learn if Firestreak really worked.

This scene was to be repeated over and over again until there was no longer any competition amongst the crews to make the interception and it became a question of sending anyone who did not have his personal photograph of the enemy at close quarters. Through the Australian Embassy in Jakarta, which stayed open for business throughout the drama, we learned that our Badger was used for navigator training. When the monsoon was affecting Sumatra in their western training area, they switched to an eastern route. They had always done so and "confrontation" was no good reason to change.

During the Hunter detachment to Labuan there occurred the only flying fatality during my tour at Tengah. Bob Shields, the senior pilot on 20 Squadron and a father figure to all the sprogs, took off with Peter Riley as his number two. Soon after becoming airborne, Peter saw flame in the area of the air-brake, under the fuselage of Bob's aircraft. He called to warn him, but Bob had already lost his radio and could not hear. After some violent manoeuvring to attract his attention, it became clear that Bob had realised that he had a problem, and soon after, the powered controls reverted to manual. Having practised manual landings many times in his 1,500 hours on type, Bob set himself up for a landing at Labuan. He punched off the drop-tanks which went on one side but hung up on the other, giving him a badly out-of-balance aeroplane, particularly difficult in manual. Trying to turn for final approach, Bob realised that he was not going to be able to line up with the runway and ejected. To complete his misfortune, the parachute failed to deploy. Even so he was alive when the rescue vehicles got to him and was able to tell Ian Pedder that his injuries "only hurt when he laughed," the line made famous by Bob Hope. He succumbed soon after and was deeply mourned. He was a salt of the earth character, quiet and undemonstrative, but a pillar of strength in the squadron.

Confrontation became a way of life, never reaching a climax but causing a great deal of frustration. It proved again that "action stations" with no subsequent action is extremely debilitating, particularly for an air force. Maintaining high-readiness states is hard on the crews, and after a very short time flying skills become dulled if they are not exercised, and yet training flying seems frivolous in the circumstances.

Thus it was that in the middle of this tense, but unresolved period of political turmoil, I was informed that I was to attend the next course at The RAF College of Air Warfare, starting in July 1964.

I became involved in a final VIP visit to the station by General Curtis LeMay, the retiring boss of the United States Air Force, who was on a world tour in Air Force One, the President's Boeing 707. He was being transferred from Seletar to Tengah in a Belvedere helicopter, not the most reliable mode of travel ever invented. The General's trademark was a fat cigar which he smoked in all circumstances and sure enough he boarded the Belvedere with the stogie going at full blast. The crewman asked the General's aide if he would get him to extinguish the cigar because there was a danger that the helicopter would catch fire. The aide replied: "It wouldn't dare!" The station visit was a success and the General, like so many others of formidable reputation, was most friendly, but then I did not work for him.

My imminent departure signalled a round of farewell parties, each one enjoyable, but one memorable – that given by the locally-recruited Station Police. Their catering assumption was that, being British, all the officers drank Scotch whisky and a reasonable ration to accompany Chinese dinner was a bottle each. It was a marvellous occasion, with local accents becoming more impenetrable as the evening wore on, and the presentation of my farewell address left something to be desired.

For my formal dining-out night I was able to invite the Station Commander (Changi) as my guest. He was Group Captain W. J. McLean RAF, the Australian who had spared me the full rigours of the law at Camden NSW some 18 years earlier.

I was driven to Changi to catch a Comet for the trip home and my change in status was impressed upon me at the check-in desk by the airman on duty. My driver deposited the baggage, saluted smartly after I had shaken his hand, and left the departure hall to return to Tengah. The duty clerk said: "Put the baggage on the scales, will you?" and I did; I was just another passenger going home.

CHAPTER XV
BLUES IN THE NIGHT

Lincolnshire is dotted with airfields, many of them made famous in war. Manby, near Louth, was a long-established prewar airfield which had latterly been home to the RAF Flying College. This major course was for senior officers who, it was assumed, were going on to better things in the operational (as opposed to administrative) side of the Service. At some point, and I am unclear as to exactly when but it must have been in the early 1960s, the aircraft were taken away and the establishment became the College of Air Warfare.

The course that I joined was composed of people like myself, between jobs and uncertain of what the future held, and one or two faces were familiar. Glen Lloyd was a graduate of ETPS and, although I did not know him well, our shared background drew us together. Wyn Roberts was on the staff, and we had soldiered through Staff College at the same time, so that the place was not totally strange, although it had its moments. One real pleasure was to find amongst my fellow students Jock Moncur, who had commanded the Scimitar squadron embarked in "Ark Royal."

The College was the major part of an academic complex which included a specialist navigator course and a course for space studies, all under the overall command of John Topham, a nephew, I believe, of the Aintree racecourse owner. He had as his deputy a Group Captain, Butch Baker, but the work was done by a few wing commanders of whom the said Wyn Roberts was one.

I must state frankly that I did not expect to enjoy the six months that the course was to last, suspecting that the transition from the hectic life of Tengah to the calm of academe would not be easy, and I was right. The first jarring blow was the summons to a church service, presumably designed to start the course on the right note, as it were. I had thought that church parades were things of the past and, although I have respect for the religious views that anyone holds, and envy of those who gain strength from their beliefs, religion had not been a big factor in my life for a long while.

My restlessness was not eased by one of the very early lectures entitled "The Principles of Radar," which struck me as an odd choice for a bunch of operators fresh from the front. There were some interesting discussions on the laws of probability as related to warfare until working through one of the tactical problems produced the "correct" answer that two 2-kiloton nuclear weapons were required to render an airfield unusable; this gave me pause to wonder if we were living in the same world. On the other hand, weapon-firing accuracies were assumed in some exercises which the best squadron in the world would have been proud to claim. We had found in the

Hunter force for example that, firing air-to-air against a flag for the first time in six months, hardly anyone registered a strike. At the end of a two-week armament practice camp, everyone was getting good scores but at the expense of air-to-ground bombing accuracy.

Bombing would improve after a bit of practice, but air-firing skills would decline. The fact is that hitting a modern aircraft (of the day) with gun armament was very difficult and needed constant practice. Without practice, as the immortal and somewhat inelegant phrase has it, most people cannot hit a cow in the ass with a banjo. Similarly, hitting a moving ground target with a conventional bomb when flying at 450 knots was not easy. Add to that the target firing back and it would be a brave man who assumed, even for an academic exercise, the sort of effectiveness that we were credited with. These realities kept intruding on my thinking and, with the best will in the world, I found it difficult to take the thing seriously. To be scrupulously fair, most of the directing staff did not take it too seriously either. The atmosphere was very relaxed, and some of the local golf courses were good, but I had a distinct feeling that I was spinning my wheels.

At the halfway point in the course we were invited to write a critique of the content, to state honestly how we found it, and to make recommendations, I suppose to help in future course planning. I thought long and hard about my submission because my true feelings were better not expressed and yet how could I pretend that I was enjoying every waking hour in the pursuit of knowledge? Having written the truth, I toyed with the idea of destroying the paper and writing the kind of anodyne generalities which I am sure would have been more acceptable, but I resisted the temptation. When we assembled to discuss the replies I could see clearly from my front-row seat that my handwriting was on the first paper to be reviewed. What I had said in essence was that in my view they had constructed the wrong course or were selecting the wrong people to attend it, using as an example the lecture on "principles of radar." I maintained that if anyone attending the course needed such a lecture he should not have been selected. If nobody required to be instructed in such a basic tool of our trade why have such a lecture? There were no cheers of support from the rest of the student body although several said in private that they wholeheartedly agreed. I thought that I gave due weighting to those aspects of the training that were good value, but stated that a serious injection of realism would lift the course to an altogether higher plane. Although I did not say so, I thought that the course was stuck in first gear and that the leisurely approach to problems bore so little relation to reality – as I had so recently seen it – that there was no teaching value at all. I sensed that my views were not welcome to Butch Baker and perhaps others who had designed the curriculum.

The highlight of the second half of the studies was a visit to an overseas operational command and for my course it was to be Far East Air Force. Thus within six months of leaving Tengah I was on a Comet of Transport Command heading back there. Hector MacGregor had handed over his Command to Sir Peter Wykeham (formerly Wykeham-Barnes, my early choice for CAS from Boscombe days). Tengah had been taken over by Ted Hawkins, a charming man who was very popular with those on the station that I knew. His appointment had been delayed because he was not jet-qualified, causing Tom Pierce to have his tour extended. I do not know how many group captains were not jet-qualified by 1964, I like to think not many, but the Appointments Board had found one. The station briefing was comprehensive and, since I recognised most of the slides that were used, I did not respond when questions were invited. There is an adage that it is a mistake to return to a place that you have enjoyed because it is always a disappointment, and I believe it to be true. Even after such a short time Tengah was different and I was a stranger. However, I was able to make my contribution to the course as a tour guide and shopping adviser.

Having dinner on the station with Jack Jacobs, the Wing Commander Admin. I learned something that for some reason had not filtered back through the grapevine. On the day that I left Changi, Peter Martin was demonstrating the Hunter to some visitors and was forced to eject when the engine stopped. Although we worked together for years later on, I never had the nerve to ask him how long he had been inverted when the motor quit.

Shortly after our return to Manby it was time to learn our immediate destinies. I had, as ever, invited the authorities to send me to Boscombe Down, Farnborough or (a new one this) to Rome as Air Attaché. I was summoned in my turn to be told that I was to join the Directing Staff of the Royal Air Force Staff College at Andover. My disbelief must have been evident because I was asked how I felt about that. I explained my dis-enchantment with staff college as a student, just for a year, and could only imagine that a tour as an instructor was a cruel joke, with me as the victim. There followed the guff that I had heard before, career post, easy to extract you on promotion, probably will not be for long and so on, none of which I believed. This time there was to be no accident to change the official mind as had happened on my return from Canada.

I had completed the first (and as it turned out, only) six months of my time in the Royal Air Force without flying myself in some sort of aircraft.

CHAPTER XVI

LET'S TAKE IT NICE AND EASY

The Royal Air Force Staff College at Andover, founded in 1922, was the original and, it must be said, it looked like it. The buildings were single-storey of very basic construction, but appeared mellow since they were ivy covered, as befits a centre of learning. In its final years it differed from Bracknell in that half of the student intake were foreign, a non-pejorative term which included American and Commonwealth. The balance were RAF officers who, rightly or wrongly, saw attendance at the college as a vital stepping stone to the advancement of their careers.

I arrived to take up my tutorial duties (we were called Directing Staff or simply DS) in January 1965, at the start of No. 23 Course. (How, after 40-odd years, the course number was 23 I cannot explain and, even more curiously, the much younger college at Bracknell started Course No. 55 in 1965!). There were 8 of us directing staff pitted against 42 of them, them being the students, but since we knew in advance the answers to all the set problems it was really no contest.

There was a German who, in common with other members of the Luftwaffe that I met, fought only on the Russian front. We had a pair of Iranians and two Iraqis, with singletons from Italy, Peru, South Africa, Bolivia, Norway, Philippines, Thailand and Uruguay. This unlikely mixture assembled in a snowstorm on the evening of the 11th January and, aided by their RAF companions with a strong assist from the Directing Staff, saw off a barrel of beer which was the traditional opening event.

I was able to welcome Alan White, who had been a flight commander on the Hunter squadron at Tengah, and to meet Paddy Hine, who was my third selection as future Chief of Air Staff; he very nearly made it too. The two Iraqis, Niamat Dilaimi and Fahim Jalal Abdul-Razak, were both Hunter pilots who had spent time at the conversion unit at Chivenor, and had ferried the first of their aircraft back to Baghdad from Dunsfold, the Hawker airfield. Pepe Guerra, the Peruvian, was also a Hunter man and with a sprinkling of Hunter pilots amongst the RAF element, common ground was quickly established. One of my great favourites was Pete Los Banos, the Filipino, a charming man of considerable talent who stayed on as Air Attaché in London at the end of his year at Andover.

One of the very early exercises was a vocabulary test, clearly designed for English speakers, which many of our students found impossible since their familiarity with the language was confined largely to aviation terms necessary to fly the world's airways. At the first staff meeting that I attended I pointed out that this test, humbling for a British officer and likely to drive him to wider reading, was totally demoralising for a foreign officer struggling with "good morning, sir." Furthermore, it showed nothing that we did not already know. I count it as my greatest, possibly *only*, achievement at Andover to have persuaded the planning staff to drop the exercise for future foreign students.

The Commandant, Vic Willis, informed me that amongst my other duties I should be editor of the college magazine, as a warning to keep diary notes for the summary of the year's activities which I should have to produce. Amongst the first was the composition of an obituary for a member of the staff who had died in Wroughton hospital. I had never met him, knew nothing about him and protested that one of his friends should write the piece. To absolutely no avail: it was the editor's job and would I please get on with it. Sitting at the back of the auditorium listening to my first lecture as a DS, the Commandant passed me a note on which was written: "Please give the vote of thanks at the end." Perhaps he had observed that I was not totally absorbed in the subject but in any event it compelled me to listen to the last bit. These were not very friendly acts, I thought, but they served to make me aware that a rigid structure existed in the establishment of the college, far removed from the "all hands to the pumps" atmosphere of an operational station. The second note for my diary was the Commandant's departure, to be replaced by Derek Hodgkinson. Directing Staff came and went with regularity, some to retirement, others resuming their normal careers. One newcomer was Brian Carruthers, who had commanded 45 Squadron at Tengah during my last year there.

The college year followed the same pattern as Bracknell with guest lecturers of mixed quality, syndicate discussions and administrative or operational problems for the students to solve and hand in within a set time. As at Bracknell, the time allowance was generous and we, the staff, reckoned it was a bad week if we played less than 72 holes whilst the students were slaving away. We also played cricket and softball against Bracknell, home and away, so that it was not all graft, but the light moments were few and far between.

During the 'industrial' phase of the course we spent a week based in Whitley Bay, visiting factories and mines in the Newcastle-upon-Tyne area. I had never been down a mine and, always ready to try something new, I went with my syndicate to the colliery. Having coffee in the Manager's office on arrival, my attention was caught by a board with a chalked message on it, displayed prominently above his desk. The message said something like: "We have all had a good prayer and sung a hymn together." It was written by a miner, one of more than a 100 who perished in the very pit that we were about to descend and had been found by one of the rescue team recovering the bodies. I suddenly thought of all sorts of things that I would rather be doing but there was no turning back. We changed into flying suits and boots which we had brought for the purpose and descended to the main gallery some 2,000 feet below. We walked through smaller and smaller galleries to the working face which was about 18 inches high, then crawled to where the miners were actually working. It was hot and dirty and most unpleasant. Poor Pete Los Banos was suddenly overcome by claustrophobia and began struggling to get past the rest of us who were quite unable to move out of his way. I was conscious that we were two miles under the North Sea, that the hydraulic props holding the roof were not plentiful and, furthermore, I could hear creaking. I was never more relieved than when our guide informed us that there really was nothing more to see and we might as well return to the surface. We were wearing helmets and lamps, with batteries in a waist belt, connected to the lamps by cables. Our exit was via the conveyor belt, thoughtfully cleared of coal for our departure. The belt was moving quite fast, and the miners with us, who were coming off shift, threw themselves on it and travelled forward on all fours. Like all good professionals, they made this little exercise look much easier than it was. Having seen the rest of my group on their way, I leaped and the battery jumped out of the waist belt and caught in the conveyor driving rollers. Under threat of strangulation, I whipped off the helmet just as the batteries freed themselves, saving me the embarrassment of losing the kit with which I had been issued. Our guide said that it often happened.

In the pit-head shower there was a tough looking little chap in the next stall, back and shoulders covered in black blotches, the battle scars of years in the pits. As we were drying ourselves he asked if I was one of the air force people visiting. I confirmed that I was and he told me: "You'll never get me up in one of those things." I had to tell him that, as far as I was concerned, his job was not under threat either.

Some of the debates that we had in syndicate were illuminating, especially with the Iraqis. We were discussing air defence systems and inevitably the fighter aircraft that represented the backbone of every air defence force. The Iraqi Air Force had begun to acquire Soviet aircraft in some numbers and, out of interest, I was keen to learn the factors which had led them to turn away from Western equipment. One of their main considerations as operators was that the Russians gave them the most up-to-date version of whatever they wanted in contrast to the British, for example, who always degraded the aircraft that they supplied. This puzzled me and I asked how this point related to their Hunters. "You would not give us the radar version," said Fahim Jalal, which puzzled me even further since there *was* no radar version of the Hunter. After some probing, I discovered that they had heard about radar-ranging, an advanced form of gunsight which was intended to take the guesswork out of assessing the distance from the target in air-to-air combat. They had heard half the story and were convinced that a radar-equipped Hunter was in service with the RAF and that the Iraqis were being sold the primitive and no-longer-required version. I could imagine an unfortunate Air Attaché in Baghdad, arguing vainly that there was no such mark of Hunter, being condemned as a liar because the Iraqis had heard about radar-ranging from somewhere. Both Iraqis were conditioned to distrust everything that they were told, read or heard in the non-socialist world, although this did not extend to those of us that they grew to know well. For example, the young son of Fahim Jalal contracted tonsillitis and the station doctor advised them to have the boy admitted to the RAF hospital at Wroughton, just down the road from Andover, for the tonsils to be removed,since they were otherwise likely to be the source of endless trouble. I was consulted and persuaded them that this was not a plot to have the boy killed, subjected to torture or kidnapped. Now these were two well-educated people (his wife was a dental surgeon), and they seriously harboured such suspicions, perhaps because in their own country such a thing could happen, or their briefing before departure had filled their minds with some pretty uncharitable thoughts about us. The quite excellent treatment that their son received in the RAF hospital converted the family into staunch anglophiles and greatly increased their enjoyment of the rest of their stay.

As the end of the course approached, the great and the good came to lecture the students and, for the RAF members, to boost their morale during a period of socialist government not favourably inclined towards the military. The Air Secretary, with several of his staff, spoke about the future with so little conviction that the unease amongst his audience was palpable. In questions afterwards he answered none directly, but passed the questioner to one of his group captains who cobbled together a reply, sometimes a not very convincing one. For the first time in my service life I became deeply conscious of a change in outlook among the younger officers, who seemed more concerned about pay, promotion and pensions than the challenge and excitement that were ahead of them. This was doubtless due in part to the very poor presentation about the future that they had been given by the highest authority on the subject in the Royal Air Force, but only a few seemed able to think for themselves that the outlook could not possibly be as bleak as had been painted. It was a dismal performance and only later was it clear that the man was extremely sick, and indeed he died shortly afterwards.

That particular lecture, combined with the lack of satisfaction with the job that I was doing, started the worm of doubt in my own mind and I began to wonder if I really wanted to be an officer in the RAF for the rest of my life. In Singapore I had studied our obligations and commitments and tried to match them to our resources, but without success. This caused me such concern that I went to see the AOC, Frank Headlam, to make sure that I had not misread the situation. He reassured me to the extent that I relaxed, safe in the knowledge that the position was clear to him too, and probably many other people. This further doubt was unhealthy, and I began to feel like a priest who has lost his faith, questioning things which I had always taken for granted. I must not give the impression that I was cast down, and filled with despair I was not, but some of my firmest convictions had been shaken and I began to look forward to my departure from Andover. Unfortunately that was still 18 months away and, with insufficient to keep me occupied, my unease grew.

Andover as an address has one great advantage; it is only just over the county boundary from Boscombe Down where many of my friends were serving in 1966 as we welcomed the new intake of budding staff officers to the College. Through discreet visits, I left my telephone number so that any time there was a spare seat in an aeroplane I was known to be available. This was to prove a lifeline.

For the next course the student mixture was enriched by two Saudis, two Ethiopians, two Ghanaians, a Greek, Indian, Ceylonese, and Chilean. Once again, for an extraordinary religious and ethnic mix, they got along well together. I have a theory that, when all else has failed, the nations will each pick an airman to be their representative at the UN and the world's troubles will be over.

The academic year had hardly started when the commandant was whipped away to become Director of Operational Requirements at the Ministry of Defence. He was replaced by Oliver Green, just off the Imperial Defence College course, and made an Acting Air Commodore in order to take command. This was another masterstroke by the appointments people. Oliver Green must have been the only chap of that seniority looking for a job who had not graduated from a staff college, not necessarily the RAF Staff College, but *any* staff college. Paradoxically, his new deputy was not only a staff college graduate but had just ceased to be an Acting Air Commodore as our Air Attaché in Moscow. This rather confusing business caused me further doubts that the people in the "Head Shed" knew exactly what they were doing.

I threw a small party at which the Saudis were guests and, aware of their religious rules, went to some trouble to ensure that every kind of fruit juice was available. On their arrival I asked what they would like to drink and they answered: "Dimple Haig or Black Label will do nicely." They settled for Bells. They both lived very simply whilst they were with us, with no show of ostentation, and were popular members of the course.

The Norwegian, Olaf Aamoth, like most of his countrymen, spoke perfect English and was quite evidently pretty sharp. He also bore a

138

startling resemblance to Jimmy Durante although he did not act like him. Vincente Piccio, the Filipino, was a much more robust member of his race than his predecessor, and associated closely with the Americans on the course. The Greek, Peter Diakoymakos, had terrible troubles with his English initially, but it improved as time went on and he finished the course with distinction.

Two former members of No. 60 Squadron, the engineer officer Eric Sharrock and the nav/rad leader Peter Borritt (who succeeded Frank Jolliffe), were the only familiar faces amongst the intake. Nevertheless, after the initial shakedown, we all became absorbed in the work.

At least one week of the year was spent in the study of "The Appreciation," an extremely formalised method of problem solving in the military. The rules are strict and the route to a conclusion and recommendation is tortuous in the extreme. In fact, the rules seem more important than the problem: the perfect vehicle for a staff college exercise. As I entered, there was a heated debate going on in the DS office about the way in which the college's solution to the exercise had been reached and harsh words were being exchanged. I was invited to referee but, rather than do that, I asked each DS how long he had spent in staff appointments. The answer in total was about 60 years. I then asked how many Appreciations they had written or seen in that time. The answer was none and this seemed to stop the argument. The exercise was a good lesson in clear thinking and disciplined writing but was surely no reason for a fight.

When the summer break came along I sneaked into Boscombe and had two weeks with the squadron now commanded by one of my old ETPS students. He very kindly gave me access to the Andover, Argosy, and VC-10 in which I flew with someone in current practice, and a Meteor which they felt I could be trusted with on my own. That was better than any holiday and I returned to my professorial duties refreshed in mind and spirit.

In the autumn we had an open day for the London Attaché Corps which was extremely well-attended. They were told about the work of the college, and sat in on some syndicate work in the classrooms to gain an impression of the instructional routine. In the evening they were our guests at a dining-in night in the Mess, and it was with some unease that I took my seat between a Colonel of the Soviet Air Force and a Commodore of the Indonesian Navy. They were most agreeable dinner companions and far better behaved than many young RAF officers that I know. Also in the party was Fahim Jalal, now Iraqi Air Attaché and a paid-up member of the Chelsea Supporters' Club. His Saturdays were spent on the terraces at Stamford Bridge, complete with blue and white scarf and flat hat. He was addicted, almost to the point of becoming a bore, reeling off statistics and goal averages of the leading clubs.

139

During our industrial studies period we were lectured by the head of the Trades Union Congress, Vic Feather, a man who had built a considerable reputation by appearing to be much simpler than he was. I remember he was asked which disputes caused him the most trouble in the sense of being most difficult to solve. He answered that any concerned with principle were a nightmare. "As long as we're arguing about tuppence an hour, I know that we'll get it settled, but when a Union says it's a matter of principle, my heart sinks." In the end, he said, it was deciding how many pence an hour would overcome the point of principle: the root cause of all disputes was money. By the time that we set off for our northern tour I had persuaded one of the new DS that he should do the coal mine and I would do the shipyard.

As the year closed it was apparent that Andover's days were numbered. An ambitious building programme was about to start at Bracknell to enlarge it and allow the closure of Andover, with a consequent saving in the annual budget. Previous attempts to close the place had been frustrated mostly, it was said, by the Foreign Office who saw the academic year as a great hearts and minds exercise for the visiting officers. Bracknell had a higher security grading and the fear was that some of the foreign officers, welcomed to Andover, would be shown the Bracknell door. The amalgamation was not going to happen in time to save *me*, but I was cheered by the thought that, with full remission, I should be on my way in six months.

The assembly of mixed, if not united, nations that made up the third and last course that I saw at Andover was again evenly balanced between British and Foreign. The Indians and Pakistanis had just concluded another of their disagreements and we had one of each in the student body. The Pakistani had been quite successful in a Sabre and it was a matter of some interest to see how he would get along with his fellow resident of the sub-continent. It goes without saying that they became firm friends, not only in the professional sense, but also formed the outstanding bridge partnership of the year. If only the politicians would leave it to the airmen. For the first time we had two officers from the newly-created Royal Malaysian Air Force, both on their first visits to Britain, both unable to stop shivering. One confessed to me his astonishment that Andover was part of a rural community. Throughout his schooling he had been told that the United Kingdom was a very small place with a large population and consisted of London, with suburbs stretching to Scotland and Wales. He thought that there were no trees or fields and that we all lived in high-rise apartment buildings. On reflection, there are probably lots of English children who believe that Malaysia is all jungle.

We had only one Saudi and at some point early in the year he and his family went missing, much to our alarm. Finally, contact was made with the Saudi Embassy in London, who confirmed that he had taken refuge there.

"Refuge from what?" we asked. Refuge from the reprisals he feared after an Englishman had been flogged in Jeddah for breaching the very strict liquor laws, we were told. Needless to say, those of us that had seen the report in the newspaper felt that the man had been treated no more harshly than anyone else who broke that particular law. Major al-Ankari was taking no chances on mob rule breaking out at Andover.

Very soon after this bizarre incident, the commandant told me that he had my posting notice, to Farnborough. This sounded like good news and I asked what I was to do there. Briefly, the government were uneasy about the number of flight test establishments in the industry, the way they were run and some of the people that they employed. As a result, a post had been created with the title "Officer Commanding, Flight Test Operations," responsible to the Director of Flying, Ministry of Technology. The first incumbent was Red Evans and I was to take over from him. It was March 1967.

As was customary, I was dined-out with some ceremony and departed for the place which by now was becoming my second home.

CHAPTER XVII

THERE'LL BE SOME CHANGES MADE

My new offices were integral with the headquarters of the Empire Test Pilots' School, now under the watchful eye of Bill Straker, close to the mess but far removed from the flight line. However, there was a faint whiff of kerosene in the air, and already I felt better. I spent a few days with Red, establishing precisely what I was supposed to do, before he left to take up a new job in Scotland, an overseas posting as far as he was concerned. I had a deputy, John Waterton, and a secretary, Alwyn Wood, so that not too much time was taken up in getting to know the staff. Best of all I had official access to aircraft of the Royal Aircraft Establishment in order to carry out my duties.

One further surprise awaited me in the form of Tom Pierce, formerly commanding Tengah, now Director of Flying and for whom I should be working. Tom lived in ETPS Mess during the week, commuting to his office in London. I went to High Holborn to see him, to be told that we (he and I) were off on a tour of North American flight test establishments in two weeks' time, passport details to the travel office. I had not been in North America for 13 years so that this was a pleasant prospect.

We travelled to Washington by VC-10 and the embassy produced our itinerary which was comprehensive, coast to coast and north to south. On our way to Eglin AFB in Florida, our aircraft landed at Dothan, Alabama where I had completed my advanced training. It was not only the same town, it was the same airfield, and even the barracks were still there looking much the way they had 25 years earlier. At Eglin we were given a review of all the programmes going on, mostly in connection with the war in Vietnam. As is usually the case, aircraft were being mis-employed and required to operate in ways that the designer had never intended. The F-4, that splendid interceptor, was being used for ground attack without much in the way of modification. Fortunately (and as we found with the good old Hunter) it was many times stronger than it need have been and stood up to the task very well. We were shown a film of iron bombs being carried as underwing stores and dropped at various attack speeds to ensure that they did not interfere with the aircraft. Some bombs clearly struck the aircraft as they were released and I asked (reasonably, I thought) what limitations they had put on the 500 lb store concerned. I was told: "none." Yes, the bombs struck the aircraft but they did no damage, so why impose an operational limitation? The need for a clearance was urgent and there was no time to be finicky. This was a good example of the approach that the American services took to urgent operational problems.

On to Los Angeles in order to visit Edwards AFB (originally Muroc Dry Lake) in the Mojave Desert. We were treated royally and shown everything that was fit to be seen although there were doubtless one or two very secret items that we bypassed. I was intrigued by the XB-1 being flown by NASA, looking very like the production model that finally emerged, but having had an obviously hard life. There were patches on the fuselage, not particularly neat ones either, giving the same impression as those redundant aircraft that the apprentices practise on at Halton. But this was no redundant aircraft, it was in the middle of a Mach 3 test programme. The pilots were interesting to talk to because they were routinely flying for long periods at speeds quite beyond my experience. One of them said that, returning to Edwards from the east at the end of a trip, they started to decelerate over Colorado, which may have been an exaggeration but made a point about flight planning that I had never considered. We were also shown the famous "Skunk Works" where so many exciting development aircraft had first seen the light of day. The Lockheed SR-71, about which little was known at the time, was quite the most awesome, futuristic aircraft that I had seen until then. The one that I sat in was also showing its age and, for a working aircraft spending its time at very high altitudes and speeds, looked well overdue for overhaul. Cracks could be seen in the windscreen sandwich, with small patches of discolouration, but the aircraft was not grounded, indeed it was being prepared for flight.

At the time, a lot of work was being done on vehicles which might have a space application, and some were very odd shapes indeed. A "lifting body," not dissimilar in shape from a fairground dodgem car, came to grief on landing whilst we were there. The attempts to put it down looked exactly like a stone skimming the water, touching and sailing off again until inevitably it ran out of energy. There can be no better place in the world for that type of research flying because the landing area is, for all practical purposes, infinite.

Having completed our official duties in the area we stayed as guests of my great friend Stan Hubbard, who had tutored at ETPS with me, and who had made the dramatic arrival at Dunsfold in the Hunter. He had retired from the RAF and taken a job with Douglas at Long Beach who were Hawker's partners in the promotion of Vertical Take-Off and Landing aircraft in the USA. They wanted him for his knowledge of the subject of course but, by a supreme irony, he could not be given a security clearance because he was an alien. This problem was overcome by Stan becoming a citizen and so this archetypal Englishman, born to stride the moors with a dog at his heels, is now an American. It was from Stan, lounging by his swimming pool, that I learned that, after an earth tremor, the first call is to make sure that the family is OK and the next is to ask if the pool has cracked. That was a most enjoyable interlude and maintained the contact between us that has held for more than 40 years.

From Los Angeles the next stop was St. Louis, Missouri, the home of the McDonnell company who were producing re-engined Phantoms for the Royal Navy. My hope was that I should get very close to one of them because the first batch were due to fly whilst we were there. Because our carriers were smaller than the big American "nukes," it was decided that more power was needed to allow the aircraft to operate safely and that Rolls-Royce Spey engines would do the trick. I have no idea what went wrong, but during the ground-running of the new aircraft, a bucketful of compressor blades came out of the back end and terminated any slim chance I had of flying one. The aircraft on production flight test flew from the factory on one side of the civil airport and were fed into the traffic pattern with the commercial services landing at St. Louis. As far as I could establish this had worked successfully for years even though all my instincts told me it was a recipe for disaster. Production aircraft are tested because, whilst everyone believes that they have been assembled perfectly, until they have been flown, nobody is absolutely sure. In the circumstances I should prefer not to have other aircraft around for a first flight.

To see the production lines, we climbed aboard motorised golf carts and by the end of the tour I was relieved that we had not set out to walk. The passageways seemed endless and I was surprised to see that many of the operatives were female, black and of generous proportions. Every production operation was mechanised until final assembly which was completed at the extreme end of the hangar so that the finished aircraft could be towed out to the flight line for inspection before flight. At peak they were producing 75 aircraft a month from the facility, which made anything that I had seen before seem like a cottage industry. It was impressive.

It was a quite different case at Fort Worth, Texas where General Dynamics were producing the F-111, a small number of which had been ordered for the RAF following the cancellation of the TSR.2. The programme was not going well; the US Navy had already cancelled its order and, unknown to us, the RAF was about to do the same. There was an air of depression about the place with large numbers of people laid off and a slump in the housing market following the departure of so many workers to other companies. Driving around the town in the evening we saw entire 'executive estates' deserted and every house with a "For Sale" sign outside. The mobility of labour in the United States is often held up as an example to the British workforce, but only by people who do not understand the vastness of that country and the huge geographical spread of the aviation industry.

At the factory the next day there was good news and bad news. The bad news was that the F-111 aircraft were all grounded so there went my chance of a trip. The good news was that the Chief Test Pilot was Richard Johnson whom I had hosted at Boscombe Down some years before, soon after he had established a new world speed record in an F-86. He was not a happy man because he could see that the programme was in trouble but he nevertheless spent time with us to talk about the project.

General Dynamics, which had absorbed the old Convair company, had acquired with it a lot of valuable research and practical data on high-speed flight. The F-102, and even more the F-106, broke new ground in the "weapon system" concept and they were very high-performing fighters. The B-58 Hustler was a very advanced bomber and the Convair 880/990 series were the fastest passenger aircraft before Concorde, and yet commercial success eluded them. Maybe they tried to incorporate too many new ideas into their designs to be acceptable to the conservative civil and military procurement authorities. Whatever the case, the F-111 had all the makings of another aeronautical lemon. There were half a dozen aircraft on the flight line, not available for close inspection, but from a walk-around I was not impressed by the standard of finish, and was especially shocked to see tell-tale marks on the side of the fuselage where the flying tail had removed the paint over the small arc of its travel. This looked like "close-fitting" taken to an absurd extreme.

We returned to Washington in order to visit Patuxent River, the United States Navy Test Centre and home of the US Navy Test Pilots' School. We were escorted by Mr Denis Higton, formerly the head boffin of the naval test squadron at Boscombe Down, now attached to the Embassy as Chief Scientific Officer. We had a marvellous visit to Pax River, with the chance to see all the projects in hand and to ask any questions that we chose. They had just lost their second instrumented spinning Phantom, although the pilot had escaped, and this led me to ask how quickly it could be replaced in order for the programme to continue. They had decided that this was a losing battle and had simply declared that the aircraft should not be spun. We were guests at an informal party in the Club in the evening and several of the residents sought me out to say how much they had enjoyed their time at Farnborough as students at ETPS. It is a very select union as I have discovered.

Our final call was at the Pentagon to talk to the procurement division. I raised the question of the Phantom spinning, not to be critical, but simply to point out that we could not give such a clearance without completing the trial and recommending a recovery procedure, as required by AvP 970, the "Boscombe bible." This document, which I have mentioned before, was first produced years ago and, although amended to take account of the rapid changes in aviation, remained the bench-mark against which all new aircraft were measured. To my surprise, the naval authorities showed great interest in my general description of the publication, saying that they had no similar document. I promised to send copies on my return.

At our embassy debrief I was able to renew acquaintance with Danny Norman, the RN Phantom project pilot, who had been a student at ETPS in my time there. Danny, an irrepressible character, was full of confidence for the future of the aircraft in RN service and was undaunted by the slight difficulties being experienced at the time. His confidence was, in the end, fully justified.

Before heading for home we were scheduled to drop into Ottawa to see what the Canadians were doing at Uplands, their experimental establishment. I had got word to my old friend Russ Janzen that I was visiting, and he arranged a training flight with a student from Rivers, Manitoba to Uplands, so that we could have an evening of reminiscence. That was the highlight of the Canadian sector of the trip except for a view of the experimental Canadair tilt-wing project. The theory was good; it took off like a helicopter but, having translated to forward flight, it was no longer subject to the laws which govern the restricted forward speed of the helicopter. It looked extremely hazardous to me.

On return to Farnborough I started to get to grips with the real job and set up a visit programme to the manufacturers' airfields. Much of this was new ground and I have to say that there was deep suspicion of our motives from some quarters. Fortunately, I knew most of the test pilots, and was able to use them to reassure their respective managements that I had not been appointed to close them down. The visits were all of a pattern. We flew in, reported to the Chief Test Pilot, looked around the facilities and usually spoke to the design staff to see what future commitments they had. Generally, we night-stopped, had a meal in the evening with the flying staff, rounded off the visit the next morning and flew back to Farnborough. When setting up the visit it was made fairly clear that we should be happy to join in any flying that was going on and this often bore fruit.

Towards the end of March 1968, I was surprised to receive at my home an official telegram, surprised because most official communications would have been sent to my office. The message was to report to Biggin Hill on the 1st April to record a programme for French television. I knew of course that it was a significant date, the 50th anniversary of the founding of the Royal Air Force, but it also looked like the perfect set-up for an April Fool joke, especially when it added that I was to call the Station Adjutant for further information. I racked my brains to remember who I knew that was currently serving at Biggin and recalled that Frank Jolliffe had recently been appointed to the aircrew selection board based there. That must be it, I thought, and I was damned if I would give him the satisfaction of yelling "April Fool" down the telephone.

I waited for 24 hours for the perpetrator to realise that his scheme had misfired and then made a very tentative call to the number I had been given. A greatly relieved adjutant thanked me for calling and asked if I could be there the next morning for the recording to be made: it was not a hoax. The short film was made with Peter Townsend, former equerry to the late King George VI, recounting his memories of the Battle of Britain, a young flying officer discussing his hopes for the future and with my story acting as a bridge between the two. This all came about because on the infamous Annual Confidential Report there was a section for foreign languages spoken and degree of proficiency, in which I had always admitted practical French and German. The computer had thrown up my name when searching for a suitable representative of those officers of a certain age.

As in all other jobs, occasional diversions occurred. ETPS lost a Hunter T.7 during a spinning exercise over Lyme Bay and I was detailed off to chair the Board of Inquiry, assisted by John Waterton (my deputy) and Duncan Cooke, a practising test pilot in 'A' Squadron at Boscombe. The pilot, Lieutenant Chris Wheal RN had survived with the usual post-ejection back injuries, and was in the Military Hospital at Tidworth. Having a survivor made the investigation so much easier of course, which was as well since the wreckage was not recoverable. The hero of the incident was a local fisherman who was out in the Bay when he heard the ejection seat gun fire, which caused him to look up and to see the parachute deploy just as the aircraft hit the water. The parachute canopy collapsed on top of the pilot and he was set fair to drown when the fishing boat reached him and the fisherman dragged him into the boat, wet canopy and all. Rushing to the rescue had done his boat no good, and it was leaking like a sieve after the battering had sprung the planks; nevertheless, they reached the shore without further incident.

Quite a lot of pilots jumped out of spinning Hunters, usually, it was thought, because they failed to wait for the spin recovery action to take effect, or they inadvertently held on a trace of outspin or inspin aileron. In either case, the aircraft would spin until it hit the ground. For these reasons, deliberate spinning was prohibited but at the Test Pilots' School it was a training exercise of considerable merit. In the T.7, with two side-by-side seats, the pilot sat in the left-hand seat when flying solo which aggravated the difficulty of deciding precisely when the wings were dead level. We concluded that this was probably the cause of this accident after speaking to Chris Wheal in his hospital bed. He was very grateful to the fisherman who had rescued him, as you would expect, and supported my recommendation that he should be awarded an MBE, which he was. To rather more practical purpose, I also pressed the Ministry to buy him a new boat which, I am happy to say, they did.

Because I was already there, I was appointed to the Flying Committee of the Farnborough Show, together with Duncan Simpson, Brian Trubshaw, Roly Beamont and Bill Morrison who, as head of the Experimental Flying Department, had charge of all flying from the Establishment. One of our responsibilities was to watch each individual flying display before the show opened, to see that it was flown in accordance with the well-defined safety rules. In 1968, we were in position on the balcony of the control tower to watch the arrival and display rehearsal of the Red Arrows. As always, they arrived precisely on time, and as they rushed in from the west we were looking down on the canopies of the formation. It fell to Bill Morrison to point out to the leader that they were too low, even for the Arrows, and would they try again. Red Leader made a telephone call and Bill soon found himself summoned to the phone to speak to a very senior officer who told him that special rules were in force for the Arrows and would he please not interfere. The worst thing that can happen at a big airshow is for the participants to start competing with each other and, in seeking to enforce the rules, that is what we were trying to forestall. It follows that if the national aerobatic team is getting away with murder, other entrants are going to object, and with justification. If proper control is not exercised, look out on the final day, when 10 days of frustration will prove too much for some performer. In the same year, the heaviest rain of recent times fell on Hampshire and Surrey, causing the rivers to rise and actually cutting off the centre of Guildford. At Farnborough, a small stream at the western end of the airfield burst its banks and when the runway was being inspected in the morning a fish was found in the runway threshold, trying desperately to get back to the main stream. For the only time in my memory of the event, there was no flying that day. As the show finally got under way, the flying was of the usual high standard, and the committee began to relax. At pre-show briefings, the visitors with language problems had found interpreters, and a smooth routine had been established. The Breguet Atlantique, a maritime patrol aircraft still under development, was being shown making a majestic fly-past and then repeating the procedure with one engine feathered. Whilst not very exciting to watch I had sympathy for the pilot called upon to demonstrate an essentially dull aeroplane which simply did not lend itself to attention-grabbing manoeuvres. On the third day however, he caught my full attention: with his port engine feathered, he was making a left turn to line up with the runway when it became clear that he was not going to make it. Feeling slightly exposed sitting on the balcony of the air traffic control tower I could only watch as he tightened the turn getting lower all the time. Inevitably, he struck the ground beside the black sheds at the eastern end of Farnborough runway 100 yards from our viewing platform, killing the crew. We then learned that the crew whose display we had cleared had gone home to be replaced by others who had not rehearsed at all. So much for our careful vetting procedure.

Time rolled on: Tom Pierce retired and was replaced by H.A.C. Bird-Wilson. Universally known as Birdy, this gallant officer lived in Farnham, just down the road from Farnborough, and found endless reasons to visit me and to go flying. He had a reason to visit BAC at Warton and the only available aircraft was a Canberra B.6. This was perfect for the task except that Birdy, who had not flown a Canberra before, wanted to fly it and there were no dual controls. It was agreed that I should fly it to Warton and he would fly the return leg to Farnborough. The trip north was without incident. He stood behind me and I pointed out what I was doing during take-off and settling in to the climb. Power settings for the cruise, descent and circuit were established and I showed the effect of the flaps which were 'in' or 'out' – there was no intermediate setting. The flaps appeared to do nothing as they were lowered until the last few degrees brought a sharp trim change and reduction in speed. Apart from that, the aircraft was like a big Meteor, and Birdy had lots of Meteor time.

Our departure Warton was quite sporting. There was a crosswind and for a brief moment we were heading for the air traffic control tower which was disturbing, especially since I could take no action other than to advise, as none of the engine controls were within my reach. That was sorted out and the cruise home was uneventful. We joined the Farnborough circuit and it was one of those autumn days with the sun setting and a little mist about which meant that overhead, the runway was clearly visible, and even downwind it could still be seen. The difficulties started as we turned into wind, when the combination of haze and low sun caused the runway to disappear. In the circumstances I would have swallowed my pride and called for a Ground Controlled Approach, but my gallant leader chose not to. After years of flying in the area I knew the ground features so well that I could give him heading corrections, which he was happy to follow. What I could not do was persuade him to slow the thing down because, in spite of its size, the Canberra approached at about 90-95 knots, and floated for ever if it was any quicker. We were still at about 120 knots when we crossed the threshold first time and I told him to overshoot and have another try, which he did. The second attempt was better but we were still too fast and used every yard of the Farnborough runway to bring the aircraft to a halt. This reinforced my long-held view that piloting modern aircraft was something to do regularly or not at all.

I continued to enjoy my visiting as the "Queen's Inspector," and was conscious of the privileged position that I held in being shown the companies' development secrets. However there was something unsatisfying about the life. I had long ago been reconciled to the fact that my days of making my living by putting on a flying suit were behind me, and with time on my hands, I began to speculate on what the future held. It was clear that I was not going to be Chief of the Air Staff although another promotion or two was not out of the question. Deeply aware that my total time at Air Ministry totalled six months, I could not escape forever, and the thought of commuting to London for an infinity of years was daunting. Because society was changing, and rarely for the better (these were the swinging sixties), military personnel were mocked and abused by politicians so that the whole ethos of the officer corps was being destroyed. Pondering these weighty topics and wondering what the hell to do for the best, an opportunity occurred to join the Hawker Siddeley Aviation military marketing team, based at Kingston in Surrey. The team, headed by Bill Bedford, recently retired from the Chief Test Pilot slot, was a new departure for the company. Sir Sidney Camm had always stated that his aircraft sold themselves and, rather in the manner of a prewar would-be Rolls-Royce owner, anyone wishing to buy Hawker aircraft was carefully vetted. The Harrier was such a revolutionary design that customers were no longer beating a path to the Kingston factory and it was felt that the concept had to be sold by people who appreciated its significance. I knew that I could not sell vacuum cleaners to save my life, but I felt that I understood enough about aircraft and air operations to be able to talk about the Harrier with conviction. I was taken on, and applied to retire prematurely from the Royal Air Force in order to undertake this task of national interest.

This proved to be rather more difficult than I had expected because Birdy, trying not to be obstructive, said he would forward my application on condition that I found someone to take my place at Farnborough. Fortunately, I learned of one of my old ETPS students who was between jobs, and practised my selling technique on him, successfully.

So, after almost precisely 28 years, I took off my uniform for the last time, with many fewer regrets than I would have expected, and launched on a new career.

CHAPTER XVIII
SAND IN MY SHOES

The Hawker factory at Kingston-upon-Thames (still referred to by many as Sopwiths) had been producing aircraft for more than 50 years before I arrived. The splendid façade facing Richmond Road concealed a working area stretching down to the river, which must have cost far more to maintain than to rebuild. It was an historic place which had seen the birth and development of some remarkable aeroplanes, the latest of which was the Harrier. It is no part of my brief to recount the immeasurable part played by the factory and its personnel in the history of British aviation; the story has been told elsewhere by authors more knowledgeable of the subject than I could ever be. However, it will do no harm to outline the events that had led to my arrival on that spring morning of 1969.

In 1965, it had been announced that development of the P.1127 (RAF), later to be named Harrier, would proceed for service with the Royal Air Force. This excited the interest of the United States Marine Corps, to whom an aircraft that could give close support of the kind that they enjoyed from their A-4 Skyhawks, but with the basing flexibility of their helicopters, was the answer to all their prayers. The marines had no research and development budget of their own since all their procurement was done by the US Navy, and they therefore were not represented in the tripartite evaluation squadron. Nine intermediate-standard aircraft had been built to be flown and assessed by a mixed bunch of British, American and German pilots operating as a unified squadron. In 1965, starting on April 1st (always a significant date for the Royal Air Force), this interim aircraft, labelled Kestrel, was thoroughly wrung out and the team produced a joint and favourable report. The USMC had access to the report, because the US Navy had supplied one of the pilots, and they liked what they read. We now fast-forward to the Farnborough Show of 1968 when Hawkers were somewhat surprised to be confronted by two USMC colonels stating that they wished to fly the Harrier. The rest, as they say, is history and the following year the USMC placed its first order for 12 aircraft. This unexpected and historic event encouraged the company to think that once again they had a winner and required enthusiasts to promote it around the world.

My first day at the new job was not auspicious. I had no idea of how long it would take to drive the 15 miles from Guildford, where I lived, to Kingston during the morning rush-hour. Determined not to be late I allowed an hour and a half and in consequence arrived before anyone else in the factory. Furthermore, when asked to identify myself by the policeman on the gate, I realised that I no longer had my RAF Identity Card, Form 1250, a document that had served me well in banks and passport offices around the world. My third, and least forgivable, mistake was to use the Directors' car park. I hasten to say that the park in question was not identified in any way, it was just one of those things that people were expected to know. I was driving a rather smart Daimler/Jaguar at the time and when I returned to it in the evening I found that it was one of several in the car park. I learned that most Main Board Directors of the Company favoured the model as their company transport and so I quickly disposed of mine. Rank or standing within the company was made clear, not by badges, but by the model of car that the executive was offered.

I had expected to report to Bill (Bedford) but he was abroad on some jaunt and had asked his secretary, Angela Lindsay-Smith, to look after me. I met the rest of the Department in the form of John Crampton, an extremely large old Harrovian officer who was titled "Technical Sales Manager," but who was in fact Bill's deputy. Later the same morning the department expanded even further with the arrival of Colin Downes, formerly of the Royal Air Force and, more recently, Handley Page. After some fairly desultory chat I asked for some manuals on the Harrier in order to fill the gaping holes in my knowledge of the aircraft. It was then that I realised that no provision had been made for the newcomers to be accommodated and, if all four of us were ever at Kingston at the same time, it would be standing room only. For some time I occupied the office of anyone that happened to be away for the day but eventually the organisation clicked.

When Bill returned I asked how the department was set up and what part I should be expected to play. From the little information that I had gleaned, Bill and John darted off to any part of the globe in response to evidence of local interest unearthed by our man on the spot. It seemed plain that, with four members now, the department should develop an organisation that allowed each of us to establish a close rapport with a region of the world. Shrewdly, Bill asked me to work something out, which was how I became Kingston's man for the Middle East; I lacked the nerve to give the area to anyone else. John Crampton had made it clear that his interest was closely focused on Europe while Colin Downes had looked after the Far East for Handley Page. Bill wanted to retain a wandering remit, to become involved in any country where he was well-known for either his Hunter work in the past or his P.1127/Kestrel/Harrier work in more recent years. Middle East required liberal interpretation since my patch started in Greece in the west, and extended to Pakistan in the east, and then south to cover the whole of Africa. My geography improved rapidly.

I was barely settled into my studies when Frank Murphy, former test-pilot and now the military Marketing Director, asked me if I had ever been to – I thought he said – Gatow, which I knew to be the old Berlin airport. I replied, as I usually did to questions about places in Germany: "Not on the ground." I had misread him. He was actually saying Qatar, which is a small, oil-rich Emirate in the Arabian Gulf. I had to admit that I had been denied that pleasure, an omission quickly to be rectified.

The Middle East, never the most placid region of the world, was beginning to generate problems quite outside the perennial Arab/Israeli dispute. Colonel Gaddafi had assumed control of Libya, and there was a growing hostility towards those that had oil from those that had none. This led to small, indefensible countries acquiring organised defence forces to declare a price of admission, just in case their Muslim brothers were entertaining any take-over notions. Qatar was one such state. Thus it was that I found myself extolling the virtues of the Hunter to the Emir and his police chief/air minister, neither of whom had the least idea of what a military aircraft could or could not do. I quickly realised that it really did not matter if the Hunter was a good, bad or indifferent aircraft as long as it was on offer at the right price. The order for three aircraft that derived from these discussions (to which a fourth was subsequently added) was unlikely to keep the factories very busy, but it was a start.

This was my first meeting with our Regional Executive for the area, John Kielder Brown, with whom I was to share many an adventure in the years that followed. We called on him in Beirut on the way home, Frank Murphy having decided that we might as well look up a few business acquaintances whilst we were in the area. Frank, a man easily distinguished by his silver hair, had been ploughing the Middle East furrow for the company for many years and knew a lot of people. It was unnerving for me, but not unusual, for our walk down a dusty street to be interrupted by a local grasping Frank in a warm embrace and kissing him on both cheeks.

The huge explosion of new hotels in the area had not yet occurred and the Saint George in Beirut was the best place to stay, a fine hotel of the highest international standard. I was to get to know it well. However on this, my first visit, I was bidden to meet Frank in the bar at 7 o'clock for a drink before dinner. I had been seeking to establish a regular tipple which would be refreshing and slightly alcoholic and had recalled Bacardi and coke from Singapore days. There was a hidden advantage here in that if I felt that a long and liquid evening was threatened I could have plain Coke with no one being the wiser. As we entered the bar the barman welcomed me warmly, nodded to Frank and asked what I would have. He produced my Bacardi and Coke with a flourish and set it in front of me. He then turned to Frank and said: "Black Label with water and no ice for you, Mr Murphy?" which was precisely what he wanted. It went through my mind that, when the head barman in the Saint George prepares your drink without asking, you have been accepted into that select band of Middle East travellers. In the restaurant the treatment was exactly the same. Emile, the

153

maitre d'hôtel, removed a Reserved sign from one of the best verandah tables, and ushered us to it. Over the years that followed, until the collective fit of madness overtook the Lebanon in 1975, I received the VIP treatment whenever I went to the Saint George, simply because I was known to be an associate of Frank Murphy and Johnny Brown.

The organisation of the aviation part of Hawker Siddeley needs to be explained in order that constant reference to certain people makes sense. Each of the factories had a small marketing team, expert in that factory's products. In each geographical region of the world lived a company employee titled Regional Executive (RE), covering several countries and functioning as an ambassador, ear to the ground for any hint of a civil or military re-equipment programme. Each RE appointed and controlled a string of agents, local businessmen with good connections, likely to hear of requirements and funding as soon as decisions were taken to proceed with a project. The agents made initial introductions for the appropriate factory teams and accompanied them until contacts were established and self-sustaining. They also made hotel bookings, provided transport and, in the case of the Kingston team whose only interest was military, arranged the vital passes which allowed us on to military establishments in order to meet and brief. I should add that Rolls-Royce had a similar system of correspondents who performed the same function on their behalf. Since everything we made was Rolls-Royce-powered, we were invariably working as a team in our marketing efforts.

At my first meeting with Johnny Brown we agreed that I should prepare myself for a tour of the area to meet all the people likely to become involved with my activities over the next few years. Quite the most daunting part of the preparation was obtaining visas, which involved hours of waiting in hostile or indifferent embassies in London for the consular section to open and for the right man to find the right stamp to grant me a visit to his country. The Foreign Office was remarkably understanding about the problem and allowed some of us to have two passports specifically to ensure that, if for some reason a passport was stamped by the Israeli authorities, thus invalidating it for the entire Arab world, we should not be stuck. The danger of this happening was confined to a diversion of a British Airways aircraft on which we happened to be travelling, a danger that seemed so remote (there would almost certainly be Arab passengers aboard) that I reduced the waiting time for visas by circulating both passports. An irritating side-effect of the need for a visa for every visit was that a normal passport lasted on average six months, and applications for renewal were a constant part of commercial life. The introduction of the business traveller's passport, with 90 usable pages instead of the previous 25, was a boon.

The Grand Tour, which lasted for 6 weeks, covered the Lebanon, Jordan, Iran and the Gulf States with J.K. Brown, and Pakistan with Maurice Brown (no relation), who was resident in Nairobi. This left vast areas untouched but it was appreciated that the Harrier was not a practical proposition for the majority of the African nations except those to whom we were forbidden to speak. At the conclusion of this tour our agreed position was that two or three of those visited had the operational need, the technical capability and the financial resources to make the Harrier attractive and affordable. The ability to operate off-airfield was a huge attraction to those states that had very few aerodromes, all of which could expect to be blasted within minutes either side of hostilities breaking out. The uniqueness of the Harrier was a deterrent to the immature air forces who, aware that the RAF had only just received its first squadron, and furthermore that it was the first and only V/STOL squadron in the world, were inclined to wait to see how things developed. The exception in my area was the Indian Navy whose only carrier was inadequate for aircraft more advanced than the Sea Hawks which were embarked, but whose planning staffs could see the life-extension that V/STOL would give to the ship.

The Air Wing of the Abu Dhabi Defence Forces, manned and led by former RAF and RN pilots, were also staunch advocates, quick to appreciate the added effectiveness that the Harrier would give them. During frequent visits I became well-acquainted, even friendly, with Twinkle Storey and his happy band of mercenaries flying the Hunters. They comprised quite the most effective force in the area. It was much the same situation in Kuwait where a small Hunter force was absorbing local recruits as pilots and ground crew, although much of the engineering expertise was provided by expatriate members of the Pakistan Air Force. This drift away from British to fellow Muslims was quite natural on several levels but did not improve the standard of maintenance.

The on/off relationship between Iraq and the UK was going through one of its better phases and, using my lapsed contacts with the Iraqis that had attended Andover Staff College, I went to Baghdad to give the headquarters staff a briefing on the Harrier. I was met on arrival by Brigadier Fahim Jalal, former Chelsea supporter, now Chief of Staff for Air Defence of the Iraqi Air Force. He made the arrangements for the briefing, introduced me to his colleagues and was generally most agreeable and helpful. Over coffee I asked what had happened to Niamat Dilaimi, his fellow student at Andover, and he brushed the question aside. Sensing that he was embarrassed I said no more but, when we were alone, he told me that Niamat was in jail. As station commander at Habbaniya he had led his Hunter wing in an abortive strike on the Presidency and when they landed back, the plot obviously having gone badly wrong, he was arrested. I was surprised but relieved to learn that his punishment had not been more condign.

The briefing was listened to with rapt attention by the audience, mostly pilots, who had been brought to Baghdad from outstations around the country. Using slides and film it was possible to demonstrate the capabilities of the aircraft even where a language barrier existed, and especially to pilots who could easily comprehend the differences in operating technique that defined the aircraft. Questions after such a presentation followed a predictable pattern and allowed the presenter to expand on specific aspects of the aircraft which were difficult to grasp at first hearing. As an example, fuel consumption during a vertical take-off was always assumed to be horrendous, based on their knowledge of the effect of reheat in their Russian aircraft. The Pegasus engine in the Harrier has no reheat and full throttle uses the same amount of fuel whether the aircraft goes forwards or upwards. Not infrequently someone would ask the maximum height at which the aeroplane could hover (which was dependent on weight and atmosphere), and until I became used to the question I wondered what was in the questioner's mind. Almost none realised what a useful tactic in air-to-air fighting was the ability to stop, so that the adversary overshot and offered a firing opportunity, but many saw being stationary as a chance to drop bombs accurately!

The Regional Executives in the vast area for which I was responsible were never idle and, I think, used the novelty of the Harrier to gain entry to politicians and military commanders who generally would not see them, simply because there was nothing to discuss. This was the case in most of Africa where the Harrier was beyond budget and, if we are frank, beyond the capability of the young air forces. Nevertheless, we were encouraged by our government to establish and maintain contacts and this we did, using Harrier briefings as the way in. For this reason I found myself in some strange places talking to enthusiastic if not very knowledgeable airmen.

During one of my early wanderings I felt obliged to visit Egypt since its air force had the capability to operate the Harrier and should have learned by experience the need to disperse when threatened by attack. Arrangements were made, not without some difficulties, for me to be met on arrival in Cairo by our man, Mahmoud Miligi. Egypt was, and in many ways still is, a police state where men in a mixture of uniforms carry guns, and are much in evidence at the international airport. I was surprised therefore to be met at the aircraft steps by a charming, cultured man who introduced himself as Miligi and who led me through passport control to await the arrival of my baggage. As we walked he was greeting people everywhere, clearly giving orders to some and shaking others warmly by the hand. He spoke to me in perfect, unaccented English but I was unable to follow any of the rapid

Arabic which was of course the language that he used with everyone else. He had absolutely no truck with the queues at immigration or customs, simply leading me to the front, speaking to the official and breezing through. Only later did I discover that he had learned to fly with the RAF, retiring from the Egyptian Air Force as an air commodore in order to become chairman of the national airline, the unfortunately-named Misr Air. In this capacity he had been influential in the purchase of Comet aircraft by the airline and had become known to the de Havilland company, by now part of Hawker Siddeley.

We achieved nothing on the visit except that I gained a passing knowledge of the political situation from Miligi and from the staff at our Embassy. There was a general air of gloom over the entire place as realisation dawned that the late President had not wrought the miracle that the man in the street had been led to expect if he embraced Islamic socialism. I was happy to cross Egypt off my list of duty calls for the short term and was relieved to be delivered to Cairo Airport by Miligi to return to London.

Check-in time was three hours before departure and it was important not to be late because reserved seats were sold within minutes of the deadline passing. Having a reconfirmed, confirmed seat meant nothing when money was to be made by selling the ticket to a traveller without one. When the formalities were at last completed and I was sitting in exquisite discomfort on a broken chair surrounded by shouting Arabs (they rarely converse quietly), all the doors were closed. I feared the worst because the armed guards were much in evidence and, with no one allowed in or out, it seemed possible that a search was about to start for someone trying to leave the country illegally. The truth was less dramatic. Having sealed the area designated Departure Lounge, a small tractor appeared towing a tanker of about 500 gallons capacity, the sort used for moving engine oil around the flight line. A generator fired up and, with absolutely no attention to the passengers in the overcrowded room, DDT was sprayed everywhere from floor to ceiling. Visibility reduced to zero and the atmosphere became unbreathable. In the middle of the ensuing chaos my flight was called and I made my way into the open air to board the waiting aircraft. It was an event that made me rather more tolerant of the highly-tuned inefficiency of Heathrow and Gatwick.

Travelling to Abu Dhabi from Beirut on my own (I think Johnny Brown was unwell), I had telexed my arrival time, flight number and confirmation of reservation to the Al Ain Palace Hotel, at that time the only one in the Emirate. It was a night flight and, after a busy day in Beirut, I was looking forward to a rest before my early morning appointment with the Air Wing. I pitched up at the hotel at midnight to be told that my room had been sold since I was late in arriving. Threats and even bribes were to no avail, as whoever had my room had paid a bigger premium than I felt Hawker Siddeley could afford. There was literally nowhere else to go and I spent what was left of the night in a chair in the lobby of the hotel. In the morning, when the Greek manager of the hotel came on duty, he was full of apologies, but the power of their monopoly was such that, furious though I was, I was forced to make light of the incident.

The Indian interest in Harrier soon became known to the Pakistani authorities and with Maurice Brown I travelled to Peshawar to brief the air force on the aircraft and its capabilities. I was accompanied by Michael Miles of Rolls-Royce (Bristol) and Jim Summers of Ferranti (Edinburgh). It was fairly clear from the extended question period after the presentation that an intelligence dossier was being prepared. Fortunately for us, if not for the Indians, none of the aircraft's performance was secret and there was no reason for us not to respond to the third degree to which we were subjected.

Together with Jim Summers, who became a close friend and most agreeable travelling companion, I made my first visit to the Khyber Pass and was deeply moved by the event. The road, of dubious construction, is cut out of the hills above, but parallel to the old camel track. Our transport was an ancient Chevrolet taxi, hired for the day, and driven by an old pirate who seemed to be high on some substance frowned upon by our society but freely available from the street stalls in Peshawar. His natural homicidal and suicidal tendencies were bad enough and the mechanical condition of his vehicle, particularly the tyres which were bald as an egg, did nothing for our morale. He attacked the blind curves with enthusiasm, heedless of the 200 ft drop if he got it wrong, and answered any questions concerning conflicting traffic with a confident "too early for other cars."

The Pass itself reeks of history with familiar regimental badges carved into the face of the rock bordering the roadway. It seems fanciful to say so, but from time to time I was sure that I could hear the skirl of the pipes. Any tribesman seen in the area was armed, usually with a genuine or replica Lee Enfield rifle. Notices at the entrance to the Pass, repeated at intervals along its route, warned against taking photographs, especially of tribal women. We asked our driver what the penalty was for any breach of the law, and from his answer it seemed clear that there was no law, except for the gun. He said that he could arrange the death of an enemy for the equivalent of 50p, unless of course the target was well-known in which case the fee went up to £5. I believed him.

We went to the border and looked over into Afghanistan, which looked remarkably similar to Pakistan. On the return we diverted to the smugglers' village where merchandise, not seen in the stores in Peshawar, was on abundant display. Each stall seemed to be selling the same mixture of cloth, radios, children's toys and cigarettes. On the adjacent track however, the armourers were busily at work manufacturing and selling guns of every type and description. The external standard of workmanship was extremely high although how many of the guns misfired or had breech explosions history does not relate. It was all very educational but I was quite relieved to be back in our broken-down transport and even more relieved to be delivered safely back to Brown's Hotel (not to be confused with another establishment of the same name in London's West End).

Maurice Brown, who had been a frequent visitor over his years as an RE, was a mine of information on the changes that had occurred since the construction of Islamabad, which forced the relocation of many of the military offices and civil ministries from Rawalpindi and Peshawar. Certainly, Peshawar had the run-down and neglected appearance of so many towns on the sub-continent, where maintenance of roads and buildings has long disappeared from the agenda.

The company had Bill Reed as agent in Karachi and I felt that, having been on his patch, I should report to him on the way home, out of courtesy, and to establish a personal link in case further questions arose from the Pakistan Air Force. He was an elderly gentleman who had lived in India/Pakistan for many years running his small trading company. He was a member of the Sind Club and had arranged for me to stay there for the short time I was to be in Karachi. He very kindly met my flight at the airport and conducted me to the cub in the ancient Morris Minor which was his executive transport. Karachi traffic makes the average banger race appear orderly and our progress through it was nothing short of miraculous. Much of the time Bill was looking at me rather than the road and it dawned on me that he was deaf as a post, and had to look at me to lip-read if our conversation was to mean anything. As is not uncommon with the seriously deaf, he tended to shout, which made my attempts at confidentiality when debriefing him in the bar of the Club pretty pointless. He also put to me, and anyone else within 100 yds radius, searching questions concerning Indian interest in the Harrier which I felt unable to answer in the circumstances.

He invited me to have dinner at his house in the evening, which provided a small cameo of life after the raj. His residence was a bungalow of the kind seen in any part of the tropics where the British have been in significant numbers: single-storey and surrounded by a garden filled with trees and shrubs. I was met by a uniformed servant who asked my name and said to wait, which of course I did. I was then led to the drawing room where Bill and his wife plus 6 or 7 dogs were waiting to greet me. The dogs were family pets, scruffy and with free access to the furniture, each occupying his favourite spot and making it quite difficult to take a seat as I was bidden. The shouting match went on as Mrs Reed and I tried to include Bill in the conversation, whilst he fiddled with his hearing aids to no apparent avail. There were no other guests, which made me wonder why I had been announced on arrival, and it was an extremely testing evening since there was no one to share the light-hearted banter.

Mrs Reed ran a riding stable and trained horses, quite aside from her main interest in dog-breeding, and would have been perfectly at home in any of the southern English counties. However, she would have missed the servants, none of whom I am sure would have found employment elsewhere.

The Sind Club itself had started life as part of the colonial order, decorated with trophies of long-forgotten chases which had represented the members' best efforts to reduce to zero the indigenous fauna. There was also a huge billiard room with half a dozen tables which seemed to be in constant use. Had I been led into the place blindfold, the voices and the slang might have led me to conclude that I had been transported to an army mess on Salisbury Plain, circa 1920. Earlier traditions were certainly being kept alive even though the language was stuck in a time-warp.

During brief spells back at the factory, digesting what I had learned and preparing to launch on another massive exercise to cover, in the most perfunctory way, the rest of my area of responsibility, I witnessed some of the incidents that were making the Harrier famous. The London–New York city centre-to-city centre air race was won by Tom Lecky-Thompson and Graham Williams of No. 1(F) Squadron. The departure from a disused coalyard at St. Pancras station in London was well worth watching. The aircraft took off vertically in a cloud of coal dust, leading some wag to remark that the aircraft used it as fuel instead of petrol or kerosene. Tom was rightly upset when, reaching for a sandwich to sustain him on his journey he found that the wretched dust had penetrated even the well-wrapped food.

I was detailed to attend the Paris Air Show to assist Bill Bedford, John Crampton and Colin Downes in fielding the stream of questioning visitors who would witness the Harrier demonstration. The last Paris Show that I had attended had been as a day-tripper and I was quite unprepared for the rigours of nearly two weeks of constant attendance. Quite apart from being on hand at the exhibition hall throughout the working day and available to conduct VIPs around the static aircraft, short notice calls to host a table at lunch were common. The day was rounded off with a dinner for a putative customer who, generally speaking, had no need to work the following day and furthermore, no intention of doing so. Kingston had a PR man of enormous charm called George Anderson who in less frantic days had signed contracts with overseas customers on behalf of the company. If he asked for help in any of his endeavours he was impossible to refuse and for that reason we found ourselves working for very long hours and starting each day as an assembly of zombies.

Bill Bedford had always had some carefully calculated eccentricities, one of which was to fall asleep at dinner, quite often snoring loudly. This was disturbing and slightly embarrassing to everyone except Bill, but it was at Paris, more precisely at the Lido, that I discovered that it was an act. Our man in Kuwait, Abdullah Al Rifai, was hosting a party of Kuwaiti Air Force officers and had arranged a large table at the Lido which we were invited to join. The table abutted the stage so that we had a first-class view of the performance; this helped to take our minds off the food, which was awful. I was in little doubt that A.W. Bedford would fairly quickly tire of this, and such proved to be the case. His snores were drowned by the very loud music as the chorus performed but it was clear that he was far from attentive. The girls completed their part of the show with a cancan, at the end of which they slid across the stage in the splits, one immediately above the Bedford head, by now cradled in his arms. With hardly a glance upwards, he reached for a felt-tip pen and wrote on the sole of her ballet shoe: *"Vive le Harrier!"*

In those late sixties/early seventies days, even more than now, all other activity ceased when the Harrier demonstrated, and only partly because of the noise. I think that half the audience did not believe what they were seeing and the other half deliberately closed their minds to its military capabilities and possibilities. It was such a challenge to operational orthodoxy that few were prepared to think their way past their prejudices and to consider its potential. I do not exclude my former service, of which I am fiercely proud, from this general observation. Much of the foreign resistance stemmed from the NIH (not invented here) syndrome although the USMC were honourable exceptions.

At my first Paris with the company I was hopelessly unprepared for the financial freedom that industry enjoys when compared to the fixed daily allowances issued to the serving officer on overseas visits. The RAF worked on the premise that you were jolly lucky to make a duty visit to Paris and should expect to be out of pocket as a result, which always struck me as fair. Not so in industry. Unforeseen entertainment commitments occurred and I quickly learned that senior members of the company did not expect to be inconvenienced by mundane things like paying bills. As a result, at the end of the show I found myself with insufficient funds to pay my bill at the Hotel Scribe and an unwillingness on the part of the hotel to accept my sterling cheque for the small balance. The banks were not yet open and I was not sure what to do next except await their opening, cash a cheque and catch a later aircraft back to London. I was therefore standing there, bemused, clutching quite a lot of francs and the unpaid account when George

Anderson asked if I had a problem. I explained and he roared with laughter, snatched my bill from my hand, produced a roll of money that would have choked a horse, peeled off the necessary amount and paid the bill. It was an important step in my military-to-civilian conversion programme.

As part of the general campaign to persuade the Royal Navy, or more correctly the politicians responsible for RN procurement, that the Harrier would allow the RN to retain organic air power even after the big carriers had gone, a weekend was set aside to fly the aircraft from the helicopter deck of HMS "Blake." The flying was in the hands of Hugh Merewether, who arrived at the ship in the early morning to carry out whatever flying or deck handling had been requested. Those of the ship's company who had shore leave, together with observers from the Ministry and the company, were ferried out to "Blake" from the King's Steps in Portsmouth Dockyard. It was the weekend of Chappaquiddick, an event that terminated the life of Mary-Jo Kopechne and Senator Kennedy's chances of becoming President. The Sunday papers were giving the story great prominence and a petty officer in the pinnace taking us out to the ship was carrying a large selection of broadsheets and tabloids, one of which he carefully unfolded to read. He had given another paper to one of his shipmates, who handled it with equal reverence. Not a word was exchanged as they read. Without apparently having paid any attention to our progress towards the ship, they simultaneously stopped reading and folded their papers with great care so that they appeared untouched, just as the pinnace came alongside. The petty officer, straight faced, spoke to his mate for the first time: "That's it then. Having it off in the back seat, foot slipped and knocked the handbrake off." I concealed my amusement as best I could, scrambled up the ladder and was led below to the wardroom. Having dumped my coat I sat at a dining table and was approached by the same petty officer carrying two silver pots and asking if I would like coffee or tea. The papers clearly belonged to the wardroom.

Hugh demonstrated take-offs and landings into wind, downwind and crosswind from the helicopter pad at the stern of the ship, an area slightly larger than the length and span of the Harrier, with the sea on three sides and the sheer face of the helicopter hangar on the fourth. It so happened that the sea south of the Isle of Wight was calm over the weekend, and to simulate rough conditions the captain steamed at full speed with the stabilisers operating out of phase in order to induce, rather than stop, a rolling motion. Even the most sceptical observer must have become aware that the conditions really did not greatly affect the operation of the aircraft. One valuable lesson was learned however, thanks to a quick-thinking young sailor. After landing in the most extreme conditions of roll that the ship could generate, Hugh was in the cockpit with the throttle closed and the

162

nozzles pointing aft, waiting for the chocks to be positioned. As the ship rolled, the aircraft nosewheel, (which had no brake and was free to caster), turned in sympathy with the rolling motion and although the main wheels were braked, the aircraft began to swing and skid on the very small and damp deck. Hugh could do nothing about it and just for a moment or two it seemed likely that he would go over the side still strapped to the aircraft. The naval airman holding the chocks appreciated the situation and quickly jammed a chock on each side of the nosewheel, stopping all further movement. It is the unexpected in development flying that makes it so interesting and keeps all concerned, not just the pilots, on their toes.

It was evident that there were just not enough very experienced operational pilots to man the Harrier squadrons that were to be formed and that a two-seat aircraft would ease the conversion task that confronted the RAF. In 1970, therefore, the first two-seat Harrier made an appearance in response to the need to convert novice pilots to V/STOL. Although equipped with dual controls, the aircraft was required also to retain a full operational capability. Its early days were not encouraging and Duncan Simpson was lucky to survive an ejection when the engine failed at low level. Remarkably, having had his broken neck repaired, he was flying again after a few months. Barry Tonkinson had another failure under similar circumstances and, by skilled flying, landed it "dead stick" on Boscombe Down. The aircraft was very badly damaged but the engine and its control systems survived so that the cause of failure was established. A modification was produced that allowed the very complicated fuel-control system to be bypassed in emergency, and for the pilot to feed fuel directly to the engine to keep it going, with none of the niceties of controlled flow that the primary system provided.

Whilst the RAF order for trainer aircraft (Harrier T.4) was being filled, sufficient spare bits were made for the company to cobble together its own demonstrator which was eventually registered G-VTOL. Rolls-Royce provided the engine, Ferranti the nav-attack system and other suppliers contributed their specialised parts. For the first time therefore, vertical and short take-offs and landings could be experienced by visiting pilots under instruction from a company pilot. It also signalled the opportunity to take the aircraft to the customer and to let him fly it in his own country under controlled conditions.

The extraordinary performance of the Harrier, quite aside from its party tricks of dancing on the spot, bowing to the crowd and flying backwards, led many to believe that it could only be flown by supermen. The fact that the demonstrating pilot had only two arms and one head seemed to come as a shock to the VIPs who subsequently met him. Remembering always that military aircraft, generally speaking, are not bought by pilots, the ability to take the aircraft to the country where we hoped it would be used, to be seen by ministers and politicians to be within the competence of their own pilots, was important. It was decided that the first tour to be undertaken by G-VTOL would be to India to fly from INS "Vikrant," their carrier. This was ambitious for a first attempt but, with some interest in each of the countries that the aircraft would transit, the plot was approved by the Hawker Siddeley board.

There was one false start when the lead pilot for the demonstration tour overran the runway at Dunsfold causing considerable, though not fatal, damage to the aircraft. It may well strike the reader as odd that a V/STOL aircraft could overrun a 7,000 ft runway, and I have never heard a reasonable explanation for it either. This set-back to our plans was not a total disaster since it allowed a more thorough preview of the planned route and the logistic problems associated with the enterprise to be made. It was clear that we would need to carry with us the routine and predictable spares such as wheels and tyres, radio and avionic equipment peculiar to the Harrier and so on, but we had also to be sure that much more fundamental requirements like fuel and lubricants were available. The only serious problem that loomed was a supply of liquid oxygen at some of the planned stopovers, refuelling and flying demonstration points, where despite repeated assurances from the local airfield contractor I was not actually shown the LOX tanker. My anxiety on this score was subsequently to prove well-founded.

At each demonstration site, and anywhere else where we might be asked, it was planned to give a briefing on the aircraft and its equipment before the flying. Michael Miles of Rolls-Royce and Jim Summers of Ferranti were therefore part of the briefing team and agreed to act also as part-time administrators. Because the primary aim of the exercise was to show the aircraft to the Indian Navy, A. W. (Robbie) Roberts, recently retired RN Observer, was part of the Kingston group, to add the necessary nautical slant to our briefings. Our escort aircraft was a 748 with crew, hired from the Manchester Division of HSA, which would carry our 5-man ground crew and essential spares around the route.

Since the ground crew had to prepare the Harrier for flight and see it off on the first leg of the day before boarding the 748, it was clear that the support aircraft was unlikely to be seen again until the end of the flying day. We therefore planned that one of the administrative team plus a fitter would always precede the main party in order to clear the Harrier's arrival, organise the ground facilities required for turn-round and/or check the accommodation plan if it was to be a night stop. Our route preview had shown that on some days when our advance party needed to go ahead there was no airways flight to the required destination. Some members of our very small team were thus departing two or even three days earlier than was necessary, greatly increasing the load on the others, simply because the airline schedules did not match our plan.

Amid all the frantic preparations I persuaded John Glasscock, the managing director of the Kingston Division, that it would be prudent, in the light of the inevitable stomach upsets and other minor ailments which confronted us, for me to get some Harrier experience so that I could at least navigate and act as "pilot's mate" if one of the two assigned pilots was unwell. As a result, I enjoyed the best day that I had had for years, flying with John Farley in G-VTOL.

The aim of this exercise was to take the aircraft to INS "Vikrant" steaming off Cochin, and everything else was subordinate to this aim, except for Kuwait, where all the VIPs were going to be in town during our stay, a rare opportunity not to be missed. Less rare was a strike by the air traffic controllers in France, which meant that I spent an anxious morning in Naples awaiting news of the aircraft.

The message came that G-VTOL was ten minutes out of Capodichino requesting landing instructions. We were using the US Navy Facility for our turn-round and overnight hangarage, and I was in the Commander Air's office when the aircraft first appeared. From the window I could see the fire and rescue vehicles parked on the hardstanding and it was interesting to see them all start to move forward as G-VTOL appeared, nose-high at about 75 knots, in their eyes in an attitude from which recovery was impossible. This was very much the effect it had on experienced military personnel who happened not to have seen it before. It was the first time that I had seen the aircraft carrying its two huge ferry tanks which were so big that they looked like two extra fuselages. No demonstrations were scheduled but there was such obvious interest that the rest of the day was taken up with briefings to the USN and to an Italian Air Force detachment that was based there. Also at Capodichino was the Aeritalia factory, which had the contract for the overhaul and repair of the Italian F-104s, and the resident chief test pilot was Enzo Cauda who had soldiered through ETPS under my tutelage. I was able to get close to a 104 for the first and only time and I have to say that it was a most extraordinary aeroplane. The wing seemed too small to support even a club aircraft and, watching a take-off which seemed to take for ever in spite of the noise and flame, I had the distinct feeling that it could have used a bit more.

I should explain that we had meticulously obtained diplomatic clearance to overfly and, where appropriate, land, for the entire route. It was at Naples that I discovered, not for the only time, that clearance and flight numbers obtained in London did not necessarily carry much weight with the Civil Aviation Authority on whose behalf they had been granted. The aircraft were authorised by the High Commission in London to land and overnight in Cyprus at RAF Akrotiri, the Sovereign Base. The authorities in Nicosia agreed that the Harrier could land at Akrotiri but insisted that the 748 escort had to land and stay at Nicosia. In vain A.W. Roberts, who had gone ahead of us, protested that the ground crew were in the 748 and nobody else could service the aircraft. Suspecting that the Cypriots felt that they were being swindled out of a landing fee, I told Robbie to pay for a landing at Nicosia, but get clearance for the 748 to land at Akrotiri. Not a chance, and he is a most persuasive character. Suddenly we needed transport for the ground crew to commute between the two bases, with more vehicles standing by to take forward any spares and equipment from the 748 found to be required during servicing. I went to see the man responsible, taking with me a model of G-VTOL as a peace offering. He was totally unmoved and thoroughly unpleasant so I took the model away again. As always, the RAF stepped in to help and loaned us vehicles for practically nothing "for recreational purposes" so that we were able to function.

The departure from Cyprus was less slick than we had hoped for the reasons given above but the party was eventually reunited in Tehran which was our next stop. On arrival, the Harrier was still carrying the same unserviceabilities, and our tentative plan to demonstrate to the Shah had to be abandoned because he was in England watching a Harrier demonstration at Boscombe Down. In his absence, nobody was prepared to fly in the aircraft or even give clearance for a flying display, and another part of our plan crumbled. The fact that we could therefore ground the aircraft for 48 hours was welcome since we had work to do on it before proceeding. The avionics man was able to fix one of the radios, which thereafter functioned perfectly, and to suggest probable faults on the other which allowed us to request the necessary spares from Kingston. I had also received a warning from the factory that Rolls had introduced an urgent safety modification to the engine, to be installed before the next flight. This was just the news I wanted to hear, sitting in Tehran, with no prospect of installing the modification which we did not have. I should have had more confidence in Rolls-Royce. Roger Cresswell arrived, carrying our essential spares as hand and cabin baggage, and was waltzed through customs by Johnny Brown before he had time to shake hands. The bits were all fitted and reduced, without overcoming completely, the serviceability problems that we had. It was my turn to go ahead of the main force so that I left for Kuwait with a relatively light heart, believing the aeroplane and its crew to be fully fit for the first time since leaving Dunsfold.

Our plan to demonstrate to the Kuwaiti Government, and to fly as many as possible of the pilots of the Kuwait Air Force, came unstuck early on and for the most unexpected reason. The sterling area had collapsed. With their

166

vast holdings of sterling the Kuwaitis were understandably concerned and their undertaking to attend a demonstration of the world's first operational V/STOL aircraft was quickly set aside. Of only slightly less interest to me was the fact that the vast number of traveller's cheques that I was carrying to pay the running cost of the tour were now quite worthless. I signalled Kingston to send more money to Bombay for me to collect on arrival.

The Kuwaitis that flew in G-VTOL were very evidently impressed, particularly by the hovering and manoeuvring close to the ground. They so enjoyed it in fact that two of them burst the tyres, which required wheels to be changed on the flight line at an outside air temperature of +45°C, not the best way to pass an idle hour.

The Rolls-Royce engine ace who was normally based at Dunsfold and therefore a natural choice to join our caravan was Frank Ashley. He was a small man, dentally challenged, who could work miracles on a Pegasus engine and was a vital member of the crew. Frank was a great tea man and, not trusting anywhere *en route* to have his favourite blend, travelled with his own supply. He would brew up in the most unlikely places, and appear at the elbow of a harassed fitter with the cup that cheers just as tempers were fraying and things threatening to get out of control. Even in the most unpleasant conditions of heat and humidity he continued to wear a sleeveless sweater in order, as he put it, "to have something to take off when it got really hot." Finally, with his help, we had done all that we could and prepared the Harrier for its transit to Bombay, via Masirah, which meant refitting the big overload tanks, and again we had a transfer problem. The crew worked nearly all night to remedy the defect (it was a broken seal which prevented the tank from being pressurised), but turned out again to launch the Harrier in the early morning. All except the pilots, who had been shielded from the long hours spent in the hangar, were worn out by now so that we returned to our hotel to await news of the arrival of the Harrier in Masirah and, we fervently hoped, Bombay.

CHAPTER XIX

SONG OF INDIA

Given a free choice we would not have gone to India during the monsoon season, but for reasons given earlier we had already been delayed, and could no longer defer the arrangements made with the Indian Navy. When we arrived in Bombay, the Harrier had already been on the ground for nearly 24 hours and was saturated, lacking even the basic protection of canopy covers and engine intake blanking plates. Rainwater was pouring from the trailing edges of the wings and tailplane and the aircraft stood forlornly in a puddle of water four inches deep. There was little we could do immediately except fit the protective covers that we had and retire in a dripping mass to our hotel to meet the pilots, get a debrief on their transit from Kuwait and assess the work to be done before proceeding to Cochin. The Harrier was carrying one or two minor, and by now familiar unserviceabilities, but nothing serious enough to delay us. Mr Chatterjee of the Indian Oxygen Company had already taken the spare liquid oxygen tanks to recharge them, and at eleven o'clock called at my room to tell me that his filling plant could not produce sufficient pressure to force LOX into our containers. With only an hour left in that last day of June 1972, I consoled myself with the thought that nothing further could go wrong until tomorrow.

By the morning things showed signs of improvement. It was still raining heavily but, having acquired some paper umbrellas, it was possible partially to protect the vitals of G-VTOL when access and inspection panels were removed to allow the normal servicing functions. Mr Chatterjee, demonstrating commendable initiative, had taken our LOX tanks to the local steel works which used LOX under high pressure and, by slowly filling an empty vessel, was able to bleed off the liquid at the correct pressure to refill our tanks. The LOX was chemically pure and perfectly safe to breathe and was in fact exactly what we had been promised during our preview of the route, but achieved in a novel way. Events were to show that this was our only source of LOX throughout our stay in India.

As far as we could tell, the Harrier was serviceable and there was nothing more we could do at the airfield before our departure planned for the morrow. Whilst everyone else retired to the hotel, I hopped in a cab and headed for the local bank where, according to the accountants at Kingston, a king's ransom in travellers' cheques awaited my collection. Like most banks except in Britain, this one was heavily guarded and with me probably not looking my best and carrying a near-empty brief case which could have contained anything, I suppose, my reception was slightly underwhelming. With some difficulty I persuaded them to allow me access to the manager. I produced my telex from Kingston telling me which bank to go to, which was examined in detail. The manager then found a fat file in which a similar telex was lodged giving my name and passport number. By now we were getting along famously and the pile of travellers' cheques was withdrawn from the safe for me to count, sign and receipt. At this point, simply as a formality, it was pointed out, he needed my passport which of course I produced. I have referred earlier to the understanding shown by the F&CO in allowing some of us to have two passports and the next few minutes caused me to curse their generosity. Kingston had given the number of my first passport and I was carrying the reserve. The money was snatched back and returned to the safe whilst I launched on a long explanation to a sceptical manager and his staff, who had quickly assembled when he cried out after detecting the passport number anomaly. The problem was finally resolved when I persuaded them to speak to the British Commercial Counsellor who confirmed that I was genuine. Bombay holds few happy memories for me.

The following day we were at the airfield early in order to launch the Harrier for Cochin. We were quietly congratulating ourselves as we loaded the 748 for our own departure when the unmistakable sound of a Pegasus engine penetrated the liquid atmosphere. G-VTOL was back in the circuit and, after landing, it was evident that we had serious problems. There had been an undemanded cut-back of engine power at the start of the climb and many of the instruments were not working, critically the head-up display. This device, which is now common on military aircraft, projected on to the windscreen all the data required to fly the aircraft solely on instruments. The conventional, electrically-driven flight instruments were for back-up only, and the pilots had clearly made the right decision not to proceed into the towering storm clouds that dotted the route. Some faults were quickly located and remedied out on the parking ramp in spite of the entry of further rain whenever a cowling or access panel was removed. The pilots climbed aboard again, fired up and dashed to the runway for take-off before anything more could go wrong. This time they did not even clear the circuit but landed immediately with another daunting list of problems.

During my time at Tengah I had experienced the effect of monsoon rain on electrics and avionics, especially in the Javelin, which suffered radar failures regularly during the passage through Singapore of the inter-tropical front. All attempts to rectify the faults proved fruitless until the systems had dried out when, miraculously, most faults disappeared. I confided all this to Pat Brace, the crew chief who, reluctantly it seemed to me, agreed to stop work, secure the aircraft, replace such covers as we had and allow me to try to find some hangar space somewhere. Accordingly, I approached the foreman on duty in the blister hangar of Indian Airlines, one Mr Krishnan, who most obligingly towed out the Caravelle undergoing servicing to allow G-VTOL to be parked in the corner. There we left it overnight.

The next morning, my judgement and reputation very much on the line, we pushed our aircraft from the hangar and ran the engine. Everything worked and it had even stopped raining – briefly. Losing no time, the pilots briefed (a lengthy process in itself at Bombay), started up and taxied. There was a heart-stopping moment when the aircraft returned for a flap check because the flap on the port side had struck its drop-tank on down selection. The tank was scored but there was no sign of further damage and the aircraft at last took off. The electrical circuit which should have prevented the flap from over-extending with the drop-tank fitted must still have been wet, because the fault never recurred. After 45 minutes the Harrier had passed its point of no return, and wherever it was it would not be returning to Bombay.

Cochin was the target of the entire tour from which the evaluation flying would be conducted, at the naval air station and from the carrier "Vikrant," steaming off the coast. John Farley, who was steadily establishing a reputation as the best Harrier demonstrator we had, is also a very sharp cookie indeed. Himself quick on the uptake, he is perhaps not the most tolerant of men with those who are less blessed. I was therefore apprehensive when we were subjected to questions after briefing, because so often the questioners either repeated themselves or wandered so far from the point that considerable mental agility was needed to identify the purpose of the question. Much of this was caused by their innate politeness which avoided saying anything that might be construed as criticism of the aircraft, engine or any component but I feared that it would not sit well with Farley who tends to be direct, not to say earthy. My fears were groundless. His patience was endless, even with the most obtuse questioner, and his answers comprehensive, although frequently a rephrasing of what had gone before in order not to embarrass his interrogator. After demonstrating the aircraft to the Admiral and his staff in his customary style, he flew out to join the ship with the Director of Naval Air Warfare as his first student. That day he flew 11 sorties from "Vikrant," changing students between trips but never leaving the cockpit, and landed back at Cochin with a serviceable aircraft. The following day he completed a further 10 trips, again strapped in the whole time, and again took the serviceable aircraft back to the airfield. It was an astonishing performance and, after the miseries of Bombay, lifted the morale of the entire crew as nothing else could.

It was evident that the aircraft had proved itself to the Indian Navy for shipborne operations and such further information as they sought centred on the radii of action claimed for the aircraft. The technical data that we had with us allowed us to show how much could be carried how far and at what height, but the evaluation team insisted that we fly one of the low-level profiles so that they were in no doubt that our figures were accurate. Such a sortie clearly required oxygen for both pilots (although the company pilot had been economising by not connecting his oxygen tube when flying at low level), and we awaited the return of the 748 with our recharged LOX tanks. On the promise of plentiful and accessible supplies at Bangalore, the home of Hindustan Aircraft Industries, the support aircraft had gone there to top up. It proved to be a wasted journey since the same pressure problem prevented the tanks from being filled. The low-level sortie had therefore to be cancelled so that the remaining oxygen was available for the transit to Delhi via Bombay.

Captain Tahiliani of the Indian Navy was to fly as second pilot on the ferry and asked that the aircraft stage through the naval air station at Goa so that the sailors there could see it. This was agreed since a refuelling stop had to be made somewhere and it could only help the cause to have enthusiasm for the aircraft at all levels in the service. Trundling along in the 748 we passed close to Goa and checked on the progress that G-VTOL had made, to be told that after taking on more fuel it had not gone direct to Delhi (which was one of the options) because the weather was so bad. When we arrived at Bombay, the Harrier was already there and we had a quick conference with the crew in the Met. Office. According to the meteorologists, 10 inches of rain had fallen on Delhi in the last 8 hours causing extensive flooding, and buildings had collapsed after their foundations had been washed away. It was evident that for the time being we were not going anywhere and I made my way across the airfield to my friend Mr Krishnan to beg space in his hangar again.

The following day the Delhi weather had improved and the airfield was again open. We therefore made all haste to get there before the heavens opened once more. This time we were guests of the Indian Air Force who had provided office and hangar space on the military side of the civil airfield. Detailed preparations were made for the briefing and demonstration for the Chief of Air Staff and the senior members of the air board. The naval adviser from the British High Commission did a fine job in providing projection equipment and projectionist, and we arranged the room carefully with the still and movie projectors at the proper distance from the screen to give sharp, clear pictures. The comfortable chairs were placed in the front for the VIPs with an uninterrupted view of the speaker's lectern and the screen. We checked our slides, ensured that the films had been properly rewound and locked the door, confident that we could not improve on the arrangements.

The next morning we arrived at the airfield two hours before the first guests were due in order to recover the aircraft from its hangar and prepare it for flight. Having filed our 10-minute slot for the flying demonstration and been assured once again by air traffic that the circuit would be clear for our allotted period, we moved to the lecture room to take up posts and await the arrival of CAS.

The place was a shambles. At some time during the night, someone had realised that the CAS and other VIPs were going to be addressed in an air force briefing room that was uncarpeted. Goodness knows what effort went into finding the sizeable carpet that was required to cover the floor and to position it. What is certain is that in order to carry out the operation all our carefully arranged seating, projectors and screen had to be moved. Further-more, during the shuffling, the slide-holder for the first of our speaker's slides, carefully arranged in the right order and the right way up, had been dropped. The slides had been placed in an untidy heap on the lectern for the owner to sort out. I was not best pleased since they were my slides. Guests had been arriving whilst we surveyed the wreckage and by now, with no sign yet of the VIPs, every chair was occupied and all the oxygen in the room had been absorbed. It was one of those moments to adopt the philosophical approach and, with a nonchalance that I was far from feeling, I asked the crowd to move to the back of the room whilst we set things up again. Eventually we were back on course and the briefing went more or less as planned. We moved from the sweltering, airless room to the apron in front of the hangar to watch John Farley perform. His routine seemed unfamiliar to me, with periods where nothing much was happening, and almost out of sight to boot. When he landed he said that air traffic control had ordered him to clear the circuit whilst they landed a civil flight and, after 5 minutes of our 10-minute slot had gone, they told him to land immediately. Farley was bitterly disappointed, feeling that it reflected upon his professionalism, although the problem was explained to the CAS who seemed to be undisturbed (and unsurprised).

The senior evaluation pilot was Kapil Bhargava, another of my former students at ETPS, who was flown in G-VTOL together with many others of his team. It was usual to give a model of the aircraft to those that we flew and, having exhausted our ready-use supply, I went with Andy Jones, who had arrived to replace John Farley, to collect a further batch from the customs compound at the airport. Before starting this enterprise I had obtained a letter from the Vice Chief of Air Staff authorising me to collect this company property, and a further note from Mr Sen, Chief Inspector of Imports and Exports, approving the release of the goods. The Chief Customs Officer, Mr Jaswan Singh, had been informed by telephone that Andy and I would be calling, and that he should allow us to collect our urgent spares and models without payment of duty. We located the goods, all correctly addressed to me, and obtained the first two clearance signatures without much bother.

We then struck a serious snag in the form of Mr Dewan, whose signature was critical to the release of the parcels. On the box containing the models, the declared value was given as £200 which was what they had cost, not what they were worth in the markets of down-town Delhi. In vain the models were shown to Mr Dewan and their purpose was explained, but neither cajoling nor threats moved him. If we were not prepared to pay the 150% import duty on these luxury goods we could not have them. I finally sealed the box, obtained a freight label from BOAC and shipped the models to myself, care of our agent in Kuwait, our next port of call. As I explained to John Glasscock, my Managing Director, in my daily report back to the factory, this could be regarded as "Jaswan of those Singhs."

We were to depart the sub-continent through Bombay, a thought calculated to depress the stoutest heart. The Harrier left without further incident and, by the time we arrived in the 748, it was tucked up in Mr Krishnan's hangar. Most of us were feeling the effects of the previous night's hospitality so kindly offered to us by the Indian Air Force contingent. We had been on the road for three weeks, short of sleep, teetering on the edge of administrative disaster throughout the piece, and what most of us required was a night's rest, not Indian whiskey, tandoori and dubious ice-cream. Our relief at shaking the dust of India (of which there is an ample supply) from our feet, and the feeling that we had done a good job in spite of the obstacles placed in our path, fortified but did not prepare us for what was ahead.

As with so many of the places that I have visited, I left with the warm glow that comes from new friendships made, and the sporting chance of never having to return. On this latter point I should have been more guarded in my optimism.

A decade later, with the Hawk attracting more and more attention around the world, the Society of British Aerospace Companies (SBAC) staged a series of presentations in Delhi and Bangalore. British Aerospace were of course major contributors and Kingston were invited to present the Hawk as part of the company effort. I can only feel that some pressure was brought to bear upon me or that I was shamed into going; I might even have persuaded myself that it could not possibly be as bad as my memory told me that it was. Whatever the case, I am quite certain that I did not force anyone to stand aside so that I might take it on.

For the Delhi part of the show we were accommodated in the Ashoka Hotel where the presentations were to be staged and were therefore spared the nightmare of moving around the city by taxi. The hotel conference centre was as large as a ballroom with space for about 200 people to be seated, and had built-in all the necessary equipment for projecting slides

173

and film, together with a public address system. The organisation was good, with time allowed between lectures for the next man on to prepare his show.

The Hindustan Aircraft factory was already involved in the part-manufacture and assembly of the Jaguar airframe and its Adour engines. In preparing my talk I had to steer between capitalising on the engine commonality, which was to our advantage, and not making too much of the Hawk's operational capability which came fairly close to that of the Jaguar. For our visit to Washington we had prepared a closed loop of the Red Arrows video which ran continuously on a convenient television set outside the briefing room that we were using and attracted a lot of interest. We took the video to India and, at the Ashoka, had it running outside the conference centre, bringing all normal activity to a halt. From time to time we were forced to turn it off so that presenters and audiences could make their way into the place. I hope that I have conveyed the impression that there was a lot of interest in our being there.

For my first show, I was on in the early evening and was working on the reasonable assumption that guests who had been listening to other people all day would take advantage of the pause between acts to go home and have dinner. I was quite wrong. When I arrived half an hour before the advertised start time to check that everything was in place as I had left it, the room was three-quarters full. Fifteen minutes before kick-off, every seat was taken and the standing room at the back of the hall was seething. The smart thing to do seemed to be to get the show on the road since patently nobody else was going to get in.

I had planned to speak for 45 minutes and to leave a similar amount of time for questions which our local man had said would be about right. The planned hour and a half became two hours with no sign of let-up until I called time. I was still in conversation with one or two guests who seemed reluctant to leave when the local man approached me and asked if I would stage an encore since there was a restive mob outside, peeved that the show had started early and they had missed it. Having absolutely nothing else to do I agreed, and the scene was repeated to another packed house. I cannot say how the SBAC arranged its invitations or who the people were, but I have never seen such large and apparently deeply interested audiences anywhere else in the world. The next day was an exact repeat and I guessed that I had probably spoken to upwards of 1,000 people at the four presentations. We moved on to Bangalore where I fully expected a lot of interest because it is the aviation centre of India, and I was not disappointed.

The presentation centre was a short walk from our hotel, and a rather more public spot than the Ashoka. As I approached it, and saw the milling throng outside, I guessed that the Arrows film was being shown. I was absolutely right and, from the look on the faces of some of the young members of the audience, they were entranced and had no intention of moving.

Strolling from the hotel to the exhibition centre I noticed a curious pile of rubbish at the corner of the low wall surrounding the hotel. It was not the common-or-garden sort of garbage that is everywhere in India, but a combination of paper, wood bark and strands of brightly coloured wool. There seemed also to be the remnants of candles that had burned there. Having seen nothing like it before, when I returned later to the reception desk I asked the man on duty if he could explain. He latched on immediately and gave me a full run-down on the albino king cobra that lived there, revered by the people as a living icon. Returning to the hotel after the evening show I gave that corner a very wide berth.

During our brief time in Bangalore, one of the innumerable religious festivals occurred. In this one the young men, riding bicycles or on foot, spent their time filling their mouths with coloured water which they sprayed at pedestrians. I think bonus marks were awarded for those that spattered a foreigner. I resolved this time that no threat or inducement would ever get me back.

CHAPTER XX

PICK YOURSELF UP

During our (Johnny Brown and self) many visits to the Emirates and particularly Abu Dhabi, we had talked to most of the Defence Force personnel about Harrier, and always received an enthusiastic response. Many of the men of influence were seconded from the British forces or were there on contract, and were well able to appreciate the enhanced capability that an aircraft requiring rudimentary landing strips rather than 10,000 feet of concrete would give them. In particular Twinkle Storey, who commanded the Air Wing, was a great enthusiast and was confident of the abilities of his air and ground crews to manage the Harrier. From India therefore, Abu Dhabi was our first demonstration point on the way home.

When I arrived, ahead of the main party, I was met by Twinkle who outlined the demonstration plan that they had evolved. Since the Ruler and the Crown Prince (who was also Minister of Defence) were in the summer palace at Al Ain and had no intention of returning to Abu Dhabi just to see an aeroplane, we should have to go to *them*. Two choices of demonstration site were for consideration, the first an army camp, the second the semi-prepared landing strip some 2,000 yards long at Al Ain. The preview of the army camp quickly showed it to be a non-starter since the parade square, which would be the focal point of the demonstration, was surrounded by flimsy buildings and tents which would have to be overflown by the Harrier and would not survive the experience.

The airstrip was perfectly alright as a demonstration site and agreement was reached that the show would be staged there. On arrival by Islander on the day of the demonstration, I could not help but be impressed by the arrangements that had been made for the spectators, headed by the Ruler. Chairs were arranged, a discreet distance from the strip, with a colourful marquee to the side in which the guests would be entertained following the flying.

Operationally, they had also done a first-class job in providing a fuel tanker and rescue vehicle, which had driven down from Abu Dhabi over-night and were in position by the control tower. Al Ain is about 1,000 feet above sea level and it was of course very hot. In order to demonstrate the two-seat Harrier it was necessary to reduce the weight by burning off a lot of fuel before attempting to hover and, since that was the main point of the exercise, the aircraft would therefore have to be refuelled before the return to Abu Dhabi, 75 miles distant – hence the need for the tanker. The rescue vehicle was there because, aside from a hand-held fire extinguisher, we could provide no cover of our own.

The Ruler and other members of the royal household arrived, surrounded by fearsome-looking bodyguards. We were formally presented and accompanied the VIPs to the demonstration site where hardly had we taken our seats than the Harrier arrived, going very quickly. After some high-speed flying and manoeuvring, and with the weight down to safe hovering, the aircraft slowed and flew down the runway. Precisely in front of the Ruler it stopped, some 20 or 30 feet above the ground, making lots of noise and raising a lot of dust from the unpaved runway. With the nozzles down for hovering, almost the total thrust from the engine is directed on to the ground and seeks out any loose material that happens to be there. I have seen it lift small concrete slabs under these conditions and was not a bit surprised to see the sand and stones clouding the back end of the aircraft. I fully expected to see the aircraft move slowly forward and start the spectacular climb which usually finished the show. Instead, the Harrier began to fly backwards and was instantly engulfed in the thick dust cloud which it had generated during its hover. Almost immediately there was a thud and the engine could be heard winding down. I knew that the boss of the local Hunter squadron was in the back seat and was concerned that in the confusion he might have difficulty extracting himself from the strange – to him – ejection seat. I started to move towards the aeroplane and as the wingtip came into view through the choking dust, there seemed to be a flicker of flame. I found that I could reach the cockpit quite easily because the undercarriage had collapsed, and I was able to insert the seat-firing pins and help the rear-seat pilot to extract himself without damage. I told him and the captain that there seemed to be a bit of fire and that we should make ourselves scarce, which we did. Returning to the reviewing stand where Johnny Brown was making a valiant attempt to explain, through an interpreter, that every sortie did not end this way, I felt rather foolish to see that on closer inspection, what I thought was flame was in fact red hydraulic fluid which seemed to be flickering because of the blowing dust. There was no fire but the splendid aircraft was stricken. One outrigger and the noseleg were broken and the nose was pointing skywards while the rest of the fuselage drooped.

The Ruler was very kind and understanding and arrangements were made to clear the wreckage and organise an airlift back to Abu Dhabi in order to let the factory know what had happened. It remains my belief that the accident destroyed the very bright prospects for the Harrier in the Middle East.

From Abu Dhabi, we had planned to go into Qatar, where the small Air Wing was similarly manned by former RAF pilots who wanted to see the Harrier. I was not anxious for the misfortune that had befallen us to be the main item in every news bulletin on local radios and therefore signalled

Qatar saying that we would not be calling in but would be in touch. I commandeered the telex machine in the hotel and held an exchange of ideas with Kingston, as a result of which I escorted the unfortunate pilot back to London. He was the same chap that had delayed our departure by over-shooting the runway at Dunsfold, and the thought uppermost in my mind was that he should perhaps consider some other line of work. I left Robbie Roberts and the ground crew to organise the salvage and recovery of G-VTOL.

In Kingston I advised that we prepare another aircraft as quickly as possible and return to Qatar in order not to give the impression that the accident was caused by a fundamental shortcoming of the aircraft. It was necessary also to demonstrate to the Emir who wanted to see a Harrier. This time it had to be a single-seater so that there was no possibility of giving air experience to the local pilots. The rented RAF aircraft was freighted to Qatar and rapidly reassembled by our ground crew, many of them members of the ill-fated earlier trip. John Farley was on hand to do the flying and the local man came up with a novel idea to convince the Emir of the wisdom of owning a few of these aircraft which none of his neighbours had. He proposed that the Harrier and the resident Hunters both be at readiness, pilots strapped in but without engines running. When the Ruler arrived at the airfield, he would order a scramble and we would see who was first into the air. I pointed out that, since the Hunters would have a long taxi from the readiness platform to the runway, and the Harrier would be at such a weight that it could take off vertically, this would be no contest and widely seen as such. He insisted that everyone would be impressed and so it was arranged. He was absolutely right, and that exercise and the stirring display that followed generated enormous interest which unhappily was never translated into an order for the Harrier. The effect of the crash in Abu Dhabi was not to be so easily overcome.

The entire British expatriate colony had turned out to watch the show, mostly from the safe viewing area of the airport arrival lounge. I was quite moved to see some of the wives in tears afterwards, telling us how proud they were that Britain had produced such a flying machine.

CHAPTER XXI

THE HAPPY WANDERER

It was some time before the realisation dawned that the first tour with G-VTOL was not a total disaster because eventually the Indian Navy went on to place an order for the aircraft. However, the scars were deep and long-lasting, not least because it was so physically demanding.

G-VTOL was recovered to Dunsfold and, whilst the patient engineers set about repairing it again, I continued my efforts to cover the very large slice of the globe that was my territory. Examining and assessing the potential, it seemed clear that Greece and Turkey, as NATO allies, were well worth visiting since both were operating sharp-nosed aircraft and were pretty close geographically to the enemy. In consequence I met Duncan Fraser, our man for the region, and formerly the Rolls-Royce man in Tokyo. He was resident in Athens, which caused a certain amount of eyebrow raising in Ankara, and we were to share some adventures over the next 15 years, mostly in Turkey, but subsequently in Africa.

In Ankara our local man was Yavuz Kirec, and our first meeting is etched on my memory. I was to travel from Beirut to Ankara on the single Middle East Airlines flight that went direct between the two capitals each week, and had reconfirmed my booking in the morning. Back at the St. George hotel I had ordered a sandwich from room service to eat whilst packing in time for my four o'clock departure. I was in no hurry and even now cannot think what made me look at my ticket, suddenly to realise that departure was at 14.00 and not 4 o'clock as the airline man had said. I probably misunderstood his English, which was not very good but infinitely better than my Arabic. I called the airport in a panic, assured the airline that I would be there, finished packing, paid my bill and leapt into a taxi, to be met on arrival by passport, customs and airline officials at the foot of the boarding steps of the 707, engines running. Clearance procedure took less than 30 seconds and I was ushered aboard to the cheers of my fellow passengers.

Early autumn in the Lebanon is like high summer in England and tropical clothing is comfortable, even when not dashing at high speed from downtown to the airport. As a concession to the expected weather at my destination, I was carrying a lightweight raincoat, although not seriously expecting to need it. As the aircraft touched down, I saw through my window the blowing sand raised by the passage of the aircraft. This turned out to be my second mistake of the day because it was not sand but snow. As I stepped out of the 707, an arctic blast hit me and the short walk across the tarmac to the arrival hall was perilous with frozen, snow-covered puddles to be negotiated. I have been cold before, indeed, much colder, but the abrupt transition from late Mediterranean summer to the first grip of winter in

Ankara was devastating. After passing immigration and customs, I recovered my baggage and considered how I should recognise Mr Kirec, whom I had never met but who was planning to be there awaiting my arrival. There were a lot of people milling around the very narrow exit from the restricted area, further reducing the chances of spotting the sort of notice that meeters and greeters carry when looking for a stranger arriving. Most were muffled against the cold so that members of the same family might be forgiven for not recognising each other instantly. For a minute or two I was much more concerned with safeguarding my baggage from the desperadoes seeking to relieve me of it than seeking out Mr Kirec, but I should not have worried. A distinguished silver-haired man in a very smart black topcoat with astrakhan collar, reminiscent of my idea of the old actor-managers, greeted me by name as he shook me warmly by the hand. When I knew him better, and appreciated just how wide his influence ran, I guessed that he had told the immigration officer who stamped my passport to point me out. At the time I was very impressed, and I continued to be throughout our long association. He was a graduate of Imperial College and had lived in London for long enough to speak colloquial English as well as French and, of course, Turkish.

He had arranged for me to deliver a Harrier brief at Air Force Headquarters the following day, and meantime took me to the Buyuk Hotel halfway up the hill which is the main street of Ankara, where I was to stay on that and many subsequent visits. The following morning I accompanied Yavuz to the Headquarters where extremely smart armed guards met us and took us to the office of the commanding general. After the mandatory coffee, an aide led me to the briefing room where I was to perform after lunch. The room was purpose-built with tiers of comfortable seats catering for an audience of about 60. The modern audio visual equipment included a back projector which required that I rearrange my photographic slides as they were set up for a conventional machine. Having done that I handed the slide cartridge to the young airman operator and went through them to check that they were in the right order and the right way up. The first film, which showed how action taken by the pilot translated into reaction by the aircraft, was strapped on to the movie projector and checked. This was a most valuable teaching tool, especially for audiences not having English as first language, since the explanation of how the extraordinary performance of the Harrier was achieved tended to lose something in translation. The second and last film covering general flying, weapon carriage and delivery was fitted to a second projector and checked. Everything was set for another Oscar-winning performance!

We retired for a light lunch, joined by our Air Attaché, Ken Ryall, who had been on my staff college course. He pointed out that the comprehension

A Dove called Devon. Useful little transport which seemed to go on for ever.

The Andover, rear-loading version of the HS.748 near Boscombe Down.

A selection of the ETPS fleet in transit from Cranfield to Farnborough.

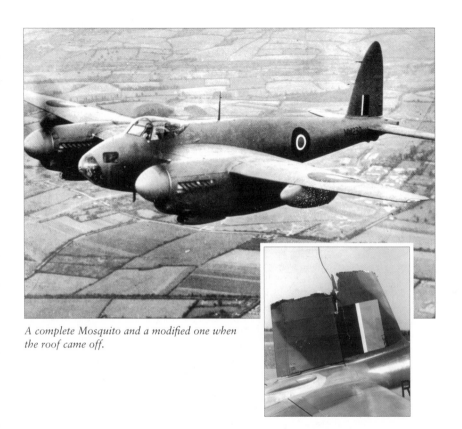

A complete Mosquito and a modified one when the roof came off.

Avro Athena at Boscombe Down. It competed with the Boulton Paul Balliol.

The Heston AOP which came to naught.

The Hornet – surely one of the best-looking fighters ever produced.

The prototype Short Sturgeon, which failed to cause a stir.

The Seamew, which looked much too frail for work aboard ships.

A Westland Welkin, which rapped me sharply over the knuckles during take-off.

Possibly the least-suitable aircraft for its designed purpose? The Blackburn Firebrand.

A Tipsy Junior provided for our amusement when visiting Fairey.

An aeroplane for non-pilots. The Ercoupe: difficult in crosswinds.

level of my audience would be very mixed. Those that had served at NATO headquarters had passable English, as did the younger officers who had gone through flying training in the United States. The hard core of those that had to be converted however would not be fluent, and I should be on my guard against talking too quickly or using RAF slang which, colourful and descriptive though it is, can further confuse someone straining hard to keep up. With this timely reminder in the front of my mind, I left the others drinking coffee and was escorted back to the briefing room. My projectionist, carrying the slide cartridge, came forward to meet me and all would have been well if he had not transferred the cartridge from his right to his left hand in order to shake hands again. The briefing room was already half-full and the clatter of my slides hitting the floor provided a diversion for the luckless group that had been detailed off to attend. Silently thanking my foresight in arriving early, I scooped up the slides and handed them in sequence to the projectionist, leaving him to insert them properly. Order was nearly restored when the Air Force Commander and his staff, with typical Turkish courtesy not wishing to keep the visiting speaker waiting, arrived and took their seats.

I prefer not to think about the next hour or so which has returned many times to haunt me. Half the slides were projected the wrong way round or upside down, so that senior and distinguished officers were standing on their heads to try and make some sense of what I was saying related to the image presented to them on the screen. Fortunately, the films were shown in the right order, and the general message was received. This initial mission led to some frantic activity back at the factory in Kingston when the Turks asked for a detailed manufacturing plan which would enable them to produce their own Harriers in a so far non-existent aircraft industry. I was introduced to a larger-than-life aircraft engineer named Yavuz Kansu, employed by the Government and clearly destined to be important in the future of the project. He volunteered the information that the US Government were offering the F-5 derivative of the T-38 trainer as a suitable vehicle on which the Turks could cut their aeronautical teeth. He however, was bitterly opposed to this offer of "the barefoot nation fighter" as he called it. It struck me at the time that, anxious as he was to leap into the manufacturing deep end, the Harrier might present a greater challenge than he thought.

The big players in aircraft manufacturing, USA, Great Britain, France and to a much lesser extent the USSR, were increasingly being confronted by governments, advised by sharp young graduates in aeronautical engineering, that saw no reason not to make for themselves whatever they needed. "Technology transfer," "shared production," "licensed manufacture" and "offset" were the buzz-words and it was obvious that a profound change was about to occur in the way that aircraft manufacture was conducted. The dilemma was clear: if we refused to share our knowledge, or tried to urge caution, a competitor nation with fewer scruples would not hesitate. Our best bet seemed to be to go ahead with whatever was proposed and wait for the partner to discover exactly the size of the task that he had set himself. It is not easy to persuade highly-motivated and patriotic engineers that they should perhaps learn to walk (by assembling manufactured parts) before trying to run (by starting with raw materials.)

There is no point in describing in detail the efforts made on both sides to bring the project to fruition before a combination of factors, mostly an injection of stark realism, led to its cancellation. However, we met a lot of nice people and established a very good working relationship with the Turkish Air Force and the Ministry promoting the industrialisation of the country.

At about this time I undertook a tour of Africa at the request of our various regional executives, not out of missionary zeal, but because as a company we were doing very little business on the continent. Briefing the air forces was seen as a way of at least keeping the Hawker Siddeley name in front of government ministers and allowing our Regional Executives to talk about power generators, diesel engines for pumping water and those other things for which the Group was the market leader. I could see nothing wrong in this since the developing air forces were at least being exposed to British technology.

Dusty Miller, a former RAF pilot, was our resident in Lagos and, although I had never met him, we were to become great chums although we achieved nothing in the way of business for the company. On my first visit he insisted that I stay at his house rather than in an hotel and, using that as a base, we travelled around talking to airmen and playing to packed houses. In some of the more remote spots there really was nothing else for them to do and we had a sort of novelty value. After completing our schedule I went on my own for some reason, which I can no longer recall, to say farewell to the Chief of Air Staff and his officers and to thank them for the arrangements that they had made on my behalf. Waiting in an ante-room for my appointment, I was joined by two young officers, in uniform and wearing pilots badges. We chatted for a while and I lightheartedly expressed the hope that their attendance upon the CAS was not for the purpose of being punished for some misdemeanour. One of them replied that they had been confirmed as suffering from sickle-cell anaemia and were in serious danger of losing their flying categories or at best being confined to aircraft having at least one other pilot. I made sympathetic noises, having no idea what sickle-cell anaemia was, but making a mental note to find out when I returned to London. I was called in, made my farewells, and left.

Dusty took me to the airport the next morning where the departure procedure was remarkably calm and orderly. At the immigration desk my passport was checked and I was asked if I was taking any Nigerian money out of the country. Since I had been a guest of Dusty for most of my stay I had some of the local currency left that I had bought on arrival, about £30-worth. The immigration officer perked up at this news and informed me that it was illegal to export Nigerian currency. The banks were all outside the customs area, and he made it clear that if I went out again I should experience some difficulty in getting back since my passport now bore his exit stamp. He was enjoying this much more than I was but I could see that Dusty was still the other side of the frosted glass screen. I asked the immigration man if I could have an elastic band and he gave me one which I used to secure the roll of notes that I threw over the screen to Dusty. The small bonus that he had evidently seen coming his way was suddenly gone. This was a not unusual ploy, I discovered. Nowhere did it say that currency could not be taken from the country, it was a local rule that everyone was meant to know.

I dropped into Ghana, where my former staff college student Ashley-Lassen was now Chief of Air Staff, and was made most welcome. He arranged for his air force to attend an evening briefing in the Mess which gave me a colourful surprise. He, and most of his colleagues, arrived in their normal off-duty evening costume which was splendid to behold. I cannot think why I was surprised but I was. The evening was one that I treasure because of the friendliness and the genuine interest that they showed, not just in Harrier, but in all the other subjects which they raised and which we discussed for hours after the show was over.

When I returned to England, I wrote to Tony Barwood at the Institute of Aviation Medicine, one of my old friends from the days of Vampire trials in Khartoum, asking about sickle-cell anaemia. He sent me a comprehensive run-down which made me aware of just what a nasty thing it is for anyone but perhaps particularly for career airmen. It is another of those diseases that those of us who live in Europe should give daily thanks for it having by-passed us, although it is now being found in our society amongst some citizens of West African descent. Its general effect is to cause a reduction in the amount of oxygen getting to the brain because of the malformation of the blood cells. It requires no imagination at all to see the effect that even slightly rarefied air would have on a sufferer flying a high-performance aircraft.

In this same time frame, President Mobutu of Zaïre visited London and was given lunch by the City, which I was detailed to attend. It was said that he had expressed interest in Harrier and would welcome a visit by someone from the company to speak to his advisers. Arrangements were quickly finalised and I found myself stepping off an aircraft in Kinshasa.

The people that I briefed were all Belgian, apparently hung over from the colonial power, but perhaps Congo-born. The sharpest aircraft in the Order of Battle was the Magister, a small, French-built jet trainer not dissimilar to our Jet Provost in terms of performance. It was against this unpromising background that the Harrier was seen as the perfect follow-on aircraft. Not for the first time in my experience I found that the planners were of the opinion that their current helicopter pilots, given a quick refresher on the Magisters, would have no difficulties in coping with this vertical take-off and landing development. It is easy to scoff, but the US Marines fell into exactly the same trap when they first started to recruit for their Harrier force.

This dilemma was never easily resolved; even though we were keen to see Harriers in all the world's air forces, we were equally keen not to have them crashing all over the place giving the impression that they could be flown only by supermen. The fact was that the small, inexperienced air force in Zaire was going to have trouble operating any fast jet unless it started a serious pilot-training system. The most useful and compelling document that I was able to devise, in order to make the point without appearing to criticise the local standards, was the training syllabus for the fast-jet RAF pilot. The simple list of flying exercises undertaken during the two years between the start of flying training until the completion of the Harrier Operational Conversion course indicated the size of the task. Unless the white ants have eaten them, several copies of a fine descriptive manual, "Harrier for Zaïre," are in the files in Kinshasa.

Coincident with the activities I have described, Bill Bedford was working away at the Swiss and in the process involving just about every member of the company, and some from outside. Between my eastern wanderings I was invited to join him in Bern in order to have lunch with the leading ground-attack, close-support exponent of the Swiss Air Force. My role would be to advise him of recent developments in the Royal Air Force, and especially the changes in dispersal policy that had been made possible by an aircraft which did not require a runway for take-off. Settled down in a very expensive restaurant, the initial exchanges completed, I started to sing the praises of an aircraft which could well have been designed to a Swiss specification, so perfectly did it match their requirements. Keen not to saturate him with information that was contained in technical documents, I stuck to the operational application of the aircraft, emphasising the fact that Harrier pilots were drawn from the Hunter force, which would suit the Swiss since they were Hunter operators. It was during a short break in my briefing that our guest asked if the four engines, which he could well understand were essential for the outstanding performance of the Harrier, did not pose some handling problems for the pilot. Suspecting that my leg was being pulled I paused, prepared to smile or even laugh out loud, but I realised that he was not joking – the Bernese rarely joke.

In common with many RAF pilots I had been led to believe that the Swiss Air Force was a highly-trained, aggressive service which would give Warsaw Pact or NATO forces a hard time if either violated Swiss neutrality. During the recent contest I knew that aircraft from both sides had been intercepted and, it was alleged, shot down. I know for sure that Switzerland was regarded as a good destination for those aircraft of Bomber Command that had been so badly damaged that the prospects of getting back to England were zero. It was the one place in Europe that could be found with the minimum of navigational skills since it was brightly illuminated when the rest of Europe was a uniform black.

However, on this my first visit, I began to suspect that all that I had been told about the Swiss Air Force was not necessarily true. It seemed clear that a long uphill struggle lay ahead of us if we were ever to promote a full understanding of the aircraft. The air staff requirement that we were seeking to fill with the Harrier had also attracted the French and the Americans, who were proposing the Mirage and the A-7 Corsair respectively. The Mirage had its supporters, of course, with a sizeable portion of the country to all intents and purposes French. Although it was a fine aircraft, the Corsair seemed to have little going for it in the Swiss context, but it did have a Rolls-Royce engine, which split the loyalties of that company's representatives who were keen to salvage something if the Harrier was rejected. The vast differences in the capabilities and performance of the aircraft under consideration illustrate the confusion in the minds of the defence planners but the company, driven by Bill's enthusiasm, launched a full-scale demonstration programme to guide the Swiss towards the Harrier as the solution to their problem. John Farley was to conduct the flight demonstrations at selected sites over a weekend. He was, and remains in my judgement, the outstanding Harrier demonstration pilot of all time, which is high praise indeed when the calibre of the others is considered. At each site he produced the Apollo take-off in which, after lifting off vertically, he stood the Harrier on its tail and climbed at an angle of incidence that would have spelt disaster for any other aircraft. This, and the final bow to the crowd, became staples of John Farley's shows and are familiar to anyone who ever watched him.

The Swiss may have been startled but they were also sufficiently impressed to continue their evaluation of the Harrier and, in the next phase, asked if one of their pilots could fly the single-seat aircraft. The reasons for this remain obscure. There was a perfectly good two-seat, dual-control aircraft in which any aspect of handling or performance could be assessed, with the comforting presence of an experienced company pilot to look after any emergencies that might arise. I do not know with what force the Swiss argued their case for the solo flight but eventually it was agreed. The flight itself lasted less than a minute when, after take-off, the Swiss pilot closed the high-pressure fuel cock instead of moving the nozzle selector lever. The effect is the same as switching off the car ignition except that the Harrier does not cruise to a gentle halt but assumes the gliding characteristics of a house brick. The pilot ejected safely and the aircraft was suddenly scrap metal in a farmer's field. The outcome of this solemn Swiss evaluation was interesting in that they selected none of the aircraft that had been assessed but instead ordered a quite large number of refurbished Hunters. I defer to no one in my affection for the Hunter but it seemed an odd choice when it was out of production and at least obsolescent.

If this all sounds rather grim and earnest it was not so. There were some hilarious moments, usually shared with our colleagues from Rolls-Royce and Ferranti who supported the Hawker Siddeley team. Jim Summers of Ferranti was an expert on the FE 541 navigation and attack system in the Harrier and had heard just about all the silly questions that could be asked about it, but even he was not prepared for the Swiss pilot who assured him that the equipment would not work against them "because our airfields are hidden in the mountains." This in reference to a piece of kit that (i) had a maximum error of one nautical mile after an hour's flight (ii) could position the aircraft for weapon launch and (iii) release the weapons on precisely the right heading, making full allowance for wind speed and direction, all with the pilot simply following guidance instructions. They did seem to live in a time-warp as far as operational procedures were concerned.

One evening we were gathered in the Horseshoe Bar of the Schweizerhof Hotel in Bern, having a pre-dinner drink. At the time, Miss Shirley Bassey had a huge hit with a song called "Something," written by George Harrison of the Beatles. Tony Lewis our Kingston PR manager was with us, a Welshman who had retained his Welshness in spite of 10 years' residence in London. In a burst of patriotic fervour, aided no doubt by some of Mr Gordon's fine product, he approached the pianist playing quietly in the corner and asked if he could play "Something." Without pausing, the pianist replied: "Anything!" There really is no answer to that.

Like Sweden, the Swiss have tried through the years to demonstrate their neutrality and independence by designing and producing their own aircraft. However, unlike the Swedes who have built some outstanding military aircraft, the Swiss have had no success at all except with niche aircraft such as the Pilatus Porter with very short take-off and landing capability. Nevertheless, they have a government-owned and run aircraft factory based at Emmen with the capability to assemble, modify and repair their front-line aircraft, and very efficient they are too. Without knowing it at the time, I was to become better acquainted with the organisation.

We regarded North Africa as the exclusive preserve of the French as far as military aircraft were concerned, although some of the more progressive countries had acquired Soviet equipment. It was something of a surprise therefore to be approached by some shadowy figures, resident at very good addresses in London's West End, expressing interest in the Harrier for Algeria. In seeking to assess the importance of this I investigated the political situation (not good) and the military situation, which might have excited their interest in our aircraft. The only reason that I could uncover was an alleged incursion in the south-west of the country by people who, one would have thought, already owned so much sand that the rest of the Sahara would have held little attraction. The trouble spots were well out of range of conventional aircraft based even on forward airfields, and a case could be made for Harriers with their ability to operate from the short strips used by the oil companies for their commuter aircraft. I went to Algiers to meet the man detailed off by his government to investigate further. He had been a "freedom fighter" against the French colonialists and operated under his *nom de guerre*. With his poor English and my rusty French we were able to communicate to the point where it became clear that I was to attend upon the Air Staff the following day and tell them all about the jump-jet. He explained that, whilst he would make sure that I arrived in the right place, he would not accompany me to the meeting as his part in the operation was as middleman and fixer. Sure enough, the next morning found me dumped at the bottom of a driveway leading to a heavily-defended government building, with assurances from my new-found friend that I was expected at the guardroom and to go ahead. I confess to some apprehension about my ability to persuade an Algerian military policeman, assuming that he was anything like ours, that I was expected by the Chief of Staff and had not arrived with the aim of blowing up the place. I need not have worried because, after an initial suspicion, I was led to the right office. I can imagine that even the humble guard could see that no one stumbling through his story in very indifferent French could possibly do any harm to anyone.

A small but select team listened with apparent interest to my briefing, occasionally interrupting to ask the English-speaking member to put a question in amplification of whatever I had said, but generally with every sign of having understood my faltering French. Fortunately, the two films that supported the briefing were available with French soundtrack, and must have helped to unscramble anything I had got wildly wrong. After an exchange of civilities I packed up my gear and returned to my hotel, the Saint George. This was not without interest as it had started life as the home

187

of an English lady who was an enthusiastic gardener, and some evidence of her skill was still visible although the gardens were less well tended than she might have wished. During the latter stages of the war it had been used as the headquarters of the allied forces preparing the invasion of Italy, and many famous names were on commemorative plaques affixed to bedroom doors. The go-between took me out to dinner to sample brique, an egg cooked in a pancake which tastes much better than it sounds, and of course couscous, a sort of stew made from semolina which seemed to have the general consistency of wallpaper paste. Fortunately I eat to live rather than the reverse so that I can get through a token amount of almost anything. I reported the meeting that I had had in the morning and frankly expected to hear no more about it. In this I was quite wrong and soon after my return to London I found myself once again on the threshold of another short tour with the two-seat demonstrator, G-VTOL.

As became routine before any demonstration tour, we did a survey of the demonstration spot, there being no need for a route survey since the aircraft would arrive direct from our home base at Dunsfold. With our nominated crew chief Len Hersey, who was also manager of the experimental hangar, I was taken to Boufarik, west of Algiers where, we were assured, we should be shown everything that we would require. I have heard hangars described as spotless, and harsh experience has shown this to be false, except at Boufarik. The hangar we were offered put any RAF station to shame and in the same way all the fuel, oil and gas vehicles lined up for our inspection were immaculate. We were very impressed especially in view of the blowing sand which was never far away.

At the headquarters we agreed the details of the visit and explained that the ground crew would arrive a day ahead of the aircraft in order to receive it, turn it around and prepare for the first local flight.

On the appointed day, the main party flew in, checked into the St. George and immediately set course for Boufarik in military vehicles supplied by our hosts. This, and all the similar drives that followed, were sporting in every sense. Lane discipline was not all that it might be and it was evident that our drivers did not expect to have their progress impeded by civilian vehicles even if they had right of way. In downtown Algiers they simply drove down the middle of the road with lights on and horn sounding giving fair warning that they were not about to stop for anyone. In the country if they ran out of road, they carved another one from the soft shoulder. It was stirring stuff.

I asked our liaison officer if I would be allowed to be in the control tower for the Harrier's arrival since I might be able to advise the pilot of any landing problems and answer any questions that he might have about the airfield. He was able to arrange this and accompanied me to the control deck to meet the duty controllers and to let them know that I should return when the aircraft was due. Shortly before the arrival time I made my way back to the tower, to be met by a new sentry, heavily armed, who knew nothing of any arrangement made for me to enter. We exchanged a few words, I handed over a Harrier pen, tie clip and cigarette lighter, and the way was cleared. The aircraft was flown by Don Riches, formerly of RAF Tengah, then Harrier Liaison Officer for Ministry of Defence and now production test pilot for the company. Five minutes before the estimated time of arrival given to the Algerians six weeks earlier, he called to say that he was at 30 miles, airfield in sight, and landed precisely on time.

The likely lads lined up to be flown were a fairly mixed bunch, mostly MiG 21 operators of presumed Algerian nationality although we had no way of establishing that and, it could be argued, it was none of our business. The thought had occurred to me that any Arab air force could slip in a pilot to do a short evaluation without our being aware of it. Furthermore, if there was no crystal-clear requirement for Harriers in Algeria, it needed no giant brain to see how useful they might be against the common Arab enemy.

The proficiency marks awarded by our pilots to their guests varied wildly from exceptional to one who, it was suspected, had never flown an aircraft in his life and could have been the squadron party political nark. They were without exception friendly, polite and anxious to gather all the information that they could. It was all quite rewarding.

We had started from the premise that any decision to order a British aircraft would be made by the President himself and we waited anxiously to see how his involvement would manifest itself. After two days of flying we were told that President Boumedienne, having now been informed by his staff of the aircraft's qualities, would come to Boufarik to witness a demonstration. This was more than we had hoped for and I quickly alerted my boss at Kingston so that he could arrange to be present.

By this time our entire party was on friendly terms with all the Algerian airmen, most of whom now wrote with Harrier pens and lit their cigarettes with Harrier lighters. All pretence of barring access to air traffic control, or indeed, anywhere else on the station, had disappeared. When word of the President's visit to the airfield got out however, there was a visible tightening of security and specialists moved in with sniffer dogs to check anywhere that he might pass close to and particularly the viewing base where he and his entourage would sit. He was said to have many enemies, not necessarily Algerian and, for example, never stayed in the same house on successive nights. How true this was I cannot tell but they certainly did their best to ensure that he would come to no harm during his visit to Boufarik. The airfield had major roads on two sides, carrying heavy traffic heading west along the coast, or south-west toward the Atlas Mountains.

We were the only people flying from Boufarik and, when the Harrier had left the circuit, the constant hum of traffic was very noticeable. The President was due to visit in the late afternoon and at sometime around midday the roads must have been closed to all traffic because there was a sudden and total silence; not even a bird sang.

The calm was broken by the wail of sirens as the President and his police escort approached from the city. As they swept on to the airfield, the guard of honour snapped to attention as Boumedienne stepped from his car. Imprinted on my memory is the image of a tall, terribly pale man, wearing a long black cloak of the kind that cultivated Arabs customarily adopt whenever the temperature falls below about 90°F. He was enormously dignified and I instinctively bowed when he shook my hand. As he turned to take his seat on the viewing stand and I saw him in profile, my somewhat irreverent thought was that, had he been wearing a felt sombrero, he would have looked exactly like the figure used to advertise Sandeman's port.

The Harrier was parked facing the President and perhaps a hundred yards from him, on a short piece of connecting taxiway. Don was strapped in, waiting for the signal to fire up and start his display. The big Pegasus engine is started by a small turbine which itself is started by the aircraft batteries. There is therefore no ground equipment required, nor is there any need for ground crew to be on hand. Whilst this is no longer unusual with military aircraft, it was uncommon in the 1960s, and it always gave great pleasure to watch the faces of those who had never seen it before as this wicked-looking aircraft, totally isolated, not only sprang into life but immediately leapt into the air straight up. I watched the President closely and was not disappointed. Don Riches flew a very nice display finishing with the usual hover, bow to the guest of honour and settling down again on the precise spot from which he had started.

For whatever reason, negotiations went no further although we had several more meetings and answered lots of questions. I had the strong feeling that HM Government were never going to approve the export of Harriers to a country fairly firmly in the Soviet orbit and, for all I know, the Algerians may have been told that on the diplomatic net. And so I said farewell to sunny Algeria with no great wish to return. However, I did.

John Parker, one of my colleagues, had responsibility for the Americas and had generated considerable interest in Harrier in Brazil and the Argentine: less, it must be said, amongst the airmen than the naval aviators. The reason for this was that the Royal Navy was about to go out of the carrier business and, in order to retain organic air power, was fighting hard for a naval version of Harrier to be flown from a ship called a through-deck cruiser, drawings of which bore a startling resemblance to a small carrier. Both Brazil and Argentina operated former RN carriers and, because they were unlikely ever to acquire one of the nuclear-powered carriers coming into vogue, or perhaps just for old time's sake, they were interested in this naval activity. With the limited deck run on their elderly ships and the waning efficiency of their catapults, they were stuck with first-generation jet aircraft, difficult to maintain and not very cost-effective. Against that background, G-VTOL was again prepared for touring, only this time without me. The tour was a success although no sales followed which, in the light of subsequent events in Argentina and the Falklands may have been just as well.

I have recorded earlier that another colleague, John Crampton, was not NATO standard size at all and stood out in a crowd. He looked after most of Europe and, when word was received that someone in Rome would like to discuss Harrier at a secret meeting, it was decided that an envoy of more normal proportions with less chance of being spotted – to the embarrassment of everyone – should investigate. The rules were that our agents were not to be told and all arrangements would be made by the man who, in some mysterious way, had made contact with the company. I was told that I should register at the Rome Hilton where I should be contacted.

Sure enough, on the evening of my arrival I was met by a most pleasant former air force general who said that he had been told to arrange the meeting. I was conducted to the rendezvous, armed with all my briefing material and performance data, ready to give of my best for Queen and Hawkers. I need hardly have bothered since my audience of two had no knowledge of or interest in aircraft but simply required me to return to London with the message that, for a considerable sum of money, it could be arranged that a contract for Harrier aircraft for the Italian Navy would be placed. The company had previously spent a lot of time and effort in persuading the Italian Navy, who by law were not allowed to operate conventional fixed-wing aircraft, that they should join the Royal Navy in their search to acquire ship-borne Harriers, and the clear implication of this meeting was that all that was a waste of time because the procurement machinery had not been oiled. I may say that the God-like figure able to work this miracle was never named, and indeed the whole thing may have been a hoax, but it did not seem so to me.

I hastened back to Kingston to debrief with John Glasscock, my Managing Director. As always, he listened with great patience, put the occasional probing question and finally asked if I thought the approach was genuine. The certainty was that this was no normal procurement process but more likely a powerful political figure seeking to cash in on a perhaps transient opportunity, and I had to say that, unlikely as it seemed, we could easily make an enemy if we ignored the approach. John said that he would ponder the question and consult the deputy chief executive of the Group,

Eric Rubython, before sending for me again. Shortly afterwards I was called to report to Rubython's office to join John Glasscock who had already outlined the story. I confirmed the detail of the meeting, described the opulence of the apartment in which it had been held and the easy authority with which the case had been put. At about this point there was a respectful tap on the door and Leslie Johnson, a member of the purchasing department, poked his anxious head around the door. Quick as a flash, Rubython said: "I think you must have the wrong Rubython," which had to be the kindest way of telling this other Johnson that there had been a mistake. How on earth he ever passed the formidable Miss Black who sat in Eric Rubython's outer office I cannot say, but he did.

The outcome of our deliberations was that both John Glasscock and I returned to Rome to investigate further, but nothing ever came of it. Interestingly, more than 20 years later, the Italian Navy took delivery of its first Harriers acquired by the conventional procurement methods.

The other abiding memory of the time is the fuss and bother that we were put to by an enthusiast in the F&CO who had decided that Uganda represented the last chance of our retaining some influence in East Africa. The other former colonies had all turned left, but the jovial President Idi Amin remained loyal to the United Kingdom, probably because of his earlier service in the Army. Or so the argument ran. Maurice Brown, our Regional Executive for East Africa, persuaded Kingston that the Harrier was very much on the mind of the President and that meant that I should gird up my loins. (Africa, it may be remembered, was part of my parish).

In almost no time I found myself flying into Entebbe, to be met by Maurice and conducted into Kampala in order to meet and brief a mixed group of airmen and politicians. My studies had revealed nothing to encourage me to believe that the infant air force was ready for an aircraft of Harrier complexity and capability, but that was not my immediate concern. The briefing was well attended and they all enjoyed the films but, as so often happened, there were no questions and I had the strong feeling that there was a huge hill to climb if progress was to be made. Nevertheless, the President had been invited to visit London as a guest of the government, and during his stay was expected to spend some time in Scotland with his old company commander in the African Rifles, now a retired general. This presented an opportunity to show the aircraft to Amin without mounting another grand tour, and was too good to miss. Accordingly, we arranged with our friends at Ferranti to make use of their facility at Turnhouse in order to show off the Harrier to the putative purchaser.

A strong team assembled in Edinburgh the night before the demonstration, with a single-seat aircraft to be flown by John Farley pre-positioned on a short piece of taxiway well away from other traffic. The visitors arrived, led by this huge man beside whom everyone else looked puny. He was wearing the uniform of a field marshal, with Israeli parachutist wings on his left breast although to my disappointment not the VC, DSO, MC and other self-awarded decorations that were allegedly usually on display. The military ensemble was slightly spoiled in my eyes by the white shirt and what seemed to be a club tie which were the rig of the day. We shook hands and, although his grip was surprisingly gentle, my hand completely disappeared as though it had suddenly been amputated.

I engaged him in conversation about the wonders of the Harrier, although frankly, it was rather one-sided, and sought to include the young man wearing the uniform of a group captain who accompanied him. He might well have been a deaf mute for all the reaction or even interest that my brief monologue inspired. Not for the first time, I was saved by the characteristic rumble of a Pegasus engine as Farley lit up. As always with those getting their first sight of the aircraft, they become aware of the noise but are quite unprepared for the violent action that quickly follows. A photograph taken at the time shows me pointing towards the aircraft which I knew was about to scream past us in a very short take-off, seeking to avoid a serious diplomatic incident by ensuring that the visiting head of state at least saw what brought on his heart tremors. John Farley, as ever, flew a superb demonstration and parked the aircraft close to us so that the visitors could meet him and examine the aircraft. This was always a tricky moment if the people doing the examining were unfamiliar with the Harrier which, immediately after landing, has one or two very hot spots. In a breeze too, anyone handling a reaction control valve attached to the rudder could easily lose a finger if the control moved whilst he was probing. On this occasion there was no cause for concern since none of the guests showed much interest in the aircraft although they examined Farley closely to see that he had the normal ration of heads and limbs.

There was some more rather desultory dialogue with the Ugandan authorities, but it was evident that they expected any Harriers that they acquired to be a gift from the British Government. In this they were doomed to disappointment since at the time we were having a tough time paying for our own defence equipment, and in no position to be generous to anyone else. I am certain that, if political expediency had dictated that the Ugandans should have Harriers, it would have led to an operational disaster of cosmic proportions because they had neither the pilots nor the engineering support to cope with a modern aircraft.

This fiasco was almost my last fling with a Harrier campaign, discounting forays into Libya soon after Colonel Gaddafi had tentatively established his regime. It was usual on first briefing visits to take one or two table-top Harrier models which could be used to illustrate aircraft manoeuvres, especially when answering questions, and subsequently be presented to the senior men attending the briefing. Our model-maker produced outstanding and very authentic models in the livery of the country concerned but, for Libya, the amended paint scheme following the overthrow of the King had not yet made it to his reference books. In all innocence therefore, after all discussion had finished, I handed the models to the two most senior members of the audience. One immediately separated the model from its stand and, using the steel pin upon which the model usually rested, attacked the now-superseded markings with great vigour. My first thought was that he was seeking to discover what sort of material had been used in its manufacture but it soon became apparent that the old royal symbol had caused him to flip.

CHAPTER XXII
VOLARE

One fine spring day in 1972 I was minding my own business in my office at Kingston-upon-Thames, pondering how best to spread the Harrier gospel to the unbelievers, when the telephone rang and a female voice asked if I would present myself to the main board meeting of the Hawker Siddeley Group at St. James's at 2.30 that afternoon. I suspected a joke and therefore asked if I could have the caller's name and promised to call back as soon as I had made certain that I could cancel my other appointments for the day. This sounded very grand but of course I knew that if the invitation was genuine, it was a parade, and any other plans that I might have were immediately null and void. It was genuine and I checked in at the appointed time wondering what on earth I might have done to incur of the wrath of the *main board*!

The story that unfolded was almost beyond belief although at this meeting my role as escort to the chairman was made plain: much later I was able to assemble all the pieces of the jigsaw.

President Sadat of Egypt had decided that the close association with the Soviet Union so favoured by Colonel Nasser, his predecessor, was not in the best interests of the nation. The promised development had not occurred, the people were no better off than they had been under the monarchy and, in short, the USSR was bad news. This was all exciting stuff but its immediate impact on a large, general engineering group that made aeroplanes was not self-evident. Sadat realised that he had to prepare the ground before cutting himself adrift from his Soviet allies, and his prime concern was keeping his air force, consisting exclusively of Russian aircraft, serviceable and able to fight. A break with the Soviets meant automatic separation from other operators of Russian aircraft who could supply spares and engineering support. The United States, whilst welcoming the political decision, would find it difficult to assist practically because they had no access to MiG spares, and politically they were close allies of Israel, the Arab enemy. Poor President Sadat must have spent many troubled days and nights trying to square this circle. At some point he sent for the leading aeronautical engineer in government service to seek his advice and, presumably, to gauge the effects of the decision that he wished to make.

The man was Khaled Shishini who was managing director of the aircraft factory at Helwan, just south of Cairo. When asked for his advice, Shishini told the President that he had graduated in aeronautics from Imperial College in London where his Professor was Arnold Hall. Following graduation, the young Shishini had been deeply involved in the plan to build Vampire aircraft in Egypt, a plan which collapsed when the Suez war occurred. He had worked in the de Havilland factory at Hatfield, visited other sites where parts were manufactured and generally had a quite wide experience of British industry. He was able to tell the President that de Havilland was now part of Hawker Siddeley Aviation, itself a part of Hawker Siddeley Group of which the Chairman was Sir Arnold Hall, his old professor. All this I learned in the months that followed when I knew Shishini well. At the St. James's meeting, all I knew was that I was to accompany the Chairman on a visit to Cairo which was not to be widely advertised.

Travelling with the Chairman was a great incentive to promotion. A company-owned 125, flown by John Cunningham, was the only way for the Chairman to get to Cairo and it also offered the opportunity to stop over in Cyprus, where Sir Arnold and Lady Hall had a holiday home in Kyrenia. We broke our outward journey at Nice in order to collect a friend of Lady Hall who would keep her company in Kyrenia, whilst we went on to Cairo. During our trip eastward, Johnny and Barbara Brown had made the short journey westward from Beirut, so that the ladies could entertain each other when the chaps went on to Egypt.

Sir Arnold had been the director of the Royal Aircraft Establishment at Farnborough and, in that capacity, had been the guest of honour at a Mckenna Dinner at the Test Pilots' School during my spell as President of the Mess Committee. I had therefore met him and spent most of the evening sitting between him, as chief guest, and Sammy Wroath who was then the Commandant. Furthermore, at that time one of my naval students named Don Camm was about to marry his daughter, Judy. None of this was known to Lady Hall of course, and it gave us something to talk about *en route*.

Aware of my aide-de-camp duties I had ordered from Hertz at Nicosia airport the best and biggest car that they had in order to transport the chairman and his party. The car turned out to be a venerable Audi in bilious orange which was not quite what I had in mind when I made the booking. On arrival I dashed around, secured the car and positioned it at the airport exit ready for the road to Kyrenia. I was just in time to see the Chairman and party leaving in the Morris 1100 that he had ordered for himself.

Cairo appeared much as it had on my last visit. No one looked very happy, for reasons which were clear to anyone who recognised desperate poverty when he saw it. The city simply could not accommodate the thousands streaming in from the countryside in the hope of a better life, only to find that their prospects were not improved by the move. For the Chairman, it could not have been an auspicious start to a business visit but, if he was shocked, he did not show it.

When the President revealed his plan and asked how Hawker Siddeley could help, and perhaps more importantly, if he could rely on our assistance, it was rather a lot to take in in one go. He understood this completely and invited us to return to our hotel and consider the matter which quite clearly required careful consideration. There was no doubt in anyone's mind that we could provide the necessary technical help if politics were not allowed to get in the way. Maintaining the present fleet of aircraft was only Stage One of the grand plan. The wealthy oil states had promised to provide financial backing for the Egyptians, the only Arab nation with the technical capability to manufacture the arms that they all felt they badly needed. This arrangement, the Arab Organisation for Industry (AOI), was said not to be specifically aimed at armaments but the reality was that the ambitious plans that they had would preclude anything else. Stage Two was to be the manufacture of aircraft and their associated power plants under licence at the already established, but sadly misused, Helwan factories. My interest quickened on behalf of the Kingston facility, where the new trainer was already under construction, which would make an ideal first project for the Egyptian factories. First though, all this had to be carried back to London and communicated to the government, happily not my job.

I understand that the news conveyed to the government by the Chairman was greeted with disbelief, to the point that in a moment of weakness it was agreed that the Egyptians could be offered the manufacture of any aircraft, present or future, which Hawker Siddeley might have in mind. This was an important concession because it would be necessary in negotiation to make clear that we could foresee a long association with gradually more testing projects. I quickly returned to Beirut to collect Johnny Brown and together we marched on Cairo.

With our man Mahmoud Miligi we called on the politicians, who directed us to the Air Force Headquarters and the Commander-in-Chief, General Hosni Mubarrak. Our discussions covered a vast range of topics including, at one stage, his description of the training that he had been given by the Soviets, which was hilarious. He was never allowed to go solo on the Badger, nor was there ever enough fuel in the aircraft to allow more than local flying in case the Russian crew defected. When I described to him the Hawk and its performance he constantly asked how I could possibly know when so far the aircraft had not been built, never mind flown. His questioning was gentle and I believe genuine; he really did not understand how fairly simple sums, experience and wind tunnel tests could produce such confident predictions. His staff were equally outspoken and friendly although it was clear that the odd one or two felt that a dreadful mistake was being made in switching political allegiance.

The Egyptians first interest was of course to establish a spares supply line and to replace the Soviet technical support teams which had advised on all major maintenance and repair tasks. My visits to Helwan, in company

197

with the Rolls-Royce team that had agreed to provide matching support for the Soviet engine overhaul programme, were aimed at identifying the main problem areas in order to assemble from the departments at Kingston the best people to help and advise. During the first year of this activity, I made 13 separate visits to Egypt, usually with a different group of Kingston colleagues.

For a fairly recently-retired RAF pilot there was something eerie about walking through a hangar full of MiG 19s and 21s. The factory at Helwan had been downgraded from manufacturing to what we would call a maintenance unit, carrying out overhauls and fairly simple repairs. I saw everything that was going on and my first and abiding feeling was of sympathy for all the people working there. Conditions were appalling with hangar doors open to create some air circulation and filling the place with sand, fine as talcum powder, which covered every surface. Men with simple brooms rearranged the dust from time to time but there was no equipment to extract the dust even from the designated clean areas.

The machinery which had been installed 20 years earlier for the manufacture of the Vampire was instantly recognisable to the Kingston engineers as it was the same as was used in our factory. It was being employed to make field kitchens for the army and was badly in need of overhaul. The ability of the Egyptian engineers was convincingly demonstrated by the little delta fighter designed for them by Willi Messerschmitt, but made in Helwan and powered by a Bristol Siddeley Orpheus engine (borrowed from the Indian Gnat programme) which the Helwan engine factory under Dr Helmi Hagar had reheated. There was no lack of ability but lack of political purpose and desperate underfunding had led to the abandonment of the project. The aircraft flew once and, according to their reports, flew extremely well and it must have been demoralising to be told to forget it since Soviet aircraft had become available in practically unlimited numbers and on very easy terms.

After their initial suspicion we were given free access to every part of the Helwan complex including the overhaul and repair shops. For the first time I began to understand the need for the enormous Russian fleets of aircraft. Serviceability was of the order of 50%, given sufficient warning to allow a surge in availability of spares and manpower. Generally it was considerably lower. Spares were not interchangeable which meant that the simplest operation, like a wingtip suffering a ding in a minor taxying accident, grounded the aircraft for hours if not days. The replacement wingtip drawn from stores was approximately the right size and shape but had to be hand-finished to be fitted to the damaged aircraft. When an aircraft was being readied for overhaul, each panel removed was tied with string to the opening that it fitted, for the good reason that it would fit nowhere else. It was the same with all other spares. Engine life was ridiculously short and engines were usually thrown away, not reworked and returned to service as was common practice in the West.

Much of my time in Cairo was spent in the company of Mahmoud Miligi who had access to everywhere and everyone, including Hosni Mubarrak, whom he had taught to fly. Like most Cairenes, Miligi had a wicked sense of humour and kept me constantly amused with scurrilous stories of life at the court of King Farouk. He was also pretty scathing about the recently-departed President Nasser who, as an army officer viewed through the eyes of an air force pilot, gained very few marks. Driving past the late President's mausoleum he said conversationally: "The right man in the right place – at last." On a late night journey from the airport where he had met me, to the Hilton Hotel on the banks of the Nile, he drove through several traffic lights at red causing me to ask why. He replied: "Experience." Here was a sophisticated man with vast military and business background, fiercely proud of his Egyptian heritage and yet able to make fun of himself and the modern society which he hated. In September 1972 he was invited by us to attend the SBAC Show at Farnborough, an event which he had not seen for years. I collected him from his London hotel on the Tuesday of the show to drive him to Farnborough, and turned on the radio to hear the news of the Israeli athletes taken hostage at the Munich Olympics, to learn that many had been massacred. I delivered a short homily to Miligi on the terrible disservice that the terrorists did to the Arab cause by such actions and his only reply was: "How else can we focus the world's attention upon our troubles?" I realised then that if he was not particularly upset by what had happened then it was unlikely that any other Arab would be affected. It was very sobering.

Many, indeed most, of the Kingston personnel that visited Cairo in connection with the MiG support project were seeing the place for the first time and were quite unprepared for the cultural shocks which started on arrival. So desperate for foreign currency were they that the Egyptians established a duty-free shopping area for *arriving* passengers where, as long as purchases were made in pounds, dollars, francs or marks, there were no limits on the amount that could be bought. This was most useful to us because we were frequently required to entertain our Egyptian colleagues and, even in the best hotels, what it said on the label did not necessarily describe the contents. Even the so-called tamper-proof bottles proved not to be so because the enterprising thieves drilled through the base of the bottle, removed half the contents and topped it up with water of doubtful origin. Most visitors became unwell at some stage of their visit, usually by drinking something that appeared to be safe but was not. After a few days, having seen the delivery trucks touring the city with crates of beer and soft drinks exposed to a sun hot enough to make them boil, most accepted the advice to stick to bottled water mixed with anything bought in duty-free, without ice.

Everyone wanted to visit the pyramids, of course, and most accepted my advice not to go in daylight when the salesmen and beggars outnumbered the flies. The sound and light show was just about the only thing that I found in Egypt that started on time and ran faultlessly every time I saw it. The show lasted about an hour and a half and was given in different languages at different times of the week. It gave a potted history of ancient Egypt with the most dramatic illumination of the pyramids and the sphinx, timed to coincide with the story being told. I tried always to make this an evening entertainment early in the period of the visit, partially to counter-balance the pretty unfavourable impression everyone gained of the modern city.

The Egyptian Air Force had bought most of its MiG spares from Poland and other Warsaw Pact countries who offered better trade and barter deals than the Russians. The only way that we could supply the parts that they required was by a process known as reverse engineering. In brief, they gave us a part and, back at our factory, it was disassembled, the material was analysed and the dimensions of each component were carefully measured. The hope was that there would be a substitute part already in manufacture that would fit and do the same job. After all, no matter where they originate, all aircraft rely upon the same basic ingredients to work. Sometimes the part could be produced easily, sometimes it involved detailed design, mock-up, prototype and tool manufacture before production could begin – a very expensive process. When our contracts manager, Leslie Palmer, and I were invited to conclude agreements with the Air Force there was always someone on the other side ready to accuse us of profiteering by offering a part at a unit cost of say £50 for which the Poles had charged 50 pence. I lost count of the number of times that we tried to explain that there was no point in seeking to compare their costs and ours for the reasons given above, but they chose not to believe us. When an agreement was finally reached, the entire engineering staff signed the contractual documents, I suppose to fend off any accusations of corruption.

In parallel with this activity, the senior engineers at the airframe and engine factories were being introduced to the manufacturing aspects of our new trainer and its engine. The Adour engine that was to be fitted was already in service in the Jaguar and was therefore fully documented in terms of performance and maintenance. Not so the airframe which was not only a completely new design but was to go straight to production without a prototype for development. There was a great deal of head-shaking about this and their fears were only put to rest after a fairly large party visited our factories and saw for themselves that the first 25 sets of sub-assemblies had been completed and 4 or 5 aircraft were very close to first flight. Their interest and excitement quickened as they were presented with visible proof that this was a real live project.

They were delightful people to be with and, since the limited amount of travel that they had experienced was confined to the Soviet Union and its satellites, visiting modern factories and strolling around London acted as a tonic. Shishini had purchased an Austin A40 during his time in England in the early fifties and since then had contrived to keep it going by resourcefulness and good engineering. Before coming to London he had compiled a wish-list of parts that he would like for this venerable vehicle and this proved to be our biggest challenge of the entire visit. We certainly found most of them, and how he persuaded Egyptian customs to allow them into the country remains a mystery. Significantly, when money from the Arab States began to flow, my Egyptian contacts began to arrive at meetings in chauffeur-driven Mercedes. For most of them that was a fair reward for years of motoring misery.

It can be seen that Egypt dominated my activities during this period because it promised to be the bridge to further exciting prospects in the Middle East where the Egyptian Air Force was viewed as the natural leader. The political shift away from the Soviet Union also seemed likely to become a model for some of the other client states offering a huge potential market for Western, particularly British, products, if we could so arrange it. Wherever we were allowed, we began the difficult task of interesting politicians and airmen in a new aircraft not yet built and flown. This may sound like a sterile exercise but it was not. The business of aircraft procurement is slow and complex and it is almost never too soon to start sowing the seeds. Timing is critical however, since even the most patient, friendly and encouraging audience fairly quickly tires of constantly being told how good it is going to be. A new military aircraft, even a trainer, is exciting and everyone wants to see it, touch it and, if possible, fly it. Then the talking has to stop.

As the first aircraft neared completion at the Kingston factory, teams were travelling the world sounding out markets and assessing how much local manufacture could be allowed in order to seal a contract. A small team even travelled to Australia to brief on the aircraft and consider sole local manufacture of the wings, in order to grab their interest. The logistical nightmare that would have followed hardly bears thinking about but nothing was ruled out in seeking to ensure the success of the new venture. I may say that the company was already guaranteed a contract from the British Government but, with that as our daily bread, the butter would come from further contracts abroad.

On their way to Australia, the team landed to refuel at Bahrain at dead of night, and most disembarked to stretch their legs. They were surprised, as they walked through the departure lounge, to be accosted by two unshaven and unwashed Europeans who might well have been asking for a handout. They were not, but were in fact two members of the company, Johnny Brown and myself, who had spent the previous 30 hours trapped in the airport transit lounge, waiting for our flight to Khartoum. Sudan Airways had discovered that if they postponed departure in two-hour bites, they had no obligation to feed or house their stranded passengers. We had tried in vain to find a member of the airline staff who would admit that neither of their Boeing aircraft was in imminent danger of arrival so that we could go into Manama and rest, or at least bathe and change. Finally, we gave the telephone number of the Hilton to the check-in girl and asked her to call us when an aircraft was likely to appear. I was pleased that we did so because we had a further 18-hour wait before we finally left for Khartoum. I suppose that on holiday such a hold-up is a major irritation but on a business trip it can be a major planning disaster since some future appointment is immediately prejudiced.

My first visit in 20 years to Khartoum was not a great success since the tiny air force was effectively grounded, and visiting the gloomy hangars from which I had earlier flown a mixture of aircraft was a sombre experience. As a way of assessing their interest in our new, soon-to-fly aeroplane, we were offering to evaluate their technical requirements to make their present fleet serviceable, using Egyptian-manufactured spares for the MiGs and our help with the Jet Provosts. It was soon apparent that their problems were largely financial and that even the Soviets had tired of pouring resources into an apparently bottomless pit. It seemed an unlikely place for us to do business since we expected to be paid.

By good fortune I was in England on the 21st August 1974, and was able to be present when the first Hawk, XX154, was rolled out of the hangar at Dunsfold for its first flight. I had seen hundreds of drawings of the aircraft, had closely examined the wooden mockup and was familiar with the wind-tunnel models. Nevertheless, to see it in the flesh was still a surprise. The legendary beauty of Hawker aircraft had begun to fade with the Harrier which, whatever else it was, was not a pretty sight. The Hawk was the first advanced trainer for years that was purpose-designed and not a converted fighter, and every effort had been made to eliminate the shortcomings of its immediate predecessors. A primary aim had been to give the instructor in the rear seat a forward view past the student in the front seat, and this made the aircraft look distinctly odd on the ground. Whilst some saw it as Quasimodo, I persuaded myself that it was like a dolphin, designed for its environment, and dolphins do not look good out of the water. After all that has been done to it since with leading-edge breaker strips, wing fences and vortex generators, it is hard to recall how clean and pure the wing looked on that fine summer evening. The back end, in contrast, looked strange with anhedral on the tailplane and the curious boxy end of the rear fuselage. All these first impressions registered as Duncan Simpson climbed aboard, fired up the engine and taxied, following the two-seat Harrier chase aeroplane. Both aircraft left the circuit to appear some time later as a pair, difficult to pick up since both had clean engines and neither is very big. In the air, with the gear up, the ugly duckling became a swan and I admired the addition to our fleet.

As is usually the case, the early development flying of the Hawk produced one or two minor surprises, mostly of the agreeable kind. The beautifully smooth wing kept on lifting and lifting but, when it finally stalled, it was a touch violent for the student pilot and had to be tamed. As bits were added the wing looked less pleasing but the stalling characteristics became docile enough to satisfy the training requirement. Similarly with spinning. The standard need is to demonstrate a 4-turn spin that is predictable and repeatable, with no traps for the unwary and which will not prove fatal for the solo student who gets the recovery procedure ever so slightly wrong. The Hawk's initial problem was that it was almost impossible to spin, no matter how badly mishandled, although a simple and foolproof way of entering the spin was evolved. As soon as the controls were centralised, or as was claimed by some of the company pilots, simply released, the aircraft stopped spinning instantly. For one Farnborough Show a smoke generator was fitted to the demonstration aircraft and Andy Jones carried out 12-turn spins as the centrepiece of his show. It must be said that this also coincided with our learning that the Franco-German Alpha-Jet was in desperate trouble with its spinning programme, troubles which were never fully overcome.

Another agreeable problem that arose was that the aircraft proved to be supersonic. This had not been a design aim since it formed no part of the staff requirement but, as dive speeds were increased to confirm the integrity of the airframe, it became clear that the increase in drag was far less than had been predicted. Within six months of first flight we had a trainer that would exceed the speed of sound in a dive, something that was quite beyond the capabilities of any competitor.

Meanwhile, interest in the aircraft was spreading around the world, and nowhere was it higher than in the Arab Republic of Egypt. By the middle of 1975, more aircraft had joined the development programme and XX156 was assigned the environmental testing task. The first phase was to examine the Hawk's suitability in conditions that we would call hot, although my Middle Eastern friends, and especially those from the Gulf, would call the Maltese climate in summer, spring-like. Jim Hawkins and Don Riches took the aircraft there, accompanied by a support party of technical and scientific staff from the company. The opportunity was too good to miss and arrangements were made for the aeroplane to move on to Cairo when the trials had been completed.

Mahmoud Miligi arranged for the Hawk to be based at Al Maza airfield, a military base in Cairo, handy for the politicians and senior staff officers whom we hoped to attract to our demonstrations. We had asked for a cross-section of pilots to come to Al Maza to fly the aircraft and they arrived in a collection of aircraft, from MiG 21s to primary trainers. The flying was uneventful except that Don Riches experienced an engine surge, the first and only one ever seen in the Adour fitted to the Hawk, and which we concluded must have been caused by contaminated fuel. This in spite of the fact that, having been warned of the doubtful quality of air force fuel, I had arranged for Shell to bring a tanker to the airfield each day. It was something we could well have done without because the Egyptian pilot who was in the aircraft at the time quite properly reported the incident, and although the finger of blame pointed to the fuel, it was slightly unnerving to think that it could happen again, because we had no choice of fuel supplier. The only other incident that caused some concern happened to Jim Hawkins who, on landing, was forced to swerve to avoid a chromium-plated car bumper which had found its way on to the runway.

There was a good turnout for the flying demonstration staged for the top brass and politicians and for which we were promised the full cooperation of the controllers at Cairo International, whose circuit overlaps that of Al Maza. On the day they cooperated in as much as they refused almost every kind of approach by the demonstrator since they had traffic taking off or landing. As a result, the demonstration looked half-hearted and not a bit like the standard Jim Hawkins show which was stirring to say the least.

A visit was also made to the factories at Helwan so that those who had not been in the parties that came to Kingston and Dunsfold could see and touch the aeroplane. Any work that had been going on before the Hawk arrived certainly stopped as soon as it ran in for a break before landing. The Hawk was the centre of attention and large numbers of the factory employees were given, or took, time off to examine it closely. Amongst them was a distinguished looking chap in civilian clothes introduced to me by Shishini as their chief test pilot. We chatted for a while and I asked him where he had undergone test pilot training (nowhere), and told him that I had tutored Fikry Zaher at Farnborough 20 years earlier. At this he fell on my neck and explained that Fikry had taught him to fly and was regarded as his father, which made me his grandfather. It was slightly embarrassing since all the rest of the Hawker party saw was me being kissed on both cheeks by an unknown Egyptian.

The visit was regarded as a success and there is no doubt that the personnel at Helwan had been won over. Most of them were English-speakers, able to communicate freely with the technical staff from Kingston and to learn from them the steady production progress that was being made. If there was any slight doubt in our minds it was caused by the political and economic pressure being applied by the French both directly and through the other members of the AOI. The staff of the French Embassy seemed able to make commitments and offer inducements that we simply could not match and, whilst we were supremely confident that we had the better aircraft, this sometimes seemed incidental to the main debate.

CHAPTER XXIII
HIGH HOPES

Our efforts in Egypt kept most of us fairly busy, but the rest of our activities did not stop, because the Hawk was becoming known to the aeronautical fraternity through articles in the specialist magazines and press. The replacement of trainer aircraft in air force inventories usually has a modest priority and our aim had always been to give the Hawk a combat capability in order to make it attractive in a dual role for the smaller air forces. This aim was gradually being met as modest war-loads were flown to satisfy the RAF weapon training requirement, and it became evident that the aeroplane was capable of carrying substantial armament, which caught the attention of other potential operators.

Our Regional Executives kept the local politicians and air force commanders informed of developments and an early response came from the Turks, who still nursed the ambition to start a manufacturing industry, and who badly needed to replace their ancient T-33 trainers. Because of our earlier association with the Turkish authorities when the Harrier was their manufacturing target, we were quite optimistic. The Hawk was in every way a more suitable vehicle for an inexperienced workforce and our man Yavuz Kirec was full of enthusiasm.

We toured factories around Turkey where the government felt that the skills and experience existed to launch the new industry. We saw railway trains and ships being built in conditions reminiscent of 1930, with crop-haired apprentices in blue denim smocks attending classes in basic engineering. As another example of their willingness to learn and develop, we were shown a factory which made aluminium window and door frames which, it was suggested, were not unlike aircraft parts. It looked like a long learning curve.

In spite of encouraging progress with the very intelligent and courteous members of the government body set up for the evaluation tests (TUSAS), a decision was announced to proceed with the Italian MB.339. This came as a shock since, although it was patently a cheaper solution to the problem, the 339 was a warmed-over MB.326 which was not much of an aeroplane on the best day it ever had, and by now had airframe and engine technology that was well over the hill. Ralph Hooper, our chief engineer at Kingston expressed it best when he said that the Macchi design team had been asked to carry out the equivalent of an update on the Gnat, and where would that have got us? Sitting in the hotel in Ankara, searching for some consolation after this further unkind twist of fate, the only good thing that I could think of was that the Turks would not be competing with the Egyptians for Hawk sales to the Islamic nations.

However, that was not the end of the story because, with the signing ceremony arranged and the senior men from Macchi in town, the whole thing was called off. Yavuz Kirec was accused of interfering in national affairs and all sorts of other skulduggery when in truth I think that all he did was to alert the Turkish Air Force to the fact that they were about to be fobbed off yet again with aircraft that nobody else wanted. As an admittedly interested observer it certainly seemed that the evaluation committee could have saved themselves a lot of work by checking project costs and simply giving the contract to the cheapest. I was surprised that Alpha-Jet, which in Turkey was being promoted by Dornier rather than Dassault, had not received a much better hearing. Military cooperation between the two countries went back a long way and many Turks worked in Germany; indeed the funds that they sent back to their families were a prime source of the hard currency required to make the industrialisation possible. However, unless the Germans were prepared to subsidise the project, it was bound to be more expensive than the Hawk and that could have been fatal to its chances.

Although I formed some close friendships with the Turkish people involved in the Harrier and Hawk enterprises, neither of which came to anything, I was not too unhappy when my travels to Ankara stopped. The national airline THY had an appalling safety record and would have been well down anyone's list of favourite ways to travel. In order to boost income it was made difficult or impossible to fly from London to Ankara direct except with THY. British airlines terminated at Istanbul where the innocent abroad switched to a venerable DC-9 of Turkish Air Lines. Being aboard one trying to land at Ankara in a snowstorm persuaded me that I must seek an alternative. Moreover a series of accidents, following which witnesses swore that the crew concerned had been drinking in the bar before departure, caused another serious dip in my THY confidence graph. The airline, seeking to reassure potential passengers, introduced random breath-testing for pilots on duty which led to a pilots' strike. I accept that the pilots may have been so offended by the company's action that they felt compelled to take drastic action, but there is the other possibility that a well established "tot before take-off" routine was under threat.

I went to great lengths to find ways of getting to Ankara without flying THY and was usually successful although it meant travelling a day or days earlier than was necessary. The PanAm round-the-world service eastbound from London was allowed direct access to Ankara for reasons not disclosed but for which I was extremely grateful. Lufthansa also had landing rights in the capital, but it meant staying overnight in Frankfurt to catch the early morning departure, which frequently I did. More testing was to finish work in Ankara in time to catch PanAm or Lufthansa going westwards. This may give the impression that I was particularly fussy about my transport arrangements but that was not so. My anxiety about THY was well-founded and, travelling home from Istanbul with one of our contract managers, we were taking off towards the sea when, soon after becoming airborne, the aircraft slowed and swung slightly. I deduced that we had lost an engine and warned Ted Harper, my travelling companion, to brace himself. After a tense few seconds, power was restored and we began to climb away again. It turned out that the captain was having a route check from a training captain who had reduced power on one engine to make sure that the man being tested could cope. This is the sort of thing that happens to all multi-engined pilots on check rides, and so it should to make sure that they are competent, but preferably not with an aircraft full of fare-paying passengers who have not been warned. I may say that, looking around the aircraft when my heartbeat had returned to what I regard as normal, nobody else seemed to have noticed or, if they had, to be in any way concerned. As a final reflection upon flying with THY, it was usual for the passengers to applaud enthusiastically when the aircraft landed successfully, whether in appreciation or relief I was never sure.

I suppose that it was as a result of our activity in the Arab world generally that the Syrians learned about our new aircraft; perhaps the Egyptians had sounded them out as potential customers for the projected Helwan production line. However it came about, I found myself responding to a request to visit Damascus in order to discuss the Hawk with the air staff. Damascus was a difficult place to reach by air since at the time most airlines other than Air France regarded the whole area as a war zone with no attraction for tourists or business passengers. Thus I found myself in the front of a Caravelle of Air France approaching the eastern end of the Mediterranean when a sharp report rather disturbed my reverie. This was quickly followed by a steward shepherding me to the aft end of the aircraft. My immediate thought was that this was a hijack (very much in vogue at the time), and that my tranquil lifestyle was about to change, and not for the better. It was nothing of the sort; one of the cabin windows had cracked, causing the pistol-shot sound, and the crew were simply being cautious and moving the passengers as far away from the defective window as they could.

The visit, which was completely uneventful, caused me to reflect again upon the changing status of the United Kingdom in the Middle East. Many of the senior members of the air force staff that I met spoke good English and were graduates of one or other Royal Air Force training establishment. Many of the engineers had been at Henlow and the pilots had converted to the Meteor at one of our flying training schools. Not so with the younger men who, like most of their contemporaries in other Arab air forces had trained in the Soviet Union and at the same time, absorbed the political doctrine that had been fed to them. The contrast was stark and led to an uneasy atmosphere since the older men did not wish to be seen as too friendly.

I have no idea how much subsidy was required to allow the Royal Air Force to train foreign students but my experience was that every penny was well spent. The affection that most retained for Britain, the academic standard, their instructors and most of their fellow students was striking.

Back at base, the company demonstrator aircraft, No. 8 off the production line, was being prepared to the export standard that had always been the design aim. The RAF trainer was a good platform, and the standard required for flying and weapon training was fairly easily achieved, but we knew that greater range and weapon-carrying capability would enhance our prospects in almost every other market. A civil-registered military aircraft is not without problems as far as international travel is concerned and we sought, and were granted, the registration G-HAWK to go with the tail number ZA101. During transit flights we were able to file a standard flight plan since the aircraft carried advanced communication and navigation equipment, although air traffic clerks who had not seen the aircraft arrive were slightly surprised to read that there were two pilots aboard but no pax! We did not emphasise that the remarkable range of the aeroplane was in part due to the carriage of jettisonable drop-tanks, since this brought on the vapours in some parts of the world.

G-HAWK continued to work up at Dunsfold, carrying increasingly improbable warloads and showing a quite remarkable standard of serviceability. It seemed always to be available for flight and many visitors were taken flying, to their enormous pleasure and to the detriment of the test programme. Most of the development work was done by Andy Jones, with Jim Hawkins and Chris Roberts as back-ups, and all three evolved stirring demonstration programmes. Andy drew the short straw and was generally the one to fly visiting pilots on weapon-carrying flights. Many aircraft manufacturers had dummy weapons made for the purpose which appeared authentic but could in fact be carried by a child. This was apparent at the end of an air show, for example, when the public had gone home and the ground crews were packing up. It was quite usual to see a mechanic walking off with a "500 kg bomb" under each arm when only the previous afternoon the crowd had thrilled to the demonstration of load-carrying by the aircraft concerned. Not so at Hawkers. Our bombs were real in that they were genuine cases and ballasted to the correct weight and, all too often, without a workable jettison capability. Aware that sometimes weapons were not quite what they seemed, announcements of the clearance of heavier and heavier warloads were greeted with some scepticism in some circles. When the Egyptian Air Force came to fly they requested, reasonably enough, that they be allowed to watch the bombs being loaded and to fly the aircraft immediately afterwards. Since he had done it all before, Andy put the visitor into the front seat, and with five 1,000 lb bombs slung beneath the wings and fuselage, taxied for take-off. In this configuration it had been established that a lot of flap was needed to become airborne at a speed which did not impose an undue strain on the wheels, and he checked that it was properly set. The visiting pilot had flown the Hawk during the visit of 156 to Al Maza and, it was assumed, had retained some of his briefing from that sortie. G-HAWK gathered speed exactly as advertised, hauled off the runway and the man in front raised the wheels followed immediately by the flap! The little aeroplane was distinctly unhappy at having shed so much lift so quickly and a nasty accident was avoided only by the skill of the man in the back who flew low over West Surrey and quite a lot of Hampshire before establishing a reasonable rate of climb. This was only one of many incidents in which visitors were spared acute embarrassment, if nothing worse, by the skill of the company pilot who was accompanying them.

The aviation industry in Britain has a long and distinguished history, with names that are world-famous and rightly so. Most companies were founded by men of brilliance and vision who in the early part of the twentieth century could see the profound effect for good and ill, that aviation would have on world affairs. At the end of the second World War the companies had established a solid reputation for producing aircraft of their own – or sometimes somebody else's – design under the most trying conditions. Unfortunately, it soon became apparent that the impressive production capacity that existed was unlikely ever to be needed again; in short, there were too many aircraft companies.

Famous and respected names disappeared in the amalgamation into conglomerates of most of the companies. Some held out and continued to go it alone. Shorts was one, but the big hitters were divided into two groups, Hawker Siddeley and British Aircraft Corporation. I have met no one who enjoyed the shotgun weddings and the depth of feeling between the reluctant partners was clear years after the event. The engine companies suffered the same fate and with the same result, but there were fewer of them so the effect was less widespread.

To retain as much capacity as possible, factories traded part manufacture, and individual plants began to specialise in some aspect of production. Folland Aircraft for example became the experts on canopies and were never seriously challenged by any other part of the group. Factories which had aircraft "in service" were contractually bound to continue to make spares and provide repair facilities for years, and quite often it was not economical to transfer the work elsewhere so they stayed open when all common sense said that they should close. There was, in addition, the profound social problem of closing a factory which employed most of the skilled men in the surrounding area with no other place for them to work.

These worries were fortunately not my concern, but I was deeply impressed at the way the Company sought to resolve the very real problems in a fair and understanding way. When we acquired a different government they decided in 1977 that the industry amongst others should be in public ownership. The two groups would amalgamate and British Aerospace would be born, to take on the rest of the world's manufacturers. I do not know if it was a good idea or not but I thought that, where two groups had difficulty in keeping watch over their separate flocks, it was a mite ambitious for a single Government department to take on the whole lot plus, if I remember rightly, shipbuilding. All sorts of people with unfamiliar titles began to intrude into our affairs and, although we had always had a nominal liaison with a very small department, mostly concerned with the danger of us spilling state secrets to one of the Queen's enemies, we now had a full-blown department with several geographical sections running our affairs.

Another interesting aspect of the nationalisation was raised by one of my managerial colleagues when he invited me to join a staff association, the polite term for a Trade Union. I bristled at the thought and asked for what purpose. It emerged that the Minister had decided that he would consult only with Unions and Associations, and the directors of the Company were concerned that only by forming an Association could the views of the people who ran the industry be made known. I took his point and joined, although I was too often away to play any useful part in the association.

The Defence Sales Organisation that was created still exists, although under a different title. I imagine it was meant to parallel the systems operated by the United States, France and the Soviet Union, each of which had aggressive sales teams travelling the world with the full backing of their respective governments, in sharp contrast to the British manufacturers who succeeded *in spite of* our government. Any hopes that things would improve for us under the new system were soon dashed, as it became clear that appointees to the department were either time-servers or overconfident young men who were against the whole idea of selling arms to foreigners. We had no idea how our requests for clearance to visit countries to discuss our aircraft were handled but, on more than one occasion, the fleeting opportunity had gone by the time that the department responded. It worked exactly as anyone familiar with government departments would have predicted.

We were keeping the interest in Hawk alive in Cairo by frequent exchange visits showing teams of Egyptians how the aircraft were made in Britain, with Kingston and Brough teams assessing the facilities at Helwan for Hawk manufacture. At the same time we were constantly running across teams from Westland who were proposing local manufacture of one of their helicopters, I think the Lynx. The Egyptian engineers wanted to make a fixed-wing aircraft and were slightly scornful of the idea that they should make a simple helicopter. Defence Sales however decided amongst themelves to support Westlands. Since only one major project was likely to be launched and would absorb all the money, skilled manpower and factory space available, we were hopelessly divided in our efforts, and seen to be so by the Egyptians. I clearly recall the meeting in the Sheraton Hotel in Cairo at which we were told by the government men that our enthusiastic efforts in support of the Hawk were seriously inconveniencing Westlands and it would be better for all concerned if we desisted.

If some strategic decision had been taken in London that,whatever our policy was in the Middle East, it would be ruined if Hawk was manufactured in the area, it was not made clear to us. However, we all felt from then on that we were competing not just with the French and Americans for this hugely important contract.

Meanwhile, G-HAWK was continuing to expand the aircraft's capability in the light ground-attack role which was seen as vital to its promotion to the smaller air forces. By the beginning of 1978 it was ready to tour and we planned to cover Egypt and the Gulf States in one great sweep. Al Maza was again our destination Cairo airfield, from which we planned to fly the pilots provided by the Egyptian Air Force. The usual pattern was quickly established; while one company pilot, Andy Jones or Jim Hawkins, briefed and flew one man, the other company pilot was briefing the next to fly and so on. The representative flying training sorties were fully covered, with lots of spinning if the student was agreeable, because we knew that this was a serious weakness of the Alpha-Jet which they would fly at a later date.

Apparently satisfied that the aircraft would perform the training task to a standard higher than they had ever enjoyed before, the hosts asked that proof be given of our claim to carry five 1,000 lb bombs at low level to a target 160 nm distant, dash into the target at 475 knots and return at low level. We had planned for this and the bombs had been pre-positioned at Al Maza.

Our armourers loaded the weapons, watched with interest by the Egyptian airmen. The bombs were real and ballasted to the correct weight and, although our team was not greatly experienced with the special-to-type equipment, the whole operation was pretty slick. The five bombs occupied all the hard points on the aircraft so that drop-tanks could not be carried. It may have been this that prompted the air force to close the military airfields around the route so that lots of emergency diversions were available in case our claims were untrue! The sortie was uneventful, as we knew it would be;

we had, after all, done it several times before, and the aeroplane landed back with fuel to spare and still carrying the bombs. At the private debriefing with Andy Jones we learned that, watching from the back seat, he was surprised to observe men rushing to take cover as the Hawk overflew, since the aircraft was not exactly scraping the desert floor. It suddenly dawned on us that, seen head-on, the Hawk bears more than a passing resemblance to the A-4 Skyhawk with which the Israeli Air Force was then equipped. Our visit ended with a flying demonstration for the Government and Air Force VIPs and an evening reception at the Hotel Meridien. As is usual, in the foyer of the hotel was displayed a board showing guests which rooms were in use for which parties. I was only mildly surprised to see that our reception was being given by "Aerospatiale" – the French management obviously doing their best for our opponents.

The tour continued through Saudi Arabia (where instructors from the King Faisal Air Academy were flown) to Abu Dhabi, Qatar and the other Gulf States of Dubai, Oman and Kuwait. On the transit leg to Doha I had my first experience of G-HAWK with Jim Hawkins in the rear seat as safety pilot. I remember that I was not over-impressed with the ground handling; the aircraft was reluctant to taxy in a straight line, probably because of a slightly binding brake, and the tiny control column was not immediately comfortable. However these are nit-picks soon forgotten in the sheer pleasure of the performance and handling when in flight. We flew at low level and I switched on the gunsight to track a vehicle making its way along the almost deserted road between Abu Dhabi and Qatar. As we passed overhead and the driver became aware of our presence, I saw the vehicle swerve sharply as though we had provided a wake-up call!

The aircraft had an equipment container, carried on the centre-line station and shaped like a drop-tank. In this the crew could carry some personal effects to tide them over until the support aircraft caught up. I called Qatar approach at 30 miles and was given the most extraordinary clearance that I have ever heard, and never expect to hear again. After giving wind strength and direction, runway in use and pressure setting, the controller added: "You are clear to join – no minimum height." Jim was an enthusiastic low flyer and I ran in to break at what I considered to be pretty low level. As we approached the runway I heard him say that we could go lower, and felt a gentle nudge on the stick. Somewhat uncomfortably I stayed where he had put me, waiting for the scraping sound of the "gin bin" on the runway. After a good '5g' break which I felt, but which made Jim yawn, we landed and taxied quietly towards the reception committee. Allowing for the fact that he knew the aeroplane much better than I did, Jim's confidence in pushing me lower on the fast approach demonstrated the remarkable view from the rear seat which allowed the instructor to monitor every move made by the student. After leaving the Gulf, where the aircraft was received with tremendous enthusiasm, we made our way home through Amman in Jordan where we flew the Crown Prince amongst others.

During the tour, G-HAWK carried 42 pilots from 8 air forces and flew 78 sorties for a total of 67 hours and 30 minutes. No take-off was delayed by unserviceability throughout the tour and we returned to Dunsfold feeling pretty smug. As I was later to discover, remarkable though this seemed at the time for an aircraft which was only just in service, there was much more to come.

CHAPTER XXIV

AMERICAN PATROL

Things were moving on other fronts too. The revised, radar-equipped Sea Harrier was taking shape and an end was in sight to the apparently interminable discussions with the Indian Navy. Either or both of these events could have triggered the awakening of interest in the Harrier suddenly declared by the Peoples' Republic of China. For sound reasons, no member of our small marketing team was assigned to China, although strange stories of the place had reached us from Hatfield, where our old HSA colleagues had succeeded in selling some Trident aircraft. For example: the delivery of a Trident had been made, it was said by John Cunningham, and on arrival the aeroplane was in perfect working order although one VHF radio set was on the blink. The customer refused to accept the aircraft and it flew back to Hatfield to have the radio changed.

Keenly aware of the dangers of industrial espionage, the Hatfield teams never used the telephone for important discussions and were meticulous in checking their hotel rooms for evidence of bugging. One of the avionics experts was charged with clearing the room before team talks started and, having checked all the obvious places where a microphone could be planted, he lifted the rug in the middle of the room. With his finger to his lips, he pointed to the metal plate set in the wooden floor, reached for a screwdriver and started carefully to take it apart. He was only halfway through the operation when there was a crash as the chandelier in the room below fell to the floor. I repeat, I only heard these stories.

With the nod from our government, the Chinese approaches were taken seriously and it was necessary to have an experienced and senior man take over the supervision of the programme. My deputy was John Parker, a distinguished former RAF pilot with considerable experience of the Americas, his patch. Totally at ease with all comers, steeped in Harrier lore and virtually unshakeable, John was the obvious choice. Not a great deal was happening in South America at the time and the decision was taken that he should lead the company effort with the Chinese. Before he became totally immersed, however, he took me on a tour of the South American countries where something might happen whilst he was diverted, so that I could respond.

This run through Brazil, Peru, Argentina and Venezuela was my introduction to the area, rarely visited by serving RAF personnel, and well away from my day-to-day interests within the company. I was intrigued by everything that I saw, especially in Brazil, a hive of activity for a country allegedly bankrupt. The opportunity to meet the senior members of the navy and air force in Brazil was especially useful since I was to have further, rather unexpected, contact later on.

The Chinese interest in Harrier led to a great deal of activity at Kingston where documents were produced in Mandarin and films were dubbed in the same language. Parties of experts, led by John Fozard, Chief Designer (Harrier), with commercial and production men in the party, travelled in droves. They were shown Chinese aircraft factories with ancient MiG machines continuing in production, which nobody seemed to want, but which had to go on because there was no other work for the vast numbers of people employed. So many teams went to China during this period that not to have walked the Great Wall was unusual amongst the senior staff at Kingston.

I did not join in any of these trips but I happened to be on Dunsfold one day when a party of Chinese were visiting there. A man billed as the country's chief test pilot (although this may have lost something in translation) was due to fly G-VTOL, the two-seat Harrier, with John Farley. With typical ingenuity Farley, faced with the daunting prospect of flying an unknown, with no form and no English, in an aircraft which could turn round and bite, produced a series of cards with instructions written in Chinese characters to wave at his student if anything seemed to be amiss. It all seemed to work and nobody was hurt, which is the main thing.

At lunch the tiny, wizened man who was heading the group was invited to lead the charge on the buffet lunch set out in the senior mess. I may add that these buffets were gourmet feasts accompanied by some excellent wines, and every visitor that I escorted remarked on the quality of the food. The Chinese leader was given an empty platter and shown the curried prawns in a chafing-dish, the cold beef, pork, lamb and lobster, the vast array of salads and the fresh raspberries, strawberries, meringue and jugs of cream. He started with the prawns and continued around the tables putting some of everything on the plate, finishing with raspberries, meringue and cream. Nobody dared to point out that it had been intended to enjoy these delicacies in succession rather than together, and he proceeded to dispose of this mess with gusto.

As was I suppose inevitable with John Parker clocking up the air miles between London and Peking, the Brazilian Navy, which had been examining Harrier for years, suddenly required urgent attention because, they claimed, a Harrier purchase had been sanctioned and funded. In commerce I learned it was not done to express doubt at some of the wilder stories told by embassies, attachés and agents, and I therefore returned to Rio to track this one down. The Brazilians are charming people and the military are very professional. The C-in-C of the Navy was trying to preserve a capability for his old carrier which, through years of poor maintenance, could no longer steam fast enough to launch and recover modern aircraft. The catapults and arrester gear did not function and a vertical-landing aircraft was his only salvation. I could only agree with his analysis and sympathise with his aim. Unfortunately, I had no mandate to present him with aircraft without payment. There was no insurance cover (through the Export Credit Guarantee Department – ECGD) available for the sort of contract price involved, and after many hours of discussion we parted the best of friends, although both disappointed at the outcome.

The need for Brazil to maintain a powerful naval presence was not clear even in those days of the Soviet Union threat, but it was hinted that the United States, having budget difficulties of its own, was anxious for Central and South America to make a greater contribution to the defence of the area. That may well have been the case, but it is also true that admirals like ships, as air marshals like aircraft and generals like tanks and, when national times are hard, they are all disappointed.

This pleasant diversion had to end because decision time was fast approaching in Cairo. As a company we had done all that we could to prove the quality of the Hawk and we had no serious doubts that the flying evaluation of the only real competitor, the Alpha-Jet, would serve only to consolidate our position. I was in Cairo in case any of the Egyptian team wished to consult on some aspect of our proposal and was idling my time away in the company of Eric Smith, former CO of No. 1(F) Squadron, now the Rolls-Royce resident in Egypt. The French were operating from Al Maza as we had and, whilst we did not exactly haunt the airfield, we did spend some time near it whilst the evaluation was in progress. We did not witness the accident but we very quickly learned that, on one of the last planned sorties, the Alpha-Jet had suffered a double engine failure. Both pilots were alive following their ejection from the stricken aircraft but the Egyptian had been badly injured. Eric and I congratulated ourselves since surely this unhappy event must clinch the contract for the Brits. Not so.

A year or so later, after we had delivered the spares for their Russian aircraft and Rolls had an engine overhaul line running at Helwan, the Egyptians signed a contract for the Alpha-Jet. This was a superb illustration of the point hammered home to everyone involved in this project that the quality of the aircraft is just a small factor in the procurement decision. The other factors were dominant in Egypt without any doubt and, although we were desperately disappointed at the time, it may have been a blessing in disguise. When President Sadat signed the Camp David accord in September 1978, he was acting from the highest motives but his action was not universally acclaimed in the Arab world. The AOI partnership, which always hampered decision-making, was in reality very frail and the rich members were those least pleased by the accord with Israel. I do not know if the

French were ever paid for their aircraft but I do know that Westlands, who had landed a small contract, had to fight for their money.

In case it should be felt that all our efforts met a similar fate, I should record that nearly all the other nations that had evaluated the aircraft on the tour described earlier bought the Hawk. The exception, Qatar, which opted for the Alpha-Jet, has recently decided to replace it with the Hawk.

The Middle East had dominated my commercial life up to this point with a few interesting diversions that I have recorded. After the formation of British Aerospace we had expanded our marketing operations, recruiting some likely lads to share the burden and to allow us to give more time to each of the potential markets for the Hawk. After the Harrier, which many small air forces frankly did not understand, the Hawk was a straight-forward, high-performance, adaptable aircraft which conformed to all their expectations of a military jet. Where formerly it was difficult to be optimistic of say, Tunisia, being in the market for Harrier, it was a likely customer for Hawk to replace the MB.326 aircraft which they had had for years. I have used Tunisia as an example not in any derogatory sense but because our man in North Africa, Gordon Wilson, was based there. Years before, he had been the Hatfield aircraft expert in Beirut to look after the civil operators of Comets and Tridents. He shared offices with J.K. Brown and I had therefore known him for some long time. He raised the possibility of Algeria and Tunisia as military markets and, although both were seen as French satellites, it was thought worthwhile to visit them. By the time that an opportunity arose, Gordon had returned to Hatfield to head the HS/BAe 146 marketing programme and Peter Boxer had inherited the territory.

After a short reconnaissance of both countries to satisfy ourselves that the requirements for a flying demonstration were available (they were), visits were agreed. Andy Jones and Jim Hawkins arrived in Bizerte on 3rd November having flown direct from Dunsfold in 2½ hours. They were precisely on the arrival time agreed some months before.

During our short stay, five Tunisians were flown and Jim gave a demonstration to what seemed to be the entire Tunisian Air Force. I have mentioned earlier that Jim was an enthusiastic low-flyer and that he genuinely enjoyed demonstrations, which are not every pilot's favourite pastime. On this occasion the senior members of the audience were on the flat roof of a convenient building with a commanding view of the airfield. I usually had a copy of the demonstration programme showing the order in which manoeuvres would be performed, so that I could point out the high spots before they occurred. The final part of the sequence on this occasion was to be a fast low run before pulling up, rolling and joining downwind for landing using tail 'chute. Low I therefore expected, between the stubby radio masts on the adjacent roof I did not. The audience loved it but I have to say that Andy Jones and I exchanged glances more expressive than anything that we might have said.

For the short transit to Boufarik (I warned you that the name would crop up again in this journal), Peter Boxer was strapped into the back seat to gain some air experience in a military aircraft. Needless to say he thoroughly enjoyed it and managed to insert "when I was flying the Hawk" into most conversations in the next few days.

Andy Jones was reunited with Lt. Mostefa, his musical friend from the earlier Harrier visit. They flew a Hi-Lo-Hi mission profile in which the fuel economy of flying at high level is exploited to increase the distance that the aircraft can go before dropping down to low level 50 miles from the target for concealment from ground radars. After the simulated attack and low-level withdrawal, the aircraft climbs again to return to base. Andy said that Mostefa sang at high level and chased unfortunate camels at low level, so that the trip was not without interest. Perhaps because we had met so many of them before, the atmosphere could not have been friendlier and they threw a monster party for us the night before we left at which we were each presented with some very fine Algerian wine and fresh dates still on the twig: a happy visit which rounded off a busy year.

In the spring, following a lot of to-ing and fro-ing with McDonnell-Douglas, our US partners in the Harrier/AV-8 venture, and discussions with several other US manufacturers, it was decided to go with Macair in a bid for the new trainer for the US Navy. This was no lighthearted decision easily taken because it was known that whatever was selected would have to be deck-capable and, in its current form, that was not the Hawk. However, nothing ventured etc. The competition was run under strange rules which meant that we were not allowed to contact anyone in the procurement chain, sailor or civilian, but we were allowed to fly sailors and civilians who were "interested." With no one quite clear about what precisely this meant, we planned an extensive tour of navy and air force training stations in the hope of flying "interested" parties. Much of the advice on where to take the aircraft came from Paddy Harbison, a retired Air Marshal who had made a career out of exchange postings with the USAF and RCAF, and who was now our man in Washington. Leslie Tuck, the nominal bureau chief, offered his full support and provided an absolute ball of fire PR girl named Karen Woods to keep us pointed in the right direction. I travelled to Washington with John Nineham who was to be our crew chief on the tour and, with the fair Miss Woods, flew and drove to the seven flying stations that we would visit, and Andrews AFB Washington where the tour would start and finish. The itinerary was ambitious because we could not afford to miss anywhere that might serve our cause, including the headquarters of the USAF Training Command at Randolph AFB, San Antonio. This may appear to be gilding the lily but someone in Congress had offered his view that pilot training was pilot training, and all services should use the same aircraft. Even if the Air Force was not in the market for a new trainer, it would be to our advantage if they did not actively oppose a Navy procurement of Hawk, fearing that it might be foisted on them by Congress at some future date.

Karen had spoken to all the PR chiefs on the stations that we were to visit and we were warmly received. We trod the delicate path between seeking to influence those involved in the selection process and simply offering free rides to any one that fancied a flip. Mostly the Base Commander, OC Flying Wing and the training squadron commanders elbowed their way to the front of the queue and we seemed assured of an attentive audience wherever we went.

At Pensacola we had serious discussions with the USN flying training staffs who were interested in the training pattern that the Royal Air Force had adopted with the introduction of the Hawk, and their thoughts on the future as the Jet Provost was phased out. As is usual when airmen get together, normal English is lost in a welter of acronyms as approach and landing aids, flight instruments and aircraft performance are bandied about. The man with ultimate responsibility for navy and marine pilot training is, reasonably enough, Chief Naval Training (CNATRA, pronounced "Seenatra"). Miss Woods, who is no dummy, but who was slightly adrift in the technical and operational atmosphere, whispered in my ear that she knew that the famous singer and entertainer was well connected in many fields, but that she had not realised that his influence stretched as far as naval training. At each port of call she contacted the local radio and TV stations to arrange spots on their news programmes during our visit and helped us to arrange hotel accommodation and car hire. John Nineham and I returned to Kingston pondering anything that we might have overlooked but, by now, I had been responsible for so many tours that I had produced a comprehensive check list, and we had satisfied all the known requirements.

A month later, in June, we were back in Washington with our ground crew of six and a spares pack that fitted comfortably into a hired "U Move" mini-pantechnicon. The spare wheels and tyres for G-HAWK occupied most of the space with the special-to-type tools and personal tool kits filling up the corners. The van was also our technical office in which the aircraft service manuals and documents were kept.

The composition of a touring support party was one of the problems that I never cracked. Whilst at Dunsfold, G-HAWK had its own dedicated servicing crew who naturally knew the aircraft and all its foibles better than anyone else. After all, they had installed all the modifications, repaired every fault and fitted every new weapon that the aeroplane was required to carry. On one tour, the armament people insisted upon including two armourers in the party, having convinced someone that there was a serious health and safety hazard in having the work done by non-armourers. When the time came for the bombs to be hung on the aircraft, the experts battled away watched with wry amusement by the servicing crew who eventually showed them how to use the equipment. Unhappily, the power of the Unions was almost absolute and they saw overseas tours as a perk which should be shared between the entire shop-floor staff, and went to some lengths to ensure that all of them, suitable or not, were considered. This was to miss the point that the tour was an attempt to ensure continuity of production and the security of their futures (and mine). The party for the American tour was a mixture of keen new boys and veterans of earlier tours, and for most of us it was an adventure.

G-HAWK, flown by Jim Hawkins and Chris Roberts, staged through Reykjavik and Goose Bay and arrived at Andrews AFB at the forecast time. Apart from being weary after three long spells strapped into a small aeroplane, both pilots were fit, the aircraft was serviceable and after a brief inspection was available for flight.

Our first working destination was Pensacola, Florida, the home of US Navy training. Instructors and students, accustomed to the pedestrian performance of the T-2 Buckeye and the fuel limited TA-4, were excited by the high performance and carefree handling of the Hawk. Most of the instructors being flown arranged to meet a fellow instructor in a TA-4, "by accident," in order to carry out a crude comparative assessment of the two aircraft. After landing, both were expressing colourful amazement at the way the Hawk out-turned and out-accelerated the TA-4, and all this without apparently burning any fuel. We were gratified by this general response because these were aircrew representative of the intended users. G-HAWK kept going all day, flying any sort of profile that the guest pilot wanted, just being refuelled from time to time. Our ground crew kept out of the way and it was clear to anyone watching (and, believe me, there were plenty) that no servicing was carried out during the working day, and precious little after flying ceased. Sailors of all ranks were sufficiently interested to call on us to have a look at the Hawk and one was overheard saying that the aircraft was clearly brand-new and it was hardly surprising that it looked so fresh and stayed so serviceable. Jaws sagged a bit when they learned that it had first flown almost exactly 5 years earlier and had been flown intensively ever since, carrying out the most demanding tasks that confronted any new military aircraft.

The story was repeated at the naval air stations at Corpus Christi, Kingsville and Beeville in Texas, and rather less intensely with the USAF at San Antonio. Here we flew the Chief of Staff, a supremely nonchalant officer in the Gary Cooper mould, who gave the opinion that they could live with it if Congress forced it upon them. I interpreted this as a mild criticism of the aircraft's inability to go supersonic in level flight, an ability claimed by the T-38 which they currently used for advanced training. Over lunch I asked one of the staff how often supersonic flight was programmed in their syllabus, to be told that there was one 20-minute flight per student. It seemed a lot of fuss to make about a number on a dial, and a lot of dead weight being carried for one short flight, but it was none of my business and I kept quiet.

When our work was done, several of us visited the Alamo, the shrine to the frontiersmen that fought the Mexicans. I had not seen it before and my first impression was how tiny it was. Inside it is equipped for the tourist with a slide-show presentation and, of course, mementoes for sale. We tend to say in a rather snooty way that the Americans have no history, but in my experience they take tremendous pride in what they have and we should perhaps learn from them.

After San Antonio we moved to Meridian, Mississippi, another Navy station. It was here that we experienced our only malfunction of the tour. Jim Hawkins was airborne on a standard familiarisation flight when word reached us that he was having trouble in lowering the undercarriage. There could be all sorts of reasons for this to happen and, if all else failed, the wheels could be blown down using compressed air. However, this purged the hydraulic system and led to considerable remedial work to restore the aircraft to full serviceability. Jim of course knew this and, for reasons never explained, was aware that selecting down when inverted had been known to encourage reluctant wheels to drop. I realise that this defies all logic but he tried it and very slowly the wheels lowered and locked. After landing safely, the aeroplane was pushed into a hangar overseen by a chief petty officer of the old school who had seen every way that an aircraft could be rendered unserviceable. The offending undercarriage leg was removed and it was found that a seal, value 50p, had cracked and allowed the hydraulic fluid to seep away. Since we were unsure of the reason for the cracking I signalled Kingston asking for a replacement leg to be despatched immediately to Washington and hand-carried from there to us by one of the BAe office staff.

This failure was a bitter disappointment because Meridian was an important training base and, no matter how often we told our hosts that none of us could remember it ever happening before, there was bound to be some doubt in their minds.

Late at night, in the hangar where we had been left largely to our own devices, the veteran "Chiefy" came in to commiserate. We showed him our problem, admitted that we had no spare because the seal had never failed before, and told him of our recovery plan. He studied the seal for a moment and told us in a fine Southern drawl that it sure as hell looked like the seal that did the same job on the undercarriage of the TA-4. He went to his stores and produced one for us to measure; it was an exact fit and in no time at all it was installed and our defective landing gear was back on the aircraft. With some trepidation the hand pump was used to build up hydraulic pressure and there was absolutely no sign of a leak, not even any weeping around the new seal. Taking G-HAWK off jacks, we pushed it outside and ran the engine to apply maximum pressure to the leg and the seal was as solid as Gibraltar. We left it in place for the rest of the trip even though a replacement leg arrived via Concorde and Graham Weller of the Washington staff. The result of all this was that we lost only one planned sortie and were for ever indebted to an aged chief petty officer of the United States Navy.

Our final working stop was the US Marine base at Cherry Point, North Carolina. This was also the shore base of the AV-8A (Harrier) squadrons so that there were some familiar faces amongst the residents. The Marines are trained within the Navy flying training system so that the staff at Cherry Point are a mixture of sailors and marines. The thing that they had in common, aside from being sea-going, was a fuel gauge fixation in the TA-4 brought about by the high fuel flow and occasional, very indifferent, local weather. Quite often it was necessary to stop student flying because local storms were violent and there was insufficient fuel on board for the aircraft to hold until the weather had cleared. (This problem had been mentioned at Pensacola and reminded me of the Javelin in Singapore.) Most, therefore, were anxious to fly a normal training sortie, simulate a 'lost' procedure, recover to Cherry Point and check the fuel reserves. Jim Hawkins did this with several of his "students" and, having mystified one of them with the aircraft's apparent ability to fly without using fuel, asked if he would like to do it again. They repeated the entire sortie without landing and refuelling. I imagine that the story was given a fair airing in the Officers' Club that evening.

I flew the return leg to Washington with Jim Hawkins and it was uneventful except that, having arrived well ahead of our DC-9 escort, we were able to make a show of being fast asleep on the Hawk wing as they taxied past. The ground crew were not amused. When G-HAWK transferred to Dulles International in order to clear customs and immigration before returning to Dunsfold, our diminutive aeroplane looked to be in danger of being trodden on by its bigger commercial brethren that had it surrounded.

The statistics of the trip are a tribute to the aeroplane and all those connected with its design and manufacture, including of course our colleagues at Rolls-Royce. We were away for 30 days during which 100 (*one hundred*) guest pilots were flown in 108 (*one hundred and eight*) sorties totalling 118 (*one hundred and eighteen*) hours. For one who grew up with aircraft that rarely stayed fully serviceable for two successive days, it was an eye opening achievement.

CHAPTER XXV

I'VE HEARD THAT SONG BEFORE

The tension and turmoil which seem to be the natural way of life in the Middle East reached a distinct peak in the late seventies and early eighties. War and the threat of war was pervasive and, except in the Gulf, travel and communication generally were difficult. A.W. (Robbie) Roberts, who had supported me so ably on the Harrier tour to India, was now our Regional Executive and had chosen to base himself on Amman. Lebanon was a shambles and to live there was not only dangerous but stupid from a business point of view since no airline would fly in or out. Amman, though less than ideal, was therefore the best choice.

It was Robbie who had been in touch, asking if I would join him on a trip to Baghdad where we might learn something to our advantage. This seemed unlikely in the extreme to me but, since I had the most recent experience of the place – none of it very agreeable, I should add – I agreed. My old friends from Andover were both gone; Fahim Jalal shot by the administration as a spy, and Niamat Dilaimi who, after a chequered career which saw him doing time and then becoming Chief of the Air Staff, had died after suffering a brain tumour. However, during the long but ultimately fruitless negotiations for the purchase of 50 Hawks, I had met a lot of the current crop of aircrew, engineers and administrators, and I seemed best placed to investigate this new twist.

The air force had reserved accommodation for us in the Baghdad Hotel, which was a promising sign since anyone that the administration did not wish to see was simply denied a room. Such small things assume enormous significance to the person seeking to understand the way things work in Iraq. It was probably also the case that some, or perhaps all, of the rooms were bugged, which made it easier for the secret police to keep up with events.

Entry to the country was by night when aircraft from friendly countries were allowed to land between the hours of 10 in the evening and 4 in the morning. We arrived from Amman with the usual seething mass of people who were always present on non-specific duties asking for baggage tags (to save the weary traveller the bother of collecting his baggage, or offering accommodation, taxis and other services which fortunately I did not understand). At some airports these were genuine hustlers who would clear customs and immigration whilst the traveller stood around looking bored, but it was as well to know your man before entrusting him with your only safe exit from the country. Bypassing this enterprising but wholly redundant group, we made our way to immigration where, having the necessary visas, we were moved on to customs. The only thing in my briefcase that caused offence to the customs officer was the current copy of "Time" magazine which I was carrying. With the old-world charm for which all customs men are noted, he removed the magazine and dropped it to the floor to join a pile of others. No words were exchanged and I have no idea if the journal contained an article offensive to the regime, if "Time" was banned in Iraq or if the customs officer ran a bookstall on the side and was renewing his stock. On an earlier visit I had inadvertently found a foolproof way of keeping the customs' noses out of my business papers. Our Defence Attaché, a soldier, was there with a Scandinavian wife and young family and it was my practice whenever I visited to take bacon, pork sausages and salami, which they craved, and boiled sweets for the children. The customs man demanded to know the contents of the plastic bags and I told him. I have never seen a chalk mark made on a bag more quickly.

Back to this visit. We were met by a staff car and conducted in silence to the hotel, where a note awaited saying that we would be collected at 10 for a meeting at Air Force HQ. At the advertised time we were collected and whisked away to the familiar, dusty, dilapidated building opposite the statue to Ali Baba, a juxtaposition I always thought appropriate.

Several old friends were present, and after the exchange of courtesies and introductions to the civilians present, I poised my pen over my notepad and waited to hear the story. I fully expected that we would be asked to requote for the supply of some Hawks at a keener price and with better delivery than we had offered in our previous discussions. I was surprised then when one of the civilians explained the idea that had come to him, that Iraq should manufacture the weapons (including aircraft) that it needed, and become independent of those unnamed foreigners that were seeking to bankrupt the nation. This had a familiar ring and, with Cairo fresh in my mind, I outlined the size and cost of the project that they were considering. No problem, I was told, but they would need some help to get the thing started and that was where we came in. It was made clear that the French and Italians would also be invited to submit proposals.

I was not sure of the current British government relationship with Iraq for, although I had told Defence Sales that I had been invited to Baghdad and received their clearance to go, my visit could only be exploratory since I had no idea of their plans. Playing for time, I congratulated them on the scheme and told them that I was sure that the company would be pleased to assist. I pointed out however that it would occupy some of our best brains for a long time, thus diverting them from their normal duties, and that, assuming a project cost of £100M sterling, a reasonable fee would be 1%, that is £1M. Without blinking the leader said: "Done." This rather threw me because I had been hoping that he would say that a committee (there's always a committee) would have to consider this; meanwhile I would return

226

to Kingston to see if HMG and, even more importantly, British Aerospace were interested in such a venture.

There was nothing more we could usefully do but we had made no arrangements to get out and we were faced with a lengthy wait for an airline booking. Because air travel was so difficult, enterprising Jordanians were offering a taxi service between Baghdad and Amman and we saw an old American Ford with Jordanian plates parked outside the hotel. We found the driver, told him to wait, packed, paid our bills and left. I have to explain that fuel prices were much lower in Iraq than Jordan and the drivers had learned to maximise their profits by installing a 10-gallon drum in the boot of the car and filling it before leaving Iraqi territory. On entering our chosen vehicle it was apparent that the driver had already filled his overload tank because the car smelt like a garage (shades of the Dakota ferry to Australia). The journey between capitals takes about 12 hours, assuming no punctures, hijacks or serious accidents. We agreed a price, £100 sterling, and set course. I theorised with Robbie that our driver had probably just made a delivery when we spotted him outside the hotel and, after a very quick turn-round, had picked up another fare prepared to pay well over the odds to get to Amman. It must have seemed like Allah's will.

Sitting uncomfortably in the back of the ancient vehicle I was watching the driver's eyes. After our early animated conversation the eyelids were starting to droop and, having already observed that we were in a desert version of the Monte Carlo rally, I became distinctly uneasy. It was clear that we could not engage the driver in non-stop conversation for 12 hours and as we neared the Iraqi border, where we stopped for a cup of tea, we invited him to curl up in the rear seat while we took it in turns to continue the drive. We handed back to a wonderfully refreshed driver on the outskirts of Amman and, although he took our fare, he had the grace not to press us for a tip.

Thus began the project which the Iraqis called SAAD 25. It was even more ambitious than the Egyptian scheme since Iraq had no industry of any kind and, through mismanagement, had gone from being the fruit and vegetable garden of the area to importing food. Nevertheless, there were some very bright young men associated with the scheme and, given a certain amount of political and financial stability it might have worked, although not in the time-scale that they wanted and envisaged.

A large team of BAe and other industrial personnel assembled to produce a plan for this huge enterprise, fortunately being paid under the study contract. Progress was made during many visits in spite of the difficulties in extracting fairly basic information from the SAAD 25 sponsors. For a long time they would not disclose the proposed site of the factories, nor whether power and water supplies existed, nor if there was an airfield from which to fly or a railhead to use for the delivery of heavy major items of equipment. It was pretty much the nightmare to be expected.

With many of the basic planning problems overcome and with the French and Italians no longer being mentioned, we were invited to take G-HAWK to Baghdad to allow its evaluation by the Iraqi Air Force. None of our hard-earned data on performance and handling in very hot conditions was acceptable and we were offered no choice but to go to Baghdad at a time of their choosing, when the tarmac would be melting and there would be no shade.

That time happened to be the early part of August 1981 and we had barely inspected and fettled G-HAWK after our triumphant tour of the US before we were off again to Cyprus *en route* Baghdad. The plan that had been agreed was that the Iraqi Air Force would position one of their pilots at Akrotiri, the sovereign base, to fly in our aircraft on the Cyprus–Baghdad sector. This was a sort of hostage in reverse plan which we hoped would give us some protection from the Iraqi air defences. On reflection, it offered the regime a marvellous excuse for getting rid of an unwanted officer, but that thought occurred to me only after the event. Our escort aircraft was a BAC 1-11, owned by the company and usually employed on carrying personnel to and from the continent for various joint programmes like Tornado and Airbus. It was speed-compatible with the Hawk and we were able to travel as a pair, each keeping a watchful eye on the other.

A further agreed procedure was that we would be met by Iraqi fighters and escorted to Baghdad. This worked to perfection and we were intercepted by a pair of MiG 21 aircraft as we left Turkish airspace north of Mosul and led into the airport. They behaved impeccably and if there had been any temptation to show off, it was resisted.

On landing, the thermometer occupying the only piece of shade for miles around was reading +48°C. Our flying programme for the week in Baghdad was based on two sorties a day general flying, and also armament work, including gun and rocket-firing as well as bombs. It was probably a combination of the extreme heat and the heavy loads being carried that led to the failure of the undercarriage leg to lower properly, exactly as it had in Meridian, Mississippi, only this time the other leg. A replacement was hurried out to us, fitted overnight and the aircraft was ready for flight the next morning. When the post-mortem was held into these two totally uncharacteristic failures it emerged that the two legs had been returned to the manufacturer for overhaul when G-HAWK underwent inspection before departure for the USA. There can be little doubt that the seals had been wrongly installed during reassembly and if one leg or both had collapsed on landing the entire future of the Hawk would have been quite different: the twentieth century equivalent of the missing nail in the horse's shoe.

The Iraqis were extremely hospitable, reinforcing my long-held view that when they turn the running of the world over to the airmen, all will be well. We were taken to an old caravan staging post which is now a very smart restaurant (assuming it still exists) for an endless series of courses of dubious-looking dishes. We were all seasoned travellers and had learned, many the hard way, to regard all food with deep suspicion, but it is extremely difficult constantly to refuse things prepared with obvious care and presented with great charm. It was not a jolly evening and there were some wan faces the next morning. That was beside the point – the intentions were good and when things went wrong in Kuwait some years later I wondered how many of those present that night were involved.

We departed, vowing eternal friendship, with some optimism that we had convinced them that they should select Hawk for their project although I was deeply aware that I had felt the same about Egypt, in spades.

In the end it all came to nothing but not without great efforts on our part to make it work. Factories were designed, and associated power installations with layouts to gladden the heart of any production engineer who has laboured for years with everything in the wrong place. Although this project failed, somebody showed them (unless they were self-taught) how to make chemical and other nasty weapons, as we discovered later.

As we were in the area we responded to a Jordanian request for further demonstrations and moved across to Amman. I flew the Hawk, with Chris Roberts in the back, while Jim Hawkins checked out in the 1-11. I had flown a couple of the transit legs during our American tour and as I became more familiar with the little aeroplane I began to like it more and more. It is exactly the aircraft that a young aviator should meet in training. Enough performance to make it exciting, forgiving of piloting errors but just demanding enough to keep the student on his toes: super little jet.

Our organisation now included men who had visited the area with me and had established their links with our regional men and company agents. After 12 years of almost total dedication to the area, I looked forward to moving on to more general management of the marketing effort. There had been some remarkable changes in that time, especially in the development of international business which led to the opening of luxury hotels where earlier, primitive best described the available accommodation. Air travel was easy with the oil wealth of the region attracting the international carriers and forcing them to provide excellent service. The countries that felt that the standards were still not good enough started their own, very efficient airlines. Aside from the ever-present political instability, it had become a much more pleasant place, although not half so much fun.

CHAPTER XXVI

MIDNIGHT SUN

Our intensive efforts of the last few years were beginning to bear fruit with important, though small, contracts for Hawk being signed in widely-separated parts of the globe. Finland, to everyone's surprise, was the first, and showed the way that future business was likely to be done.

After an extensive, not to say exhaustive, examination of the contenders, the Finns selected the Hawk over all the aircraft which we saw as the competition in the trainer/light attack category. The Finns did not enjoy complete freedom of choice in their selection since they were bound by treaty to have an approximately 50/50 balance of Soviet and Western aircraft. It followed therefore that we were faced with the Czech advanced trainer L-39, (probably at a give-away price), as well as the usual Alpha-Jet, MB 339, CASA 101 and SAAB 105 which, although ancient, was the product of a Scandinavian neutral and attractive from that point of view.

The commercial innovation in this competition was that whoever succeeded had to provide industrial participation and compensation to the full value of the contract. No one quite understood this initially but Colin Chandler, who was the Managing Director at Kingston at the time, applied his enthusiasm to the problem. Every major British company that might be in the market for anything that was, or could be, made in Finland was approached and asked to record any purchase against our compensation commitment. I remember that British Rail needed a new car ferry which was manufactured in Finland and counted as part of the deal. Bentalls, the multiple store in the heart of Kingston, staged several "Finnish Weeks," promoting Finnish products with great success. Agreement was reached with Valmet, the government-owned company, on the manufacture and assembly of Hawk components, the value of which was also counted as part of the package. I worked for a time on promoting the new Finnish basic trainer, the Leko 70, in Egypt where its simplicity of manufacture was appealing, and other applications, crop-dusting for example, were possible. There was a tremendous company effort to meet this novel contractual requirement and it was done.

I have to admit that I had never thought deeply about Finland and, when confronted with closer association with its people and its industry, I assumed that it was probably rather like Eastern Germany before the wall came down. I pictured grey and grim buildings occupied by dour people who, with the highest suicide rate in the world, did not get a great many laughs out of life. It was thus without much optimism that I made my first trip to Helsinki to meet our in-country representatives, Machinery OY, the Finnish Air Force and Valmet.

As the Finnair DC-9 broke cloud at about 200 feet on the final approach to Helsinki, and I could see the snow-covered ground below, I wondered, not for the first time in a long life, if I had made a terrible mistake in undertaking this visit. My spirits sank further when, after disembarking, I walked with my fellow passengers to the terminal building over frozen tarmac and in semi-darkness: it was about 2.30 pm. Inside it was warm and clean and my spirits lifted when a very pretty immigration lady stamped my passport and welcomed me to Finland. At customs, the man asked to see my passport but paid no attention at all to my luggage, and waved me through with a further welcome. This was already far better than I had expected.

In the arrival hall two men were waiting, one very tall, the other less so. They were Heikki Timonen and Bjorn Schoenberg of Machinery OY and they had both turned out to welcome the first-time visitor. Both spoke fluent English (I was to discover that most Finns speak some English), and both destroyed for ever my preconceived ideas of the dour Finn. I have never met nicer people and, after many years of visiting each other, I have never been in better company.

Staying in a modern hotel, just outside the city centre, I could see from my room many of the lakes which are a feature of Helsinki and indeed the entire country. In the morning under heavy skies and never quite light, the ducks came whistling in looking for a handout from residents and visitors who fed them. The lakes were frozen, of course, although the ducks seemed not to know it and, in trying to land, went skating along the surface in true Disney fashion. It was hilarious to watch and a source of endless amusement.

My first meeting of the day was to be lunch at Machinery OY company offices to meet the Chief of Air Staff and some members of the Valmet organisation. With this in mind I had asked Bjorn where I should go to get an impression of life in the city. He recommended that I should visit Stockmans, a big department store, to look around, but to be sure to go there by the tram which stopped in front of the hotel and would drop me off at the store. I was not wildly enthusiastic about the recommended mode of transport but, willing to try anything, I did as he had said. The tram arrived and I observed that, in order to retain the internal heat, only one door opened. I entered clutching a handful of coins which I offered to the conductress, at the same time enunciating very slowly and distinctly, "Stockmans." She looked at the money and said in perfect English: "Single or return?"!

On later visits I was able to see a lot of the country and it reminded me of western Canada, a land of lakes and pines. Winters were similarly harsh but they prepare for them and life goes on normally although not much hiking is done in the winter.

Some years after this, we began discussions with SAAB when they were wrestling with their JAS multi-role project, not because the design was causing them difficulties but because the budget was under constant attack. Enthusiasts will know that the Swedes have produced some of the most innovative fighter aircraft ever seen, peculiarly suited to their natural and military environment. The budgeting problem was that they required the new operational aircraft and wished also to replace the SAAB 105 trainer which was becoming uneconomic to keep going. We produced a plan to allow them to use a Hawk as the basic airframe into which they could install the clever avionics to meet the multi-role task. As an alternative, if they wished to preserve their total neutrality for their combat aircraft, we proposed that they buy some Hawks to meet the training task which we would ask Valmet to make for them in Finland. This would provide further work for us (we made the major components) and for Valmet, which would gain us credit for any further Hawk buy that Finland might make. It was a good scheme which deserved to succeed but the Swedish government, which was going broke under its welfare programme, told SAAB and the air force that they would have to start another life-extension programme for the SAAB 105.

The Swedes had become aware that the new US Navy training programme broke with tradition in ground training by using computer programmes, which are cheap and last for ever, instead of men who are not and do not. The theory was sound: an instructor would introduce a training subject and the brightest part of the class would grasp it immediately. The less gifted would be able to select the programme on video and watch it as often as they wished until they were up to speed. All this against a background of an annual graduate pilot requirement of more than 600. In Sweden, where having an air force at all is constantly debated, the annual requirement for new pilots is less than 50, but they wanted to see if they could amend the US programme to suit their needs.

Always anxious to help, we arranged for an expert from Douglas at Long Beach, California to visit Stockholm with us, to fill in the detail of the electronic plan. His name, engraved on my heart, was Jay Swink and he was without doubt an expert. I explained the general philosophy of the programme to the assembled air force and procurement agency (FMV) personnel and handed over to Mr Swink for the technical bit. I realised after five minutes that I had not the faintest idea of what he was talking about and, looking around the audience, the same seemed to be true. He produced visual aids of what appeared to be wiring diagrams for a space probe and explained in excruciating detail the function of each microchip. At the end of it all he asked if there were any questions and, unlike the staff college where someone was primed to get the ball rolling, there was stunned

232

silence. Afterwards, over coffee, I asked some of the Swedes if they were clear about the systems but they all seemed too numb to answer.

CHAPTER XXVII

SOUTH AMERICAN WAY

The formation of British Aerospace brought some surprises, indeed shocks, to some of us at Kingston. Bear in mind that until now we had regarded BAC as one of our most serious competitors, prepared to go to some lengths to hamper our efforts in support of their own. Where we had Harrier they had Jaguar, when we won the new trainer contract from the British Government, it was against a BAC submission of a new aircraft and, in desperation, a re-engined and upgraded Jet Provost. Our relationship with our counterparts is best described as uneasy since we shared a common test-flying background with some of them whom we had known for years. Even the company amalgamation did not make things easier since we each had aircraft to promote, frequently in conflict.

The most startling change, though, became apparent in the upper echelons of the company where new, and different enough to be strange, personalities began to appear. One of them, who rejoiced in the title of "Managing Director, Marketing" was Alec Atkin, a large Peter Ustinov look-alike. The Hawker Siddeley Aviation marketing director was also an Alec, Alec Watson, and when we both happened to be at Kingston he would call and have a cup of coffee and go over the ground. We rarely travelled together because he was not keen on the Middle East and for reasons given earlier, I had been tied to the area for years. However, there were indications of serious interest in Harrier for the navy, and Hawk for the air force, in Brazil. John Parker was still extending his knowledge of Chinese food and it fell to me to accompany the two Alecs to Rio and Brasilia. At the time Air France operated Concorde to Rio and the plan was to travel together using this service, an experience I expected to be wholly pleasurable after more hours than I care to count in other commercial aircraft. Our departure was planned for a Sunday and in the middle of the preceding week the pilots of Air France went on strike. I lost my chance to fly Concorde, but gained another sound reason for not trusting the French! As it was I left on my own, a day earlier than planned, in order to be on the ground when my two directors appeared.

If you absolutely have to be hot and sticky, there are worse places than the Copacabana Beach Hotel in Rio which, as the name suggests, is on the beach looking out over the South Atlantic ocean. The hotel is old, and no worse for that, but some services are unreliable – the air conditioning for instance. The climate is very like Singapore and when it rains be in no doubt that you will get wet. I was gazing out of my window watching volley-ball and soccer being played on the beach when the heavens opened. Normally-dressed people walking along the promenade stopped, removed their outer clothing which they popped into a plastic carrier bag, and continued walking in their bikinis/swimming trunks as though it was the most natural thing in the world. It was such a practical idea that I wondered why I had never seen it anywhere else.

I met the two Alecs at the airport when they arrived by 747, both looking slightly shot at; it is after all a long way from Gatwick. I should say at this point that neither is of athletic build but Alec Atkin had informed me that he was dieting and following a strict eating regime. When he went missing the next morning as we were called for our inter-city flight to São Paulo, I looked for him all over the place before finding him in the snack bar, putting away the most enormous hamburger. It had been clear the previous evening that he was paying scant attention to the alcohol limit allowed by his diet chart and I stopped worrying about it.

We were going to São Paulo to meet the directors of Embraer, the national aircraft factory, to discuss Harrier and Hawk, and a work-sharing arrangement if either or both was selected for service in Brazil. It was difficult not to be impressed by the successes already achieved by Embraer. Just a few years before, Colonel Osirez, a serving officer in the Brazilian Air Force, had been pointed at a green field site and told to start making aeroplanes, and he had done exactly that.

Our visit did not start well. We were scheduled to meet the chairman at 11 o'clock but we were intercepted and told that something had occurred at the factory to force a postponement until 2 o'clock. Alec Atkin was not best pleased, and his irritation showed. Alec Watson and I, on the other hand, had lots of experience of delays in meetings, sometimes for good reasons, sometimes for reasons which defied belief, but which had to be accepted with good grace.

We pitched up at the appointed time and were met by the Production Director who explained that he would give us the factory tour and that subsequently we should take tea with the Chairman. I have explained before that I never found it easy to be moved by a jig-borer, routing or pipe-bending machine but I have learned to show enthusiasm for what is often the pride and joy of the man operating it. Alec Atkin by contrast knew about the machines in a factory and became quite animated when shown some of the very modern kit on display. I took this as a sign that his earlier grumpiness was now forgotten.

I knew that there was a strong Italian influence in the factory (their chief designer was Italian), and Embraer had part-manufactured and assembled the Macchi MB.326 aircraft currently in use in the air force. I was more surprised by the numbers of young people of Japanese origin in the design offices and on the shop floor. The overall impression was of youth as against the greybeards commonly found in our factories at home, and a dynamism usually missing in our work force. Remember this was before the Thatcher revolution had really taken hold.

Sure enough, at the end of our tour we were led to the very simple offices of the Chairman where we met Colonel Osirez, who welcomed us in a most gracious way, explaining that a fire in the factory had occupied his full attention at the time of our planned meeting in the morning. We underlined the purpose of our visit, congratulated him on the standard of the workshops and emphasised our confidence that Embraer could cope with any joint venture that we might conclude with Harrier or Hawk. I began to feel that it had all gone rather well as we rose to say goodbye and depart for the airport. As he shook hands at the door, Alec Atkin, with all the charm of an unmade bed, remarked how well they were doing and if they ever wanted to become involved in modern technology the Colonel should feel free to contact him. I am not the cringing type, but I cringed. I should not have worried however; the Colonel thanked him and added that if we wanted to make aeroplanes on time and on cost we were free to consult *him*!

After a couple of days in Rio meeting the navy chiefs who were based there, we flew to Brasilia to meet the Chief of Air Staff to seek to interest him in the Hawk as a trainer, and in our new single-seat version as a ground-attack aircraft with limited air defence capability. The Brazilian dream is of a combat aircraft which is efficient and easy to fly but above all has a 1,000 nm radius of action, that is, can deliver an attack 1,000 miles from where it took off and return. Roger Dabbs, chief designer Hawk, had come up with a scheme which allowed the single-seat Hawk to meet this demanding criterion. We had already flown overload tanks which effectively doubled the fuel capacity of the aircraft. With these we could carry two bombs or rocket pods, plus the gun on the centre-line station, and Sidewinder air-to-air missiles on the wingtips over the required radius using a Hi-Lo-Hi profile. Our difficulty was that the single-seater existed only as a full-size plastic model and nobody had shown any great interest in the concept, although I am delighted to see that the situation is now changed. The audience listened with polite interest but I am certain that they wanted a glitzier solution to their operational requirement.

It could be said that our trip was not a great success, something that it is necessary to accept on so many occasions, but it was not quite the end. A party of air force representatives visited us in England to learn more about us and our aircraft but there was to be no happy ending.

Since we were "in the area" so to speak, we moved on to Caracas where the former BAC had good contacts following the sale some years earlier of the Canberra to the Venezuelan Air Force. Our man there was Sir Raymond Smith whose life-style was, to say the least, enviable. The meetings that he arranged were social. He threw a splendid, well-attended party at his house at which everyone that mattered was present. Problem was they were all in civilian clothes and impossible to separate by service, name or rank. The following day we were taken horse-racing in the elegant private box style, and again we met lots of charming and important people. Neither function advanced our cause as far as I could see but perhaps this is what very senior members of a company should do, leaving the serious work for their staff.

CHAPTER XXVIII
SWINGING SAFARI

Extreme torture would not be required to make me admit that Africa is not my favourite continent. Some parts are better than others but, taken in the round, I would much prefer to be somewhere else. Michael Mendoza, who looked after the area, was a bright and diligent young man and he had well-earned success with the Hawk in Kenya and Zimbabwe. As always, the contracts were won after long and at times painful campaigns.

The Kenyan Air Force was equipped with some Hunters which were long in the tooth when they bought them and which required experience and tender loving care to keep serviceable. Although we had put a resident engineer there to help and advise, it became clear that they were waging a losing battle in seeking to keep them going.

It was one of the rare occasions when we were positively encouraged by the Defence Sales Organisation to step in and offer the Hawk, and Michael Mendoza had his first sales success. The order for 12 aircraft was the first since Finland although for reasons never made clear we were not allowed to publicise the sale. When the aviation press got wind of it we were allowed to confirm that "an unnamed African country" had indeed bought some Hawks. The fact that aeroplanes by their very nature are to be seen flying and further, tend to be painted in national colours, made a mockery of the secrecy surrounding the contract but it was never admitted.

As was customary, a company service engineer accompanied the new aircraft to assist in the routine maintenance and to advise on spares procurement. Crates of spare parts and technical manuals went by sea to Kenya as part of the original contract, the items selected in accordance with the known usage in the Royal Air Force.

A few months later, messages of increasing urgency were being received at Kingston, forecasting grounding of the aircraft unless certain spares were received. This was puzzling since the spares pack-up that accompanied the delivery of the aircraft contained the spare parts now said to be needed. As far as could be established at Kingston, all was in order. The shipping documents were complete, the shipping agent confirmed the loading and the ship had not sunk *en route*. Armed with this information and the supporting documentation I accompanied Michael to Nairobi in order to help him in clearing the company's name.

At headquarters we saw some very unhappy equipment officers who had been unable to explain to their superiors how this had all come about, and who were initially unmoved by our assurances that we had neither misled nor swindled them. When the paper chase finally ended, the spares, hundreds of them, were discovered filling the customs sheds in Nairobi waiting for the import duty charges to be raised and then paid: by whom was not clear. For some time the customs sheds were used as a technical store and as a spare was needed it was traced to the appropriate crate, removed and handed to the Air Force; it was a monumental mess.

When normal relations resumed between the British government and the newly-independent Zimbabwe, what had been the Rhodesian Air Force looked to its traditional suppliers for help. Spares were required urgently for their Hunter and Canberra aircraft as well as replacements for aeroplanes that had been damaged or lost during the period of Unilateral Independence. Our government was not keen to deal directly with the white Zimbabweans who formed the majority of the airmen and we were the go-betweens.

The Royal Air Force had a vast array of spares for the dwindling Hunter force and most of the urgently required parts were quickly supplied. Finding the replacement aircraft was more difficult since the company had none and had to ask the Ministry if they had any second-hand Hunters for disposal. One of the requirements was for a two-seater and the Zimbabweans had therefore asked for a T.7. They clearly did not realise that "T.7" precisely defined the aircraft to RAF standard with a 100-series Avon engine. We bought one on their behalf from RAF stocks together with the two or three single-seaters that were required. The Ministry must have seen this as a wonderful opportunity to dispose of some old bangers that had been around for some time; I remember that one had a starboard mainplane that was fatigue life-expired.

Before the aircraft were collected and flown to Africa, the documents were scrutinised by the leader of the purchasing commission back in Harare. A furious signal arrived at Kingston on a Sunday morning, I remember, calling into question our integrity, not to mention our parentage. The paper work had revealed that a RAF T.7 had a "small" engine where clearly the big-engined export version of the aircraft would have been preferable in their climate. My reply was carefully composed because, through a simple misunderstanding, the entire project was now in jeopardy. In the end all was well due in no small measure to the fact that they liked and trusted Michael Mendoza.

The Hawk drama was to continue in Zimbabwe. The first four aircraft were delivered to Thornhill, the main operational base, in mid-1982. Within days all had suffered varying degrees of damage when explosive charges were thrown into the engine air intakes. Three Hunter aircraft suffered a similar fate in the same attack and were completely destroyed. Three of the Hawks were repaired eventually, but the fourth was written off.

The extraordinary outcome of this was that some of the senior, white, members of the Air Force who had negotiated and fought for the new

Hawks and the replacement Hunters were thrown into jail. They were held for a long time in appalling conditions and forced to confess that they were behind the plot. Those of us that had dealt with them knew that this could not possibly be true and sent a stream of guarded letters to them whilst they were in captivity in an attempt to bolster their morale. To our enormous relief, when they were brought to trial the case collapsed and the ridiculous charges were dismissed. Most no longer live in Zimbabwe.

When the single-seat Hawk variant was taking shape, I took a small team to Harare to tell them about it and to see what ideas they had for an aircraft which would appeal to an air force like theirs. Inevitably we wound up discussing their Hawks, listening to their complaints and hearing changes that they would like to see. Generally they were very happy with the aircraft and the only modification that had their universal and heartfelt support was the installation of armour plating under the front seat. it seemed best not to inquire into the uses to which the Hawks were being put that had led to such a popular demand.

My old friend Robbie Roberts was now resident in Harare and took me into the hills at the week end to play some golf and look around. It is a spectacularly beautiful country blessed with just about everything to make life agreeable. Long may it continue that way.

At the end of this visit we made our way to Botswana to see Ian Khama, son of Seretse. He is an aviation enthusiast and welcomed our discussions on both versions of the Hawk. We were joined by Duncan Fraser, now retired and living in Nairobi, so the stories went on long into the night. Their small air force will develop, and an aircraft like the Hawk is just what they require for a painless expansion into a greater operational capability.

I had an interesting insight into the tensions which exist all over the area and which can be aggravated by the most unlikely things which just do not occur to the visitor. The hire car that I collected on arrival was a run-of-the-mill French or German vehicle, not remarkable in any way as far as I could see. It came as a surprise therefore to be stopped in transit from the airport to the hotel to be asked for papers. I produced my passport and the car hire documents, which were examined before I was waved on. Within half a mile I was stopped again by an armed patrol and again asked for my papers. After the same routine I asked if there was something wrong to attract so much attention. It was pointed out to me that the hire car had South African plates, which made the driver a prime suspect. Each time I ventured out in that wretched car the same thing happened so that I was not unhappy to leave for Johannesburg.

I have no burning desire to return to South Africa but I am glad to have seen it once. Johannesburg is a magnificent city although there seemed to be an air of unease about it, with very large men patrolling the hotel and its

RAF Tengah. A Hunter GA.9 of 20 Squadron.

A typical Canberra profile. This is a B.6.

A Javelin 9 (with re-heat). Ours developed "centre-line closure" with catastrophic results for the Squadron Commander.

The author with the boss of the visiting F-100s. We subsequently flew together.

The sad end of the Harrier demonstration in Al Ain. The thud was heard around the Gulf.

The Company demonstrators G-VTOL and G-HAWK returning from the Paris Air Show.

The author pointing out the source of the noise. Harrier demonstration for President Amin.

The author roughing it in Manila.

surroundings, for example. This was before the ending of apartheid and some very unpleasant things were going on in the cities and even more, in the countryside. It is not easy to be optimistic about the future.

CHAPTER XXIX

EAST OF THE SUN

From time to time the Japanese evinced an interest in the Harrier, and this seemed to quicken when the Sea Harrier appeared. A certain logic could be seen in this since their self defence forces were meant to be exactly that, and they were forbidden any equipment that could possibly be used in an aggressive sense. The radar-equipped Sea Harrier operating from a small ship could be used for picketing duties, protecting mainland Japan beyond the range of domestic radars. The surges of interest seemed to follow exercises in the area involving the US Marine Harrier wing and it could just have been that watching their aircraft in action inspired the Japanese. For whatever reason, there was to be a British Exhibition in Tokyo which would feature our aviation industry with the Harrier as its centre-piece. Peter Martin, who normally looked after Japan, was deeply involved in the Philippines and it fell to me to represent the company at the planning meeting preceding the exhibition.

This produced several firsts for me. During my personal piloting days my boss had Japan within his operational area and often threatened to visit but, since the country was firmly under American control, I suppose he saw other places as being of higher priority, and we never went.

I had slept through a mild earthquake in Tehran, but experienced a genuine shake during my first Tokyo visit which gave me deep sympathy for anyone who lives in an earthquake zone. It was not a pleasant experience even though it was barely reported the next day because it was so low on the Richter scale.

I did not attend the exhibition but it must have generated some interest because an invitation arrived to address the MTI, the Japanese equivalent of the CBI, as well as the Navy and Air Self Defence Forces.

British Airways flies the Great Circle route to Tokyo with a stop at Anchorage, Alaska and, although this is the quickest way to get there it still seems to take for ever. Entering the transit building for the brief stopover, I saw the Kodiak bear, standing upright with front paws extended, that dominated the foyer. It crossed my mind that any passenger that had availed himself too freely of BA's hospitality might receive the sort of shock from which it is difficult to recover.

Met on arrival in Tokyo by our local representatives, I was given a crash course on the etiquette of visiting cards in Japanese society. They also presented me with three boxes, each containing 50 cards, with my name in English on one side and Japanese on the other. Such a quantity seemed like a lifetime's supply but I was assured that I should need them all. They were absolutely right, as I quickly discovered at the MTI briefing when each of the 40 or so in the audience bowed and handed me his card as he entered the presentation centre, receiving one of mine in exchange. I do not know the origin of the custom (although it looks faintly 'Victorian Britain'), and I see no harm in it, but how it helps the visitor I am not clear. The Japanese characters on the cards meant nothing to me so that I was unable to correlate card and person when I examined them subsequently.

The presentation was tiresome because I had long since ceased to use a script when talking about Harrier; as the slides appeared, each acted as a trigger for the explanatory words that went with it. I had not realised that an interpreter would be present and would require a word-by-word script for translation and delivery. For earlier visits by the company (and the Royal Air Force who had demonstrated a Harrier in Japan) we had produced the short films which supported the briefing with Japanese sound track. These were used to augment the information already given by showing, for example, how the exhaust nozzles were moved by the pilot to achieve slow or hovering flight. These may have been a life-saver because try as I might I could not help diverting slightly from the script from time to time as I left the lectern to point to a significant part of the slide on display. The unfortunate interpreter lost the place on several occasions; when emphasising that the final attack phase was at low level I used the phrase common amongst airmen, "down amongst the weeds," which required a long explanation from me in front of the largely bemused audience. They were all very polite and apparently attentive but I felt at the end of it all that it was rather like a "Round Table" luncheon day when the secretary arranges a guest speaker to help fill the gap between lunch and tea.

At the headquarters of the Self Defence Forces, the card ceremony was repeated before we got down to business. This time there was no interpreter and I assumed that those present were English speakers, probably following training in the USA. To a large extent this was probably true but, to a Westerner, the Japanese facial expressions of understanding, puzzlement, amusement, boredom and irritation are not easily distinguished, so I really did not know how much of what I transmitted was actually received.

As was usual, at the end of the meeting I invited questions and, as is not unusual, there was an uneasy silence. Finally one of them asked how much the aeroplane cost. I answered and the supplementary came back: "Does that include the engine?"!

It now seems unlikely that Harrier will ever appear in Japanese markings but I would not be shocked if the AV-8B, the upgraded version, caught their attention because of its largely American development and production.

The Philippine Air Force was commanded by General Vincente Piccio who, as a Major, had been an Andover student during my teaching stint there. His air force was badly equipped through nobody's fault, it was just that the economy could not support large investments in military hardware, especially when they lived under the defence umbrella of the United States. Politically though, the continued presence of US forces in the Philippine Islands was becoming intolerable and Vic Piccio, who had the ear of President Marcos, was anxious to obtain some modern and affordable aircraft. They had serious insurgency problems in the north and the everlasting preoccupation with "threat" from Malaysia which had haunted them for years.

Peter Martin had done a splendid job in preaching the Hawk gospel and, when the single-seat variant took shape with its increased operational promise, he needed support.

I had been to the Philippines in my earlier life, staying at Clark AFB in singularly uncomfortable Quonset huts and living mostly on ice-cream. This time was very different. Peter, as a regular visitor, had lots of leverage with the management of the Peninsular Hotel and I found myself cossetted in one of the world's great hotels. It had been General MacArthur's headquarters before his hurried departure, and after his rather more famous return.

After long and exhausting flights to the Far East, usually arriving in the early morning, I found that I was able to work until lunch-time when physical collapse became imminent. The best solution by far was to have a couple of dry martinis followed by a light lunch and a snooze, which set me up for the evening. Accordingly I ordered a drink in the bar, and watched the Filipino barman pour the Beefeater gin into the shaker. He then took the bottle of French vermouth and, without removing the cap, shook it over the gin. I was about to tell him that I wanted it dry but not arid, when I observed that a small hole had been punched in the metal cap allowing minute quantities of vermouth to escape. Never try to tell a professional how to do his job.

General Piccio summoned his staff to hear all about the single-seat Hawk and, probably because he was there, they listened. It is difficult for people stuck in an aviation time-warp to appreciate fully the progress that has been made, much of it in very recent times, in the capabilities of small military aircraft. Some of the equipment that could be installed in the Hawk was quite new to them and variations of the same questions were asked to try to understand inertial navigation, forward-looking infra-red and laser ranging. The General, a man after my own heart, saved his questions for the golf course where we could discuss freely and without embarrassment. The golf course belonged to the Philippine Air Force and I am happy to say that I am a lifetime honorary member.

244

The Marcos regime had just about run its course and collapsed spectacularly soon after this, although I disclaim any responsibility. Another promising prospect disappeared overnight after a great deal of work by a lot of people but I had learned to accept that this was not unusual.

Making my way back from Manila I had arranged to meet Frank Bebbington in Brunei in order to talk to the young air force that was being developed there. The pilots were all expatriates, mostly British but with some Australians and New Zealanders for good measure.

Twenty years or so earlier, I had taken General Walker (C-in-C Far East Land Forces) there in a Canberra, to try and find out what the hell was going on after all communication with Singapore had been lost. There were rumours of an Indonesian invasion, but nobody knew for sure what was happening. It was a dismal place, with continuous rain, and my memories of it were not especially cordial. What a change. Where previously I had left as soon as my aircraft had been turned round because the limited tented accommodation was fully occupied, this time I was conducted in some style to a Sheraton Hotel. I have stayed in better, but it made a tent appear distinctly shabby. There was evidence of enormous wealth everywhere, most spectacularly the palace of the Sultan which is of indescribable opulence.

The young aircrew assembled for the Hawk briefing the next morning were attentive and intelligent, all anxious to learn more about the aircraft. This was in sharp contrast to so many other occasions when it was fairly clear that those present would just as soon be somewhere else. I found it very rewarding to speak to lively groups with a genuine thirst for knowledge who, at the end of it all, felt that they had really learned something that would be useful in the future. Normally, we drifted away from the narrow topic of Hawk and discussed just about every aspect of military flying, information that they absorbed like a sponge. It came as a bit of a shock to me to realise that I was becoming a sage, long enough in the tooth to be listened to with respect and interest. I had to remind myself that in my early twenties I had regarded airmen in their thirties as getting on a bit, whilst those in their forties were quite certainly over the hill. I was fast approaching 60, the age of those former squadron members who would entertain dining-in nights with tales of the Indian Frontier in the 1920s and '30s and whom we regarded with sympathy as amiable old buffers who had absolutely nothing in common with us.

CHAPTER XXX
HAPPY TALK

In compiling these reminiscences of the non-military part of my aviation life I have concentrated on the major events at the expense of many less important but nevertheless satisfying and agreeable diversions.

For example, visits to Madrid to meet the Fuster brothers, Ricardo and Nicholas who represented Hawkers and then British Aerospace in Spain, and who played a major part in the introduction of the Harrier into the Spanish Navy. The brothers are identical twins which confused my first meeting with Nicholas, some time after I had met and grown to like Ricardo. I was changing aircraft at Madrid on my way back from Rio de Janeiro when I saw Ricardo heading for the departure area to board an aircraft. I rushed over to shake hands only to have this rather startled man shy away from me as though he had been confronted by a madman. It was of course Nicholas and when I had finished explaining he shrugged and said that it happened all the time.

Both men had been sent to England in their youth to complete engineering apprenticeships in order to continue the family business. At some point they had realised, as Spain began to prosper after the turmoil of the civil war and then the second World War, that there was a future in introducing manufacturers to customers. By the time I met them their interests were broad and they were very prosperous. Just how prosperous was made clear when, as we prepared to leave his office to go to lunch, Ricky produced a small automatic pistol from a drawer, checked that it was loaded and put it in the waistband of his trousers. We left the building and climbed aboard a decrepit old motor car which bore honourable scars from a long life in the traffic of Madrid. It was much later that I discovered that this was his own anti-hijack routine. Where a smart car might have attracted the attention of kidnappers, the old banger certainly did not, and if anyone expected Ricardo Fuster to submit without a fight he was in for a nasty shock. At the time, holding prosperous businessmen to ransom was a popular Spanish pastime.

I enjoyed many days in his company, not only in Spain but also at the Farnborough and Paris Air Shows where he was a regular attender. We talked at great length to the Armada about the advanced Harrier, the AV-8B, in the hope and even expectation that an order would be placed with us rather than McDonnell Douglas. It did not happen because I think that the US Government offered terms that we found impossible to match.

The Spanish Air Force became seriously concerned at their standard of flying training as they considered new aircraft in the F-18 category exhilarating by anyone's standard and especially for a young man trained on the modestly performing CASA 101 Aviojet. This led to lots of meetings with the Air Force and the presentation of a paper on the Hawk at a well-attended symposium in Madrid. This was well received and we talked at length to the CASA company to see if there was some way that they could become involved in manufacture of the aircraft, but it proved impossible. Whilst having sympathy for their budgetary and employment problems, we were experiencing the same difficulties with a diminishing amount of work to be shared between our own factories.

With the Hawk established in service in Finland there were frequent reasons to visit the Valmet factory at Halle, where the aircraft were assembled and tested, and this was always a pleasure. They were all so enthusiastic about the project and interested in the efforts that we were making to launch their little Leko 70 trainer in other markets.

We had formed a close association with the Minister of Defence, the Chief of Air Staff and many other members of the military services and all were keen for us to see our aircraft in operation. This led to visits to the units in Pori, Rovaniemi and the Kerala wing in Lapland to talk to the operators, listen to their complaints and encourage them with trophies for the best student in various training categories. I visited many places where people not only remembered but talked at length about their experiences in fighting the Russians during the early days of the war. Although the content of most of the stories was grim, they were always told in an entertaining, not to say humorous, way. It is difficult for the Finns to ignore their very large neighbour and it must be said that industrially, it would not be in their interest to do so, but it is clear that there is not much love lost between them. Bjorn Schoenberg told me the story of a boundary dispute between the two countries which led to a slight modification of the border. Unfortunately the new boundary line would bisect the home of an old trapper and he was invited to opt to stay Finnish or become part of Russia. After some thought he said that he would stay as part of Finland because the winters were less severe. This seemed to me to say all there was to say about the relationship between the two countries.

When the last Hawk was handed over to the Finnish Air Force, a small party of us went to Pori to meet a former FAF pilot who had flown Hurricanes and had been converted to the type by Sir Dennis Smallwood, retired from his post as C-in-C Strike Command and now adviser to British Aerospace. A painting of the aircraft was commissioned and presented to the veteran by Sir Dennis in a hangar packed with several generations of airmen. It was quite moving to see how touched he was by the gift, and fascinating to listen to the tales of the war that he had to tell.

At their Halle factory, Valmet, which is a semi-public company, had pilots on loan from the Finnish Air Force to carry out their development flying. They had cleared the Leko 70 trainer for service with their own air force and, although the numbers required were never going to make them rich, the contract had held the design and production teams together. The trend towards turboprop basic trainers was becoming evident with the emergence of the Pilatus PC.9 and the Embraer Tucano (we even considered a turboprop installation for the Hawk to meet the basic training role), and Valmet felt that this was the sort of project that they could tackle with confidence.

As the design got under way the lead pilot, Major Paavo Janhunen, attended the course at the Empire Test Pilots' School, now back at its original home at Boscombe Down. We saw him often during his year in England and his natural charm and modesty captivated us all. He returned to Finland to resume his task at Halle, concentrating now on the turboprop Vinka which was approaching first flight. This was accomplished successfully and the process of data gathering began, slowly at first with careful checks after each flight, and then more quickly in the race to have the aircraft cleared for service.

At some point in the handling programme it all went disastrously wrong and both aircraft and pilot were lost. This had a devastating effect upon Valmet, the Finnish Air Force and those of us at Kingston and Dunsfold who had known Paavo. We asked our friends at Machinery OY how we should react and on their advice we commissioned a handsome gilt cup for annual presentation to whoever in the air force or industry was judged to have made the greatest contribution to flight safety. I went to Helsinki to present the cup to General Merio, the Chief of Air Staff, in a sad and very moving ceremony. Because many of those present would have only marginal English, the stalwart Bjorn Schoenberg asked that I fax my speech to him so that he could translate as we went along. I have always found eulogies difficult as the balance between respectful praise and the more light-hearted aspects of the character of the deceased is hard to strike, but critical if the tone is to be right. Should anyone be interested, I can tell him that the most carefully crafted eulogy loses a lot when the deliverer has to pause after each sentence for a translation which, he hopes, accurately reflects what he has just said. I had complete faith in Bjorn and I believe that my tribute was well received. Only when it was over did General Merio introduce me to Paavo's widow who had been in the congregation throughout.

A much happier event was the presentation to Bjorn of the OBE awarded for his services to British exports. The ceremony took place in the British Embassy with many of his family and friends present and, as is customary on these occasions, he listed all those that should have been rewarded rather than himself, but secretly he was delighted.

On each and every occasion that I visited Finland I asked myself how I could have even entertained the thought that they were a dour and unhappy race. In winter certainly they might have seemed subdued, but no snow-bound city is much fun for the inhabitants or visitors. I loved the place and the people and never missed an opportunity to visit.

At one stage it was convenient to combine trips to Finland with quick darts into Sweden to check on progress on the very ambitious JAS project. The consortium involved included SAAB, of course, for the airframe, Volvo for the engine and Ericsson for the advanced avionic equipment.

I suppose because the future of the project was so uncertain, and to keep their options open, the Swedish Materiel Procurement agency (FMV) invited us to look at the facilities of each company. If they were forced into a collaborative project through economic circumstances, it seemed that British Aerospace would be on the short list of potential partners. (In the short term this all seemed to be wasted time but, when the go-ahead for the JAS (Gripen) aircraft was given, the manufacture of the wing was entrusted to BAe.)

Together with Ted Pincombe, one of the Hawk design team, I spent a most enjoyable week or so in Stockholm, Gothenburg and Linkoping having a look at aircraft design and manufacture, Scandinavian-style. The Swedes are a pretty relaxed race it has always seemed to me, although their governments over the years have discovered the hard way that the good socialist ideas which we all applaud have to be paid for. When taxes seem to have reached a ceiling and still more income is needed, the instinctive political reaction is to savage the defence budget. In neutral Sweden, which has adroitly avoided close links with any international defence groupings, the cry goes up the loudest. The defence ministries have a difficult case to argue and any major project is under constant scrutiny. Things are made worse by the Swedish insistence that any defence equipment that they sell, to very carefully chosen customers, shall not be used in anger. This can be seen to be inhibiting.

Each of the factories that we saw was dining-table clean, which came as no surprise, but the method of working and the conditions at SAAB and Volvo came as a severe shock. The practice has now become common but in the mid-eighties it was revolutionary. There was no recognisable production line, but small teams worked on whatever they were making until it was completed, and the product was identifiably theirs. Morale was extremely high, sickness was minimal and each employee had an acute sense of achievement.

The factories were also an eye-opener. Most were carved from solid rock and, I should guess, were impregnable to conventional weapons. The subterranean roads and rail tracks for the movement of minor and major assemblies made a deep and lasting impression on me.

I had never visited Austria for business or pleasure until, against my advice because I could see absolutely no profit in it for us, the decision was taken to accept the invitation from the airport authorities in Graz to demonstrate a Hawk at the party to celebrate the 50th anniversary of the airport's opening. This rankled with me because we spent enough time away from home, *and* company money, pursuing slim prospects of sales and I could see no merit in adding to our burdens with quite hopeless excursions. As was usual for such a trip it was prudent to check what we were letting ourselves in for and, together with the trusty Michael Mendoza, I set out to preview the place and its facilities.

All the usual requirements were easily met and the air force liaison man, responsible for participating visitors, could not have been kinder. He agreed that we could have a rehearsal slot and showed that the programme was tightly scheduled in a very professional manner.

He was at some pains to make clear that our team, along with any others taking part, would be housed and fed at their expense. Not unnaturally I asked where this would occur as we required transport unless the accommodation was local to the airfield. We were advised to rent some cars since we would be staying some way away "at a place with lady monks." His English was not much better than my faltering German and I had to admit to total bafflement. We made all the necessary arrangements and returned to Kingston to admit, somewhat ruefully, that there was no good operational reason why we should not go to Graz, although I persisted in my view that it was a pointless exercise.

The usual tussle started when it became known that the trip was on, as the lads in the hangar decided how many tradesmen would be required to look after the aeroplane, which would fly from Dunsfold to Graz, carry out a ten minute show rehearsal before landing, display for 10 minutes the next day and return to Dunsfold. The answer that they came up with was crew chief plus five. In reality we could have gone without ground crew because the pilot could carry out the pre-flight and turn-round, and with two of us on the ground to receive and despatch him it would have been all too simple. If anything had gone seriously wrong with the aircraft, the proposed six men, carrying no tools or spares, could have done nothing anyway, and if spares had to be flown to us then so could men. In vain I urged the Managing Director to cancel the whole thing unless they would agree to, say, two men, neither of whom would do anything. I lost.

We travelled out the day before the event was due to start and, after collecting our hire car, met our liaison officer to assure him that the game was on and that the Hawk would arrive at the advertised time the next morning. The leg from Vienna to Graz was flown in a small commuter aircraft "without facilities" as our American cousins have it. In consequence, after several reviving cups of delicious coffee, I needed the loo and was directed to the adequate, but not elaborate, prefab on the military dispersal. I mention this only because above the trough was a half tin can fashioned into an ashtray and above that a notice which read, in German: "Please do not throw your cigarette butts into our urinal, and we promise not to pee in your ash trays." Who said that they have no sense of humour?

There was nothing more to do at the airfield and we asked to be directed to the accommodation provided for our stay. We were led to the village of Seggau, high above which was a convent with a part of it converted to a back-packer's hostel. The Savoy it was not. Each of us was allocated a cell, little changed from its original design, and exquisitely uncomfortable. Even worse, on the three mornings that we were there I found myself in a race for the bathroom with several half-naked female hikers!

The highlight of the show was the arrival in a Mystère 20 of Niki Lauda, former world motor racing champion and clearly local royalty. The Hawk performed immaculately as always and the Austrian aerobatic team, flying 8 SAAB 105s, scared the life out of me with their enthusiastic but not terribly well-coordinated display. The Hawk required fuel and oxygen, of course, and the screwdriver attachment of my Swiss Army knife performed admirably.

The Canadians have always offered training to NATO nations and, although the RAF no longer sends students, it does provide the occasional flying instructor. The unified Canadian Forces, which have become prominent in global peace-keeping, have also sought to consolidate and expand this training function, and why not? They are good at it and they certainly have the clear airspace which makes the job much simpler. Looking to the future, their Chief of Defence Staff had called on us at the Paris Air Show to ask for Hawk data and a visit to Ottawa to brief his staff. Our de Havilland (Canada) man became very excited about this and I arranged to go across to see them and talk about the aeroplane.

The visit was unremarkable. The highly professional audience was undemanding even if it took me some time to get used to the olive drab uniforms which they all wear. Thus passed a very pleasant couple of days in late summer, and I greatly enjoyed the feeling of being amongst friends.

There was one strange thing however. On arrival I had headed for the "Four Seasons" hotel where our man had made a reservation for me. It is a swish, modern place of international standard and I looked forward to some rest after the flight from London. At reception I was completing the registration form when the young man, seeing my Surrey address, asked if it was my first visit to Canada. I explained that I had been there several times, and even in Ottawa where, more than 40 years before, I had stayed in the "Bytown Inn." He informed me that I was staying there again because this was the site of the old Bytown Inn. *Plus ça change . . .*

CHAPTER XXXI

WINGS OVER THE NAVY

Our tour of American bases in June 1981 had been a great success but it was not until later in the year that it was announced that the McDonnell Douglas/BAe proposal for a modified Hawk had been selected to meet the new trainer requirement. At this point the rules of the game changed and there was a frenzied exchange of visits between the technical and financial staffs of the two companies as well as visits from Navy Project Officers charged with watching the customer's interests.

The announcement, which caused great rejoicing to us at Kingston, was less popular with some of the US manufacturers whose bids had failed. Grumman, traditional suppliers to the US Navy, employed a lot of people from the New York constituency of Senator d'Amato and the Senator tried hard to show that the selection process left a lot to be desired if it resulted in a partially foreign bid succeeding. The fact that the McDonnell Douglas Corporation was an even bigger supplier of aircraft to the USN, and would lead the consortium which planned to produce the Hawk, finally told, and the House and Senate gave their approval. This was an enormous act of faith on the part of the US Navy since it could be seen with half an eye that the deck-capable Hawk would bear only a passing resemblance to the aircraft flown by the Royal Air Force. There were obviously other wheels within wheels and our political relationships were very strong at the time but nevertheless, it was a major achievement by the company, following as it did the sale of Harrier to the US Marines.

The paperwork required to support the proposed design changes, costings and production plans comprised many volumes and must have absorbed a fair part of the annual output of a Finnish paper mill. One complete set of the submission documents stood more than a metre high and the demand for copies seemed endless. Anyone who nurses the belief that we have bureaucracy gone mad in Britain should study some other countries, like India and the USA. Happily, this was all someone else's part of ship and, although I was interested, my closer involvement was deferred until the spring of 1983. Acting on advice from McDonnell and our own people in Washington, the decision was taken to return to the capital with G-HAWK in order to fly the civil and military VIPs involved in the programme. I confess to personal doubts about this scheme because to fly a VIP in the relatively small, uncongenial environment (to those not used to it) which is a military aircraft has two possible outcomes. If he/she likes it, you have made a friend and supporter. If on the other hand he/she is sick, the post-flight report is likely to be less flattering. I was quite wrong to have worried.

The aircraft was scheduled to arrive in Washington on 29th April and, as is usual, the support team went ahead in order to ensure that all the things that we had arranged on our preview were in place. On the Navy side of Andrews AFB we had a parking slot for the Hawk with easy access to a hangar in which our spares and servicing documents were stored. Lt. Cdr. Steve Songer, our liaison officer, had arranged some office space for us and we had a corner of the VIP Lounge in which to store the flying clothing for use by guests who did not have their own. This was also the briefing room where pre- and post-flight interviews were carried out, often against a noisy background of admirals awaiting flights to all parts of the continent and some to rejoin ships using the carrier on-board delivery aircraft.

Partly to impress, but also to make the fullest use of our time there, we had asked the US Navy to programme five flights a day, each of approximately one hour. Miss Karen Wood had again been assigned to us by the Washington office and, exactly as before, had the entire US Navy contingent eating out of her hand. Not only did she check the continuing availability of the people scheduled to fly with us but she also provided a constant supply of donuts and coffee for guests and crew alike.

The guest list included 14 admirals and 3 senators as well as naval captains and marine colonels in the total of 50 to be flown in 10 working days. It was interesting for me to see how many civilians connected with the procurement system indirectly, as budget controllers or aides to members of Congressional committees, had fought their way on to the list. In one or two cases I am sure that the name of the boss or departmental head had gone forward in the first place, to be switched at the last moment to the person who actually flew. It was a successful ruse and I am sure that everyone gained from it.

Our two company pilots were Chris Roberts and Taylor Scott, who shared the flying. Whilst one was airborne, the other was briefing the next guest, and so it went on through the working day. As a souvenir of the flight, each participant was presented with a British-made pewter tankard with a rampant lion handle, neat but not gaudy and well within the financial limit placed on unsolicited gifts that American officials may accept. After the flight, the company pilot autographed the tankard using a tiny electric drill. The tankards had all been flown into Dulles International in order to clear customs and the only problem that we had came from an unexpected source. The articles were properly described on the manifest and, although customs seemed uninterested, an officer of the Food and Drug Administration confiscated them. The reason given was that the lead content was not defined and could present a health hazard to anyone using one of the vessels! This difficulty was overcome when the dedicated public servant concerned was invited to take a sample tankard for testing and another for his personal retention. We heard no more.

We were all accommodated in a Holiday Inn motel at Camp Springs, almost opposite the main entrance gate to Andrews AFB. It was adequate, although not one of the chain's finest. Its main disadvantage from our point of view was that it did not offer breakfast at the time the crew needed it, that is about 6 o'clock in the morning. Our first guest was scheduled to arrive before 7 for briefing ahead of the first launch of the day at 8 o'clock. An all-night diner down the road solved this problem and became the BAe early briefing room during our stay.

The flying programme was tight enough for us all to value a night's rest and I was not best pleased when a hammering on my door wakened me at 1 o'clock in the morning. The range of possible emergencies was so wide that I dared not ignore it, even had I been able to. The motel had a curious electricity-saving device which connected the safety chain on the door to the on/off switch. This ensured that the air-conditioning was not left on in an empty room for example, since to leave the room the safety chain had to be removed, thus severing the electricity supply immediately. Up to this point I had regarded the system as a thundering nuisance since, on my return at the end of the working day, I usually had my hands and arms fully occupied with briefcases and papers and was impatient of the need to install the safety chain in order to switch on the lights. On this occasion however, I was relieved that, in order to see, I had to leave the safety chain in position. A very large Afro-American wearing a bobble hat which covered a lot of his face was asking me something which I could not decipher, at the same time peering over my shoulders in order to see if anyone else was in the room. I politely regretted my inability to help him and shut the door. I mentioned the incident to the receptionist the next day, and was told off for not calling the desk when it happened because it sounded like the mugger that had been bothering guests for some time; it caused me to reflect how much things had changed in the southern states over 40 years.

In order to accommodate the pilots and engineers we took the aircraft to Patuxent River, the Navy Test Centre, for one day during our stay. There is a dummy deck painted on one of the runways so that deck landings may be simulated, and this provided an insight into some of the demands for changes that were being made. Where the very low drag of the Hawk makes it such a good performer, Navy pilots like lots of drag for carrier landing and found our "airplane a bit slick for the deck." Many design changes later they have lots of drag on the T-45, the aircraft that entered US Navy service. A very tall member of the staff looked vaguely familiar as he made his way over to speak to me. His accent was certainly not American and I was momentarily baffled since he clearly knew me. He introduced himself as

Chris Wheal – former RN pilot – and it suddenly clicked. He was the ETPS student forced to jump out of the Hunter, the accident which I had investigated some 15 years earlier. It was his height that had foiled my immediate identification but of course he was in hospital when I met him and I had never seen him standing up!

At the end of our second working week, Andrews was having its annual Open Day when, we were given to understand, it was usual for a quarter of a million people from District of Columbia and the adjacent States to attend. Aircraft which were due to participate caused some interruptions to our programme as the airfield was closed to allow them to rehearse. The Thunderbirds, the United States Air Force demonstration team, were usually the highlight of the day but, on this occasion, there was a change in the script.

By pure chance the Red Arrows were touring the United States at the time and had therefore been invited to take part in the Andrews Open Day. They used their arrival as a rehearsal and brought the station to a halt as work stopped, and everyone watched the immaculate display which is the trade mark of the Royal Air Force team. Where the Thunderbirds were all rush and noise, disappearing from the view of the audience for quite long periods, the Arrows moved as a unit, always in sight so that the smoothness of the formation changes could be admired. Not for the first time, I was proud to be associated with them, however remotely.

Since the professionals were giving a demonstration of the Hawk, we were not required to fly, although Chris Roberts as a former Red Arrow could have filled the bill. Instead, our aircraft was part of the static display within a roped-off area inside a hangar, loosely patrolled by navy and company personnel. At least that is how it started. We had not allowed for one of the less attractive aspects of the young American male which is to defy any suspicion of authority. We did not want people crawling over the aircraft for the obvious reason that they might cause damage, and for the perhaps less obvious reason that the ejection seat remained armed and would have spoiled someone's day if it had been activated. When the first youths were seen ducking under the protective rope it became clear that a constant guard was required. After the crowd had dispersed at the end of the show, and G-HAWK was being recovered, several empty soft drink cans were found in the engine exhaust pipe, thrown there by spectators frustrated at not being able to get into the cockpit, I suppose.

The weather throughout the day was beautiful and remained so for the reception given by the Embassy in the evening. It is a nice building with lovely grounds and, showing much more consideration than ambassadors are often given credit for, both aerobatic teams were guests. As is always the case, they got along famously as might be expected of two groups of pilots, probably the élite of their age group in their respective services. They were all flanneled and blazered but the Thunderbirds were easily distinguishable by the brutal haircuts which they sported – if that is the right word.

When it was all over, the flying target had been exceeded and we had flown 53 guests rather than the planned 50, for a total of 55 hours and 40 minutes. The aircraft had not missed a beat in that time and, with its mission accomplished, the drop-tanks were refitted and it flew back to Dunsfold via Labrador and Iceland. The fact that all this was accepted without comment is in itself remarkable.

With the Hawk now firmly sold, I could foresee no further need to visit the United States since the AV-8B (Harrier Mk. 2) was essentially a McDonnell/Douglas project with British Aerospace acting as subcontractors and consultants, a rather sad reflection in itself. Of course, those of us dedicated to the V/STOL concept maintained a close interest in AV-8B and, together with several others, I listened in on a briefing by the Macair team. The much bigger wing on the new aircraft is made of carbon fibre and I was fascinated to hear about the manufacturing process and the further applications that were being considered for this new wonder material. Thinking back to my former experience I asked what snags were likely when the aircraft moved from the gentle hands of company personnel to the rather more basic handling by marines in a hurry. What, for example, if a mechanic dropped his tool kit on the wing (I've seen it happen many times)? With a metal wing a patch may be rivetted on; what sort of repair could be done if the bonded surface of a carbon fibre composite wing was broken? The Macair presenter said: "You change the wing, sir." Even then, a wing was a 5-million-dollar piece of kit and I must say that I felt some unease.

My reason to return had nothing whatever to do with Harrier or Hawk or any derivatives thereof, but a quite different vertical take-off project of which I was vaguely aware, having read about it in *"Aviation Week."* This was the tilt-wing V-22/Osprey, exercising the minds of Boeing-Bell. The concept was not new, indeed I had seen the Canadian vehicle years before at Uplands, Ontario. This time, it was said, the US Navy and Marine Corps had identified a need for a Chinook-sized, heavy-lift VTOL aircraft for the assault role. Helicopters are alright for area intervention where no one is shooting back but, speed-limited as they are, they are highly vulnerable. For reasons which are not self-evident, British Aerospace decided that we should be involved in this research programme and, together with some of the designers, I was despatched to see what it was all about. It seemed likely to me that if the Americans had any ambitions to sell the device in Europe, they would need a partner in exactly the same way as we had to have an

American partner to succeed in the USA. Whatever the case, it seemed like an interesting scheme and I was delighted to go.

The old Vertol division of Boeing is based in Philadelphia and that was the first port of call. We arranged to stay in an hotel on the airport really for convenience because after this quick visit we were to travel to Fort Worth to see the prototype at the Bell factory.

I travelled the day before the rest of the party and was therefore on my own for the first night of the visit, which I spent quietly, recovering from the trans-Atlantic flight which I always found tiring. At least that was my plan. Having stayed awake for as long as I could, I fell into a deep sleep to be wakened – it seemed like minutes later – by the sound of revellers returning to rooms in my corridor, making noisy farewells and promising to meet in the morning. I thought no more about it and tried to get back to sleep. The next day was Sunday and I was up bright and early to investigate Philadelphia, which I had never seen before and was keen to explore. On my way to the coffee shop in the hotel I found myself passing through a crowd of the most enormous men, many of them coloured, all of them noisy. They were without a doubt the cause of my disturbed rest; they were also the Philadelphia Eagles football team and I was grateful again to whoever provided my even temperament, which stopped me from rushing to the door when they woke me up.

On short acquaintance the city was a disappointment although I enjoyed the historic sights, as always in the United States beautifully preserved. The rest of the place was run-down and badly in need of a lick of paint, it seemed to me.

Our Boeing hosts received us with great warmth and courtesy and did a first-class briefing job. They were fully aware that their aircraft would hold no interest for the Royal Navy but they believed that we might spread the word to the French, for example, who retained defence commitments to former colonies. This seemed unlikely to me but I forbore to comment.

The Osprey must take off and land vertically because its twin engines drive huge propellers which, when the wing is rotated for forward flight, would strike the ground, even with the undercarriage extended. Because it is intended to be shipborne, the Osprey must be capable of fitting on a standard carrier lift which means that the wing must also turn laterally through almost 90 degrees so that the aircraft will fit the lift. The machinery required to accomplish all this is relatively massive, complex and expensive. During our visit however, we were invited to a formal lunch at the Naval Yard where the company briefing team explained to local dignitaries how the Osprey could be used for international airport to town centre commuting. This application made more sense to me because there would be no need for it to be carrier lift-compatible, and the aircraft could be made simpler and safer. Even so, the conservative public might prefer a helicopter ride for the short distance involved since, even at twice helicopter speed, the time saved would be marginal.

Our welcome at the Bell factory at Fort Worth was equally warm and we were quickly taken to the hangar where the prototype Osprey was being constructed. Mostly made of black-painted carbon fibre, it looked pretty dull although no one said this to the men working on it. I was most struck by the large lump of machinery on the top of the fuselage for the purposes mentioned earlier, like the rotor head on a chopper but even bigger.

During a pause in the proceedings we were all hustled off to the PR office to be photographed wearing brightly coloured scarves and 5-gallon hats. The reason was obscure until later in the day we were presented with our passports for the State of Texas, beautifully produced and ordering the rest of the world to treat with due courtesy and regard this friend of the State of Texas. Failure to follow these instructions or to serve anything other than the best "sipping whiskey" would be followed by severe punishment. All signed by a Justice of the Peace. What a souvenir, and what lovely people.

CHAPTER XXXII
TOO DARNED HOT

Progress is often slow in the aviation business, no matter how fast the product, because every step forward has to be taken with meticulous care since the pitfalls are many and varied. This stately pace carries forward to aircraft procurement programmes and it is usually a long growing season between sowing the seeds and the harvest. Five years after our grand tour of the Middle East the first tentative signs of serious progress began to appear. Significantly, the interest came from Saudi Arabia, Kuwait and Bahrain, none of which was likely to be dependent upon funding from an outside source. The Saudis particularly were starting to acquire some very capable aircraft and must have realised that the aircraft in their training system were inadequate. The King Faisal Air Academy had been staffed by the British since its inception and, although relations were not always cordial, the academic and flying instruction was of a generally high standard, influenced as it was by RAF procedures. The future pattern of RAF pilot training was beginning to crystallise and would feature a turboprop basic trainer followed by the Hawk for advanced and weapon training. The Royal Saudi Air Force, also aware that the US Navy had selected Hawk, had decided to make a further serious evaluation of the aircraft in their own country, under representative weather conditions.

There was simultaneous interest from Kuwait and, rather to my surprise, rumours of a request from the Emir of Bahrain for his pilots to have a look at the Hawk. When planning one of these exercises there is a temptation to consider other places *en route* where there may be merit in staging a demonstration but, on this occasion, I knew that G-HAWK was already scheduled to return to Washington DC at the end of April, and here we were aiming to be in the Middle East until two weeks before departure for the USA. It all began to look a bit tight and the decision was taken to limit the scope to the three countries named above.

The pilots who drew the short straw for the trip were Andy Jones and Heinz Frick, former member of 20 Squadron, late of Rolls-Royce and now of British Aerospace. They ferried via Malta, where the support BAC1-11 carried us, and where we night-stopped. The journey continued via Luxor in Egypt to Riyadh, capital of Saudi Arabia and the base of the Air Academy. The enormous advantage of the 1-11 escort was clear because the two aircraft could travel together and any work required on the Hawk airframe or engine could be carried out by the ground crew on landing. The pilots were not even required to refuel and inspect their aircraft before proceeding: such luxury.

Entering Saudi Arabia for the first time is not a pleasant experience for the foreigner and, at the pre-tour briefing, I had sounded all the warning notes that I could in order to make everyone aware, without actually frightening them. Whilst I have always found the Saudis to be polite, friendly and quiet, the baggage handlers and general labourers are usually not Saudis. They are, on the contrary, rude, coarse and unfriendly and, since we had to unload the support aircraft, we were bound to see quite a lot of them. Some of the freight was delicate and would react badly to being thrown about or dropped and I was gratified to see the care with which everything was being handled. Inside the aircraft, the company ground crew, all ex-navy or air force, were to be heard addressing Mohammed, Abdulla and Farouk by name in pidgin, threatening them with the most dire punishment if they should get it wrong. All were smiling, and each seemed to understand the other in the way that only servicemen and locals can.

A "fixer" from the Academy collected all our passports and, as was usual, they disappeared into a drawer in the immigration officer's desk, never to be seen again until we were leaving. How on earth they kept track of who was where and when he was departing I shall never know but, in nearly 20 years of visiting the place, I was always reunited with my passport as I left.

In many Arab air forces the dress code, if one exists, is regarded as a general guide and "uniform" has a different meaning. Not so in the King Faisal Academy: staff and students were exceptionally well turned out and moved everywhere with a sense of purpose that was a delight to see. Our first guest pilot was the Commandant, Brigadier General Jawaini, exactly as it should be, and he flew the aircraft extremely well. His deputy, Colonel Darwish, exploiting his rank and position to the full, was difficult to remove from the Hawk and had no hesitation in elbowing others off the flying programme on the grounds that there was another important point for him to check. They were all delightful people and great fun to be with. Some were graduates of Cranwell and had done very well there, in spite of cultural and language difficulties. Indeed Prince Bandar, a member of the royal family, had won the Sword of Honour and returned to the Kingdom to argue for the expansion and re-equipment of the air force.

The flying was uneventful as far as we were concerned although operating from a major civil airport always brings some difficulties, especially when one of the guests wants to carry out some circuits and landings in a busy traffic pattern. Heinz Frick, who is a very talented cartoonist, produced each evening a sketch of one of the highlights of his flying day, much to the amusement of the Saudis and ourselves.

Whenever a guest pilot flew more than once it was naturally arranged that he would fly with the same company pilot each time. It was therefore Andy Jones who, having flown with Colonel Roki by day, found himself night flying with the same officer. As Paddy Barthropp (who hated it) used to say: "Night flying is just the same as day flying, but with the lights on." Whilst this is undeniably true, Andy had not expected to find himself looping and rolling in the dark, which turned out to be Colonel Roki's favourite pastime. When informed of this I could only observe that, if you have to do it, there is no more friendly place to do it, with a full moon and a cloudless sky.

Our working week in Riyadh passed swiftly, averaging five sorties a day and with no snags on the aeroplane. As in some other countries where alcohol is prohibited, the punishment for producing or selling it is condign and swift, as some visitors have found to their cost. However, given the right company, it would be a mistake to assume that Saudi Arabia is a good spot for resting the liver. The Embassy of course is allowed to import liquor and, by special arrangement, so is the senior resident of British Aerospace. Our farewell party was certainly not a drunken orgy but nor was it all fruit juice.

The caravan moved on to Kuwait where our local affairs were now in the hands of Abdul-Aziz Al Ghanim (known to us as trebleA-G), a jovial man who had arranged for us to stay in the SAS Hotel (owned and run by the Scandinavian airline, not that distinguished branch of the British Army). This was a perfectly acceptable hotel, almost on the beach, in a newly developed section of Kuwait City. Its only slight disadvantage was that there was only one road leading to it, and that road was easily missed since it had absolutely no distinguishing features at all. This was to prove significant later on.

The aircraft was flown to a Kuwaiti Air Force base out in the desert and we were provided by our man trebleA-G with a Chevrolet minibus to transport ourselves to and from the hotel. For some curious reason, I suppose insurance, I was the only nominated driver although, once inside the air base, any one of the party was free to use the vehicle.

We spent another working week there, flying three or four sorties a day until the midpoint when we stayed on into the evening in order to night-fly with Colonel Bader, the base commander. This went off smoothly and, after putting the aircraft to bed, we were given supper on the base by the people that we had been flying.

I should have said that the minibus was top of the range with every known extra, automatic gears, power steering, servo brakes and a fuel gauge that did not work. I had initially been impressed by the modest fuel consumption until, after a day's driving, the gauge still showed full and even General Motors could not have achieved that sort of fuel economy. As explained earlier, I was aware of the approximate number of miles that I had driven since topping up the tank but I had no idea of the mileage covered inside the base in other people's hands. Thus it was that, after night-flying and a jolly supper, we set out to return to our hotel. We were all tired, and one or two may even have been snoozing when there was a sudden hush and we were, without any doubt at all, out of fuel. Not only is there no water in the desert, there are not many filling stations either and our best bet seemed to be to return to the air base. The crew hopped out and started to push as I turned across the narrow road. They were about to start pushing the front of the vehicle to allow me to complete the turn when the lack of power – or any other – steering made itself felt and we were stranded, blocking the road. The absurdity of our position was becoming clear: out of petrol in the middle of one of the world's biggest oil producing countries, hoping for someone to drive up and assist.

We became aware of considerable traffic in the distance, coming from the direction of the air base, and it seemed that we were about to be rescued. To our considerable alarm it became clear that the vehicles approaching were tanks and armoured cars of the Kuwaiti Army out on manoeuvres, and we were impeding their progress. Showing admirable coolness, the man in the leading tank simply pulled off the road on to the desert and he and his troop drove around us. Shortly afterwards, a stream of Mercedes and BMW motor cars, driven by the pilots that had hosted our supper party, arrived and quickly supplied us with a can of fuel to return to the airfield, there to fill up from their garage. There was some relief when at last, after what was becoming a very long day, we were heading for the SAS Hotel. It seems unnecessary to add that, with no street lighting, this was the time for me to miss the road to the hotel and spend a further half hour looking for it. There was an ironic cheer from the back when, at long last, I stopped in front of the hotel. There were about four hours left of the night before we started again for the airfield. Oh! The glamour of travel.

The visit was rounded off with a couple of weapon-firing sorties which are always a bit of sport and generally enjoyed by the pilots. Some years later, when the Iraqis invaded, the capability of the Hawk in this role was fully exploited and the Kuwaiti Air Force acquitted itself well.

Our final port of call for the tour was Bahrain which has a tiny air wing, but was rumoured to be in the market for our aircraft. When trying to get to the bottom of this, it seemed to me that the plan was for Bahraini students to be trained in the King Faisal Academy, and their contribution would be some aircraft on semi-permanent loan. This certainly made more sense than for Bahrain to set up and operate its own training scheme.

The visit started well with the Crown Prince attending the flying demonstration given by Andy Jones. The four pilots that they had put forward to fly the Hawk included the pilot of the royal helicopter, who had never flown a fixed-wing jet aircraft before. He was agreeably surprised to discover that, after less than an hour in the aeroplane, he was able to fly circuits and landings without any help from the company pilot. There were no criticisms of the Hawk and we felt that a good job had been done, although we were not sure why we had done it.

Whilst we were there a C-141 Starlifter of the USAF staged through and I watched it start up and taxy for departure. Pouring from the bottom of the fin were what seemed to be gallons of red fluid, to my eye closely resembling hydraulic oil. I dashed to the tower and pointed this out to the duty controller who called the aircraft to inform the captain. After a very short pause a voice said: "Thank you sir, we are aware of the leak and plan to have it fixed when we get to Okinawa." Even after all these years they still surprise me with their Chuck Yeager-type "Aw shucks, that ain't no real problem."

The route home was through Luxor and then on to Malta for a night stop before the final leg to Dunsfold. Demonstrating far less judgement than usual I agreed to fly the Luxor–Malta leg with Heinz Frick. With his usual flair, Heinz arranged for us to be photographed in front of the Hawk before we climbed aboard. It was only when we were posing that I noticed written on the nose of the aircraft, especially for the camera, "BAe senior crew. Combined age 108." After departing Luxor and climbing to altitude, we cruised for 2½ hours before crossing the coast as the drop-tanks emptied. The whole sector took 3 hours and 50 minutes, at that point easily the longest that a Hawk had been airborne. After landing at Malta I personally felt 108 years old and was prepared to concede that the old thrill was no longer there.

The next morning, having watched the departure of G-HAWK, we piled aboard the 1-11 to return to Dunsfold. By local arrangement, HM Customs provided an officer to clear our returning aircraft on our home airfield on the strict understanding that nobody brought in dutiable goods in excess of the official allowance. This worked very well and saved us the tiresome business of landing Gatwick in order to clear ourselves and our spares pack-up through the green channel.

An hour from landing the 1-11 captain asked me if I would care to have a drive and I accepted quickly because I was not doing at all well in the poker game in the passenger compartment. I sat in the right-hand seat (the aircraft is normally flown from the left), disengaged the autopilot and tried some gentle manoeuvres. The force required to change direction seemed, and was, enormous when compared to the Hawk which I had flown the previous day. I have to say however that the seating position was much more comfortable. As we began the let-down into Dunsfold I thanked the captain, expecting him to resume control. He told me to go ahead and gave the speed and rate of descent that I should seek to maintain. It may seem odd, since the seats are only a couple of feet apart, but the entire aspect of flying is different in the right-hand seat. The line of sight is quite different and of course the throttles, which are on a central console, have to be managed by the left hand and not the right. I am happy to report that the landing was without drama and made a fitting conclusion to the tour.

CHAPTER XXXIII

CLIMB EVERY MOUNTAIN

After the strange events surrounding the Harrier in Switzerland, it was with some apprehension that I observed the growing interest by the Swiss Air Force in the Hawk. The general feeling within the company was that this would be an important scalp to hang on our belt in the face of competition from the French/Germans and Italians, all well represented in the ethnic composition of the country. This was beyond dispute but, having seen at first hand the curious – not to say bizarre – military thinking behind their earlier aircraft acquisitions, I was not confident.

Discussions had been going on in a desultory way with senior members of the air force who were beginning to feel that the Vampire Trainers that had been in service for 30 years represented diminishing flying returns for the maintenance effort involved. We supplied information and briefings to the various bodies that help to form opinion in the Service and Parliament in response to spasmodic requests. After our return from the United States with G-HAWK, we were invited to participate in the annual open day at Bern airport on the Sunday of the first week in September 1983. Before accepting, Michael Mendoza, who was taking over our European affairs, and I went to Bern to consult with Peter Arengo-Jones, our adviser, and the Swiss authorities. Our plan was to widen the scope of the visit by offering some air time to the Swiss Air Force and to the pilots of the national flight test centre at Emmen. Most of the Emmen pilots, led by Bernie Alder, were old friends, particularly of Bill Bedford, and supported our plan. Having got them on side the air force also fell in with the scheme although they emphasised that all this would be unofficial and should not be taken as any indication of official interest: it was very Swiss. Eventually it was agreed that we should position at Emmen for a couple of days and then move to Sion, an historic air force base, to allow some military pilots to have a quick handling flight. On the Sunday of the air show the Hawk would arrive at Bern from Sion, give its display and land.

I have said before that most meetings in Switzerland take place in very expensive restaurants and this series to set up the visit was no different. It came as a surprise therefore, when we arrived at Emmen with our aeroplane and crew, to find that we were not invited to share the canteen facilities but had to arrange lunch for everyone in a local café. We had all been to places where from choice we arranged packed lunches from our hotel rather than face the food on offer at the air base. In Switzerland we had no such qualms, and this registered as another example of their thriftiness. I have formed an illogical distrust of any man who keeps his small change in a purse, not just

266

to ensure that he loses none of it, but also to save wear and tear on his pocket. It is a common practice in Switzerland.

All the Emmen pilots are vastly experienced and have graduated from a test pilots' school in Britain, France or the United States. Although now civilians, each is a former military pilot and, under the standard Swiss military reserve laws, rejoins the service each year to fulfil his training commitment. In their normal jobs they carry out development trials on in-service aircraft and air-test those coming off major inspections and overhaul; they are all current on the aircraft of the Swiss Air Force which at the time included Mirage, Hunter and F-5. Four of their senior pilots flew the Hawk, including the chief, and all were happy to have a company pilot on board to act as safety pilot. This is quite usual during a preview evaluation if the aircraft has dual controls because it removes from the guest pilot any need to learn emergency drills and starting procedures.

They were unanimous in enjoying their flights and we listened carefully to their comments post-flight. Bernie Alder is a very tall man and felt that his knees were uncomfortably close to the instrument panel. He also thought that the windscreen frame was too thick and partially obscured his view in formation-flying. The first observation was not new because most admirals in the US Navy seem to be 6 feet and some inches tall and those that flew the Hawk said that they felt cramped. They seemed reassured when told that 98% of the human race would fit into the aircraft and that the ejection path was so designed that, in combination with the leg-restraining garters, there was no chance of collision between knees and instrument panel: Bernie was convinced. As to difficulties in formation-flying because of the restricted view from the cockpit, I asked if he had seen the Red Arrows recently. The point was taken and the subject was quietly dropped.

Another of the Emmen pilots asked to carry out some spinning. He was flying with Heinz Frick as safety and they clambered up to a safe height to begin spinning. When established in the spin, the GRD pilot suddenly applied full aileron against the direction of the spin. The Hawk immediately inverted and continued to spin, which is an even more uncomfortable condition than ordinary spinning in which the aeroplane stays the right way up. Heinz it may be remembered, is Swiss-born, and I have often wondered in which language he expressed his view of events. As with most unplanned departures from normal flight in the Hawk, if everything is put back into the middle, the aircraft sorts things out for itself as it did in this case: all part of life's rich pageant for a company test pilot.

At Sion, the pilots were instructors or trainees and rather less exuberant in their handling of the aircraft, which of course they all enjoyed. Who could fail to do so after the very tired Vampire Trainers that were their day-to-day diet?

Some of us returned to Bern in order to witness the demonstration, leaving some ground crew to see G-HAWK airborne and to pack up the tools and spares. The background to the demonstration area was spectacular with snow-capped mountains all around the valley in which Belp airport lies. It has only one, not very big, runway with no over-runs at either end, and any failure to stop would put the aircraft into a crop of maize waiting to be harvested. The airport had been restricted to turboprop airliners until the advent of the four-engined BAE 146, which demonstrated its ability to take off and land with large safety margins in the hands of DanAir pilots.

Many familiar faces were in the crowd waiting for the Hawk and when it arrived the audience were clearly excited. The aeroplane was still in its simulated US Navy pale grey paint scheme with red fin and wingtips. It was beautifully flown and looked most handsome against the natural background.

Using what would now be called a noise abatement procedure, Heinz wound up the speed someway from the airfield and, just before he passed in front of the crowd, almost closed the throttle so that the aircraft was moving very quickly but in almost complete silence. After demonstrating the usual airshow manoeuvres he landed and, at least halfway down the runway, opened the throttle and overshot. The Hawk leapt into the air, completed another circuit and landed. This time he surprised the onlookers by popping the drag chute which we had been carrying but not using during the earlier part of the visit. The effect was dramatic and the Hawk came to a complete halt in less than half the runway length. It was a very convincing demonstration of the versatility of the little aeroplane in a country where some of the remote airfields are difficult to get out of and into.

Although not clear at the time, this was the start of a lengthy campaign to persuade the Swiss to re-equip with the Hawk in the face of strong opposition from our industrial opponents.

In my experience, things were rarely normal in Switzerland and in the trainer replacement battle there were even more factors in play than in the usual military acquisition programmes. The budget allocation was tight, which favoured the Italian aircraft, MB.339. The numbers required were small since the pilot training programme is very modest but they had somehow to be boosted in order to make part manufacture and assembly in the government factory a feasible proposition without going over budget. The people at Emmen had decided that a minimum of 20 aircraft had to be built in order that their unit costs did not look ridiculous when compared to ours. We could show that half that number of Hawks would satisfy the training task because of the vastly improved utilisation of the Hawk when compared with the old Vampires, but we had to choose carefully where we said it.

The Swiss project leader was called Fred Lauber, a Swiss/German, with a Swiss/French deputy named Rene Bosel. I warmed to Fred on first acquaintance but I had grave reservations about M. Bosel who we knew was clearly displeased by the performance comparisons made (at their request) between Hawk and Alpha-Jet. We knew a lot about the French aircraft by this time, not least because a Royal Air Force student at the French Test Pilots' School had been given an Alpha-Jet for his evaluation exercise and a copy of his report had found its way to Kingston. Many of its shortcomings, it has to be said, referred to its weapon capability which, they claimed, did not interest the Swiss. Even so, its single-engine performance and spinning behaviour would have gained it some caustic comment from Boscombe Down.

After two or three years of sparring, with visits to and from government offices and factories, the Italian entry was dropped and we were invited to participate in a fly-off against the French. Our own aircraft, G-HAWK, was by now getting a bit tired and although it still flew well it was not representative of the latest aircraft coming off the line. The Swiss knew this and insisted that they evaluate the best on offer, which might seem a reasonable request except that we did not own one, and neither did the RAF from whom we might have borrowed. After some negotiation we rented a brand new aircraft from the Kuwaiti contract, changed the markings, sent a large cheque to the Kuwaiti embassy and set course for Emmen.

By the time that the aircraft arrived I had spent two fruitless days trying to persuade the evaluation team that there were great advantages to carrying a company pilot in the aircraft at all times to take care of the safety checks and emergency procedures. My concern was that even a minor accident would have great financial repercussions with repair costs and penalties for delayed delivery to Kuwait. In making this case I was aware that implicit in my argument was less than total confidence in the air force pilot/instructors scheduled to fly for the next month, and the hint that this trainer aircraft was much trickier than we had led them to believe. I had to admit defeat when M. Bosel informed me that the French had raised no objection to handing over their aeroplane. I should not be at all surprised if he gained control of the Alpha-Jet by telling them that we had readily agreed to the Swiss request.

At Emmen we discovered that we shared a hangar with a rough curtain separating us from the French. This was all very friendly and I was delighted to see the mountain of spares accompanying the Alpha-Jet. Our minimum kit had been driven there from Kingston in a British Aerospace Transit van, not only because we were confident of high serviceability, but also because we could call up any large item required and have it delivered within a few hours. In the month of the trial we needed no back-up from the factory.

The arrival of the two competing aircraft was stage-managed for the benefit of Swiss television. They joined up with a Swiss Vampire which led them over the airfield at a gentle pace in loose formation and in not very good weather. The instructions were clear and concise; when the cameramen had finished, the aircraft would land in turn and proceed to the ramp in front of the hangar for more pictures. There would be no demonstration flying of any kind and the authorities would take a dim view of any breach of these instructions. Heinz Frick and Chris Roberts followed the briefing to the letter and, as they made their sedate way around Emmen circuit, the Alpha-Jet rushed past with shock waves clearly apparent in the damp air. Patrick Experton, who was flying the aircraft, had apparently not understood the directions that he had been given in his own language. Oh yeah?!

During the opening mass briefing I was introduced to Rick Wenger of the Pilatus company with whom BAe had formed an understanding. We would promote their PC.9 as the basic trainer for the RAF and they in turn would promote Hawk for the Swiss Air Force. I explained how limited was our ability to influence official procurement programmes in the United Kingdom (I was already aware that the Embraer Tucano was being favoured by our government for the trainer role). He dismissed this out of hand and added that we had better make sure that PC.9 was selected because if not, Pilatus would certainly prevent Hawk getting into Switzerland. He was wrong.

Since we would not have one of our pilots in the aircraft when it flew, it was arranged that one of us was always available in the tower when the Hawk was flying to give advice in an emergency. I sought to ensure that a company pilot was on hand when potentially difficult exercises were planned since I was fairly sure that, for instance, none of the Swiss pilots had been involved in an inverted spin, but might have heard that one of the Emmen pilots had recovered from one. I therefore asked M. Bosel if I could have a programme of each day's planned flying to arrange safety cover. He agreed. The first that he produced showed Exercises A3, B4 & 5, C7 and various other combinations of letters and numbers. It is common practice in training schools to allocate code lettering to exercises for programming as a convenient shorthand. However, instructors and students both know the code, and I searched in vain for the key to this helpful document. I asked M. Bosel what it meant and he quite flatly refused to tell me even though I emphasised that I was not trying to probe state secrets, I just wanted to know what they were doing in our aircraft. We never became friends.

At a late stage of the evaluation, both aircraft were required to carry out some air-to-ground firing against targets in the mountains and I was invited to spectate from the range officer's station. Some of my enthusiasm waned when I learned that the only way to get there was by helicopter; nevertheless I presented myself at the appointed time, dressed warmly against the weather. A very small NCO greeted me at the helicopter flight office and led me to a tiny chopper into which, rather to my surprise, he climbed, inviting me to strap into the seat alongside. Whilst in transit I asked him how long he had been flying helicopters, how he liked them and the sort of things that one does ask. He informed me that normally he worked in a bank and was simply doing his two-week militia commitment. As we approached the landing site on a very small ledge, with almost no margin for error, I began to feel that I was getting too old for this kind of thing.

The firing was impressive since the targets were not easily approached because of the surrounding high ground, and some adroit manoeuvring was required to attack and escape. One of the Emmen test pilots attached to the evaluation team, a civilian named Bischoff, who had recently graduated from the USAF Test Pilots' School at Edwards AFB, killed himself in a Hunter carrying out weapon work on the same range shortly after we had left.

The fly-off was completed without any damage to anyone or anything. It had taken a long time to fly just a few hours and we were all relieved when it was over because it had not been a very interesting event. Two more years were to elapse before pen was put to contract but eventually we were rewarded.

CHAPTER XXXIV

THE PARTY'S OVER

1987 was my last full year of honest toil and I reflected on recent events with very mixed feelings. The decision had been made to go ahead with a single-seat version of the Hawk as a private venture, based on the interest that had been created in some foreign markets by our briefing team. The prototype had flown successfully and the concept showed considerable promise because, having removed one seat, there was an impressive amount of space within the fuselage for advanced avionics which increasingly were simplifying the operational task for the pilot. It was shattering for us all when, six weeks after first flight, the aircraft was lost whilst rehearsing the presentation for the press, and Jim Hawkins was killed. Even now, nobody knows what happened, but it was a devastating blow to the programme and to those of us who knew him well.

Tentative plans for touring with the aircraft to those countries showing most interest, mostly in the Far East, went on hold and the presentation team was again forced into action to try to recover lost ground. The unexplained loss of a new aircraft strikes a huge psychological blow to those services with procurement in mind because it is impossible to answer the burning question which they all have – how could it happen to one of your most senior pilots? Nevertheless, putting on the bravest possible face, we set out to reassure them.

Early in the year we visited Thailand and the Philippines, both countries anxious to acquire a modern aircraft and both greatly influenced by the success of the Hawk in Indonesia. Bill Bedford was now resident in Jakarta and beavering away on the ground to suggest to them that a single-seat version of an aircraft that they had in service made good sense. The Indonesians had caused us some grief in the way that they operated their aircraft, and in particular, the cavalier manner in which they treated their safety equipment. After one or two serious incidents we were compelled to make a film for them showing how to get properly dressed for flight, the reasons for wearing flying boots (polished or not) and correctly securing the flying helmet. The fact is that if a pilot does all these things according to the book and straps in as tightly as he should, he is not terribly comfortable and that is a sharp contradiction to the Indonesian way of life.

Sir David Evans, Denis Smallwood's successor as Military Adviser, joined us on one visit to Jakarta and his suite became the briefing room for our team talks. We had assembled at coffee-time one morning to plan our batting order and to allocate possible questions to whomever was best placed to make a sensible reply. The coffee had just been delivered when I began to feel very strange indeed because things were swaying and moving in the room. I thought this must be a dizzy spell, something that I had never previously experienced, and it took a moment or two for me to realise that *I* was perfectly well but the *room* was shaking. For those that are unfamiliar with the phenomenon, I have to tell you that being on the fourteenth floor of an hotel when an earthquake starts is not a happy experience. It is curious that those of us who do not live in earthquake zones do not immediately identify a tremor for what it is, but suspect some personal physical frailty. Even when realisation dawned it was difficult to see what self-preservation action one could take from 200 feet up with no parachute.

Our colleagues in Finland, who were monitoring events in Stockholm where the JAS project was going through another political trauma, advised that a carefully written paper lauding the versatility of the Hawk and especially the single-seat option might be sent by Valmet to their counterparts at SAAB. Such a paper was produced proposing that, if costs had to be saved, why not buy the required new trainer (Hawk assembled in Finland) and use the money thus saved to proceed with the operational aircraft which, for reasons of neutrality, could not be bought in from abroad? It was further hinted that, when Finland was seeking a MiG 21 replacement, it might look favourably on its neighbour's all-purpose fighter. It was all to no avail but it led to some interesting discussions in Stockholm and London. During his visit to London, the Swedish Minister of Defence was invited to our head offices in the Strand for lunch and discussions on our military division. To start the briefing, and knowing that the Swedes had operated a lot of Hunters in the 1950s, I had found an ancient black and white slide of a Swedish Hunter. At the run-through for the main board members before the presentation, I was stopped in mid-flow and asked, it has to be said by a former BAC board member, if I was quite certain that the Swedes had flown Hunters! As is now widely known, the JAS project came to fruition and British Aerospace became a substantial contributor to its success.

The Zimbabwe Air Force was another prime target for the Hawk 200, as the single-seater has been designated. After some initial hiccups, they were making a success of their small Hawk fleet and realising the economies that could be made, without sacrificing capability, by phasing out their well-liked but expensive-to-run Hunters. In preparing for my departure from the company I had recruited some promising younger men to succeed the old hands. When the RAF had introduced the 38/16 retirement option allowing 38-year-olds, or those with 16 years' commissioned service, to retire with honour, many sought to start a new career and were drawn to the industry that they knew best. I had several of these as well as some former company apprentices in more junior slots, learning the trade as it were. It seemed to me that I must leave a competent organisation to carry on the good work and in general I think I succeeded. One of these recruits was Terry Newman, who had been the Tornado project pilot at Boscombe Down before joining us. For his first trip with the company he came to Zimbabwe, and I asked him to make the main presentation. He prepared with great diligence and told me that he was ready to have a dummy run in our own departmental theatre. Using his considerable operational background he had produced a marvellous image of the equipment possibilities for the 200 series and it was all very well done. Unfortunately, some of the gear was totally unknown to me and, I had to assume, would be an equal mystery to the Zimbabweans. He modified his talk and I reckoned that when I understood it he had it pitched at the right level. A sure sign that it was getting time to move on.

The Malaysians had started an Aviation Exposition at which the world's aeronautical companies were to assemble and display their wares, rather like the static exhibition at the Farnborough Show. We had not been before, and there was a need to make further visits to Thailand and Singapore in pursuit of the first elusive contract for the Hawk 200, so I joined the party. The show in Kuala Lumpur was the forerunner of what has become an aviation "event," but it was not wildly exciting on this occasion because there was no flying. However there was some good golf to be had, and, through the good offices of our man on the spot I was allowed entry to some of the best courses.

We talked to the Singapore Aircraft Industries teams who were feeling ready to take on more responsible work after their great successes with Hunter developments. They sensed that a market existed for aircraft of the Hawk class, not just for themselves but also for their neighbours of the Pacific Rim. They were great enthusiasts, building a reputation for first-class work in their expanding factories and they could become formidable competitors to better-established companies in the future.

Excitement was high in Thailand where we had shown that we could easily meet their operational requirements and it looked most promising. The Thais were also interested in the HS.748 turboprop for both military and civil use and there was a great gathering of BAe (formerly Hawker) people in Bangkok after the Malaysian show was over. We were sitting in a group having a beer before dinner when somehow the conversation drifted around to amusing events that had occurred to us individually and collectively. When it came to my turn I told them about the parade rehearsal at Boscombe Down during which Red Evans' shoe had fallen apart, and its aftermath. Colin Dodds, one of my recruits, said when I had finished: "When you are gone, all this will be lost." I am sure that it was well-intentioned, although it seemed a bit blunt to me at the time, but it led indirectly to this book – so now you know who to blame.

I was due for release, without good behaviour, on the last day of January 1988. The word filtering down from the front office was that vast changes were imminent, none of them likely to be uplifting to the members of the company in Southern England. Kingston and Dunsfold would close, production being transferred to Brough and Warton. Weybridge had no future and its few remaining functions would be transferred. It was a depressing picture and, although it had long been apparent that the over-capacity in the industry had to be corrected if any of it was to survive, it was sad for a romantic traditionalist to think of all that history being thrown away.

Because of the need to talk again to the Singaporeans and to ensure that my departure did not lead to a break in communication, I made the arrangements for my last trip as a member of British Aerospace. I travelled via Bangkok and Kuala Lumpur to give an encouraging word to my merry men still slaving away there, and then on to Changi, marvelling again at its transformation since I first saw it in 1945. By way of introduction, I had invited Stephen Cochrane, one of the new young members of the depart-ment, to join me there in order to introduce him to the territory. His presence gave me the excuse to show him the island, at the same time wallowing in nostalgia. We visited Changi Village, no longer dusty streets and wooden shops but clean roads and parades of brick-built stores with accommodation above. Seletar village seemed unchanged, but deserted. We visited Kranji war memorial and I remembered standing there at dawn on ANZAC day, waiting for my Javelins to fly over in salute. And finally to Tengah. I had asked the director of Singapore Aircraft Industries if he would request the air force commander on my behalf that I might be allowed to visit the station, 25 years after I had left it. Unhappily, it could not be agreed because of the security status of the airfield, and I had to wonder what on earth there might be there that I had not seen before!

I returned from this trip on Tuesday 26th January and went to my office the next day. A young woman from the Divisional Secretary's office called on me to tell me about pension arrangements, continuing health insurance cover and all those other dreary subjects which suddenly became important. She caught my attention when she said that from my executive pension would be deducted my RAF retired pay, at a stroke approximately halving my income. I spent the next two years seeking to have this changed, or at least explained, but without success. Even the ombudsman was apparently unable to do anything other than sympathise about a rule which, he said, could be seen as unfair but which nevertheless was legal. This was not the happiest way to finish my working life.

I had a lot of friends in the company and it was with genuine sadness that I made my farewells to them. For the reasons given in the previous paragraph, it was much less difficult to leave some of the others.

It has always seemed to me that one of the silliest questions ever posed is: "Would you do it all again?" There is absolutely no chance of such an offer being made so the answer does not really matter, but I would. I am just sad that, having lived through what I regard as the golden age of aviation, those that came after me have been denied the same fun and excitement.